Karl Jaspers

An Introduction to His Philosophy

Karl Jaspers

An Introduction to His Philosophy

BY CHARLES F. WALLRAFF

PRINCETON UNIVERSITY PRESS

PRINCETON, NEW JERSEY 1970

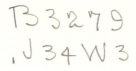

This book has been composed in Linotype Times Roman

Printed in the United States of America
by Princeton University Press, Princeton, New Jersey

To Dean Wallraff

Preface

More than a score of books by Karl Jaspers have become available in English since 1933 when, soon after the three-volume *Philosophie* appeared, Eden and Cedar Paul published a translation of *Die geistige Situation der Zeit* called *Man in the Modern Age*. And in the fifty-six years since his first book was published, this early co-formulator (with Martin Heidegger) of German existentialism, whose background in medicine and psychology resembles that of William James, and whose investigations equal in range and profundity those of John Dewey, produced a series of provocative books and essays on a wide variety of topics. Beginning with psychopathology, he contributed to the development of the psychology of world views, social psychology and sociology, national and international politics, world history, art and literature, theology, and, of course, philosophy —the subject to which he devoted most of his major efforts since the early 1920's.

Jaspers' influence in his native Germany, and in Switzerland, where he resided after 1947, has been profound. It is indicative that his recent *Wohin treibt die Bundesrepublik?* (translated in part by E. B. Ashton as *The Future of Germany*) provoked such a storm of controversy that it became necessary to write a second book nearly as long (235 pp.) to answer the critics of the first book. But this hardly begins to tell the story. His books are studied all over the world, and translations of his writings have been published in sixteen countries, including Argentina and Japan.

Nothing in the above, however, should be taken to mean that Jaspers' philosophy is easily accessible to us. Apart from his many interpretations of the writings of great historical figures, his strictly *philosophical* views appear in English only in a few brief semipopular books. In 1949 Ralph Manheim offered, in *The Perennial Scope of Philosophy*, a series of six guest-lectures on philosophical faith, given in the summer of 1947 at the University of Basel. Two years later the same translator gave us, in *Way to Wisdom*, what had just been presented to the German-speaking peoples as an "introduction to philosophy." In 1955, twenty years after the delivery in Holland of the original version, appeared *Reason and Existenz,* a series of five academic lectures, translated by William Earle, through which Jaspers emphasized the significance of Nietzsche and Kierkegaard and expatiated for the first time upon his new philosophy of "the encompassing." And in 1967 appeared two new translations: R.F.C. Hull and Grete Wels published *Philosophy is for Everyman,* "a short course in philosophical thinking," originally presented over television in the autumn of 1964, and E. B. Ashton provided, in *Philosophical Faith and Revelation,* a somewhat abridged and unusually literary version of a recent (1962) account of philosophical faith viewed in relation to the quite different faith which derives from religious revelation.

We should surely be thankful to have so many translations of Jaspers' own statements. But still, up to the present, remarkably few articles on Jaspers have appeared in English. And the big books—the youthful and exuberant *Psychologie der Weltanschauungen,* in which most of his basic ideas were first presented or, at least, adumbrated, the three-volume *Philosophie,* which he favored above all his other writings, and the eleven-hundred-page testament to truth and reason, *Von der Wahrheit*—are (except for brief excerpts) unavailable in English. Consequently, those who wish to study Jaspers' writings have to choose between attempting to assemble a meaningful philosophy from a number of translations of compendious, overlapping, and, for the most part, semipopular expositions, and working through hundreds of pages of intricate, and, at times, uncommonly idiosyncratic German.

Neither alternative is entirely satisfactory to most students. While Jaspers' books provide materials enough to engage the efforts of scholars for years to come, still those who stand on grounds alien to Jaspers, i.e., those who have concerned themselves with philosophers quite different from such Continental thinkers as Pascal and Kierkegaard, Kant and Hegel, Schelling and Schopenhauer, Dilthey and Husserl, Nietzsche and Dostoevsky, are understandably troubled by Jaspers' style and bewildered by his thoughts. Time and again American readers say of his writings that they are "agonizingly abstruse," "esoteric," "unrigorous," "unsystematic," "amorphous," and the like. Odd as this may sound to those who are accustomed to enjoying Hegel and Heidegger, it undoubtedly expresses a natural and predictable reaction. Paul A. Schilpp, editor of the *Library of Living Philosophers*, simply speaks the unvarnished truth when, in his preface to the volume of essays on and by Jaspers, he alludes to "a terminology which is peculiarly Jaspersian," stresses the indispensability of the glossary to his book, and adds that Jaspers' "style of writing . . . has led to difficulties . . . which, at times, have seemed almost (if not actually) insuperable" (p. xi). It *is*, for example, initially puzzling to read that "we are living being, consciousness, mind, and Existenz," or that "Reason is the Comprehensive in us." And we *are* astonished to find Jesus and Buddha included among the philosophers, Nietzsche lauded for his obvious self-contradictions, and, in *The Great Philosophers*, Confucius and Nicholas of Cusa given more space than Socrates and Kant.

The present book is intended to help students overcome these and similar difficulties by presenting Jaspers' thoughts in comparatively clear and straightforward fashion. While it denies that philosophy is "practical" in any cheap and obvious sense, it follows Jaspers in attempting to avoid the otiose and emphasize the relevance of philosophy to matters of ultimate concern. Those who wish a more theoretical and systematic presentation may well call to mind that, as Heidegger's followers express it, Jaspers, like Kierkegaard—and to some extent Sartre—quite deliberately spurned the "ontological" in favor of the "ontic." Following Kant he rejected the very possibility of ontology in the traditional sense, and, as a result, was unconcerned with general theories of being. His thinking proceeded largely on the level of individual decisions and acts; it did not merely tolerate but called for appeals to authentic self-hood. Like the pragmatists who previously had turned away from the idealistic "absolute" to face concrete problems in the here and now, Jaspers looked to philosophy to assist the individual in his unique and enigmatic situation. A highly *theoretical* exposition of *Existenzphilosophie* can properly be written only by a nonfollower: if written by a follower it would deny by example what it affirmed by assertion.

After a brief biographical section, the introductory chapter prepares the ground by formulating and calling into question several widely held assumptions which stand in the way of any clear and sympathetic apprehension of Jaspers' views. Then, abandoning negations, the remaining chapters expound a number of major existential themes, not with a view to weaving them into one systematic whole, for Jaspers' philosophy is essentially and inescapably pluralistic, but rather in order to elicit the significance of each one and to show how they supplement and reinforce one another.

Considerable use is made of quotations, especially when they are needed to present crucial passages hitherto unavailable in English. In translating such passages I have preferred the spirit to the letter, and ready communication to strict correctness. Furthermore I have often sought to domesticate arcane views by pointing out their similarity to currently familiar doctrines. Criticism has been deliberately omitted as premature in an exoteric exposition and downright inimical to the purposes of an introduction intended to promote communication and sympathetic understanding. I have attempted throughout to preserve what Jaspers calls the "two wings" of existential thinking: on the one hand the generally applicable concepts and judgments which form the content of scientific knowledge and much philosophical thought, and, on the other, the existential appeal to the individual reader in his unique and unrepeatable historical situation.

There are of course many today who summarily reject all standpoints that assume the relevance of philosophy to the "big questions" concerning matters of belief. And it is surely true that if philosophy must be regarded as knowledge in some more or less scientific sense, then it must scale down its pretensions and limit the scope of its activities to a few restricted and manageable areas. The problems that Socrates discussed with the Sophists have not yet been solved, and probably will prove insoluable. But granting this, it is equally true that existing individuals, who must decide here and now how to live and what to live for, will, when their problems are ignored by the philosophers, either turn for help to whatever persons or sects offer it on the most attractive terms, or, in their fearful disillusionment, lose their footing and, as it were, fall into the abyss of nihilism and despair.

It was with a view to this situation that, shortly after the war, Jaspers declared: "Philosophy must not abdicate. Least of all today" (*Perennial Scope,* p. 3). Not that he was concerned to raise standards, professionalize the teachers of philosophy, and the like. Quite the contrary. Like Kierkegaard he distrusted the comfortably situated and carefully protected servants of church and state, and like Nietzsche he feared the academic philosophers with their apologetics for the *status quo*, their insistence upon being considered right at all costs, and their consequent failure to face up to things as they are—a failure revealed chiefly through the sham, cant, hypocrisy, and downright bad faith which marred their lectures and books, and their lamentable disinclination to engage fairly in frank, open, and friendly discussion aimed exclusively at the unbiased grasp of philosophic truth.

Jaspers extolled not professionalism and expertise but greatness, and commended not the latest but the best. He referred his students, not to carefully selected and well-schooled professors, but to the several score of "great philosophers" who, during the past two and one-half millennia, surpassed their contemporaries in insight and expressed profound truths honestly and with a striking disregard for personal consequences. It is always open to us, he said, to join the small company of lovers of wisdom who, without depending upon any generally accepted creed or powerful institutional framework, use a small collection of timeless classics as a secular scripture through which to receive constant inspiration and enlightenment from a superior source. As Jaspers was heard to say in his classroom: "A single page from Plato or any great philosopher is worth more than all the writings of Kuno Fischer—yes, and Windelband too."

This timeless philosophy—this *philosophia perennis*, as it is frequently called—provides no generally accepted and indefeasible conclusions. Philosophy is, as Diotima told Socrates, the love rather than the possession of wisdom. It is always on the way, and its devotees are perpetual beginners who, unlike scientists and technicians, are never entitled to regard the results of their inquiries as definitive. It is the activity of philosophizing and not any specific philosophic creed that counts. For, somewhat paradoxically, the extrascientific *faith* in which philosophical thinking issues is, as Socrates was perhaps the first to urge, more fruitful and satisfying than the most fully verified, precise, and internally consistent knowledge. While this view is far from obvious, there is, as I hope to show, much to be said for it.

Charles F. Wallraff

University of Arizona
August 1969

Acknowledgments

Grateful acknowledgment is made to the following publishers who have granted permission to quote from the books by Professor Jaspers which I have indicated: The University of Arizona Press, *Nietzsche*: *An Introduction to the Understanding of His Philosophical Activity*; The University of Chicago Press, *The Future of Mankind*; Harcourt, Brace and World, *Three Essays*: *Leonardo, Descartes, and Max Weber*; Routledge and Kegan Paul Ltd., *Man in the Modern Age*; Walter de Gruyter and Co., *Existenzphilosophie*; R. Piper and Co., *Von der Wahrheit*; Springer-Verlag, *Psychologie der Weltanschauungen* and *Philosophie*.

What I owe to Professor Jaspers must surely be evident on every page. I am also deeply indebted to Professor J. Loewenberg, whose courses in Kant and Hegel first aroused my interest in German philosophy, and to Mr. Walter Loewey who provided the traveling scholarship that enabled me to study at Heidelberg University during the year 1934-35.

I am grateful to Mrs. Phyllis Lim who made many helpful suggestions while typing the manuscript, and to Professor Richard E. Palmer whose informed reactions to the typescript provided detachment and objectivity when they were most needed.

Finally I wish to thank the University of Arizona for facilitating the writing of this book by granting me sabbatical leave during 1966-67.

Contents

༄

CONTENTS

Karl Jaspers

An Introduction to His Philosophy

Jaspers' Life and Writings

~~

Karl Jaspers had just passed his eighty-sixth birthday when, on February 26, 1969, he died of a stroke in Basel, Switzerland. He was born in Oldenburg, Germany, about twenty-five miles west of Bremen, on February 23, 1883.[1]

His father, who descended from many generations of farmers and merchants, studied law and, after serving for some years as high constable of the district, became director of a bank. His mother came from a family of farmers that had occupied a nearby region for hundreds of years. Here, near the North Sea, he spent his boyhood with his parents—and at times with his grandparents—"brought up with a regard for truth and loyalty, for achievement and reliability, yet without church religion (except for the scanty formalities of the Protestant confession)."[2]

At the local Gymnasium a distressing altercation with his authoritarian principal reached a climax when he refused to join a fraternity "on the ground that these imitations of the university fraternities were based on distinctions of social background and parental occupation, not on personal friendship."[3] When the other students without exception yielded to the prevailing view and sided with the principal, he stood alone.

During his nineteenth year a chronic debilitating illness which had long prevented him from participating in the stren-

NOTE: Titles are referred to in the footnotes by combinations of capital letters as explained at the beginning of the bibliography given on pp. 215-19. The alphabetic order of the letters chosen is always the same as that of the German titles. English translations, regardless of their titles, are listed directly after their German originals.

[1] This account is based in large part upon E. B. Ashton's translation of the "Philosophische Autobiographie" (entitled "Philosophical Memoir") and Felix Kaufmann's translation of "Über meine Philosophie" ("On My Philosophy").

[2] UPT 132.   [3] PFT 195.

uous activities of normal youths was correctly diagnosed as "bronchiectasis and cardiac decompensation."[4] Since this illness, which was regarded as incurable and as generally fatal during or before middle age, made impossible for him the long hours of intellectual labor required of normal scholars, he was forced to follow a strict regimen and to learn to work with maximum efficiency.

At the universities he soon found himself out of sympathy with the philosophy professors, who seemed to him personally pretentious and dogmatic.[5] When their courses proved to be irrelevant to the vital issues with which philosophy has traditionally been involved, he simply dropped them. His first three terms were spent studying the humanities while attending lectures in law. Finding the abstractions and fictions of jurisprudence alien to him, and wishing to become intimately familiar with a factual science relating directly to basic human concerns, he took up the study of medicine. In 1909 he received his M.D. degree.

The following year he married Gertrud Mayer, whom he had known since he was introduced to her by her brother Ernst in 1907. From the time of their very first meeting, this remarkable woman, to whom he since dedicated many books, was *en rapport* with him to a degree that he had not previously believed possible. Since she had come of a devout Jewish family, she was able to acquaint him with Jewish translations and interpretations of the so-called Old Testament. Having faced profound crises—her sister was permanently insane, and a close friend had taken his own life—she was well acquainted with what Jaspers was to call "ultimate" or "boundary" situations. Being well trained in Latin and Greek and eager to study philosophy, she was ideally qualified to understand and share in his life work. (For years she transcribed his manuscripts, which no one else could

[4] PFT 198.

[5] *Ibid.* During his student days he attended a fair sampling of universities. We learn from WW 172 that "in 1901 and 1902 [he undertook] studies in jurisprudence in Heidelberg and Munich, and then the study of medicine in Berlin, Göttingen, and Heidelberg."

read.) Above all, their conversations attained an ideal seldom recognized as even possible: a straightforward, frank, and unreserved expression of beliefs honestly held. Even mutual criticisms could be carried on in the candid but sympathetic spirit in which reasonable and intelligent men who prefer knowledge to delusion privately criticize their own thoughts and deeds. "It was only with my wife," he says, "that I entered on the road of . . . lifelong, imperfectible, unreserved, and therefore inexhaustible communication."[6] During the 1920's it was her brother, Dr. Ernst Mayer, M.D., who contributed greatly to the improvement of his *magnum opus* by carefully studying the manuscripts and telephoning his critical suggestions from Berlin to Heidelberg.

Meanwhile, in a manner somewhat reminiscent of the career of William James, Jaspers proceeded step by step from medicine through psychiatry and psychology to philosophy. In 1909 he became a voluntary Research Assistant at Heidelberg Psychiatric Hospital—a position which provided an opportunity for the thorough studies that culminated in the publication in 1913 of the book that made his reputation as an authority on psychiatry, viz. the *Allgemeine Psychopathologie*. This book, the fourth edition of which was completely revised by 1942, though not published until after the war, undertook to clarify the various methods of psychiatry, with especial emphasis upon the phenomenology of the early Husserl,[7] and to introduce psychiatrists to Dilthey's method of "understanding" (*Verstehen*) and its usefulness within a "descriptive and analytical psychology."[8] The speculations of the specialists in the field seemed to him to be "mere talk without real knowledge,"[9] and he objected

[6] PFT 300.

[7] When, in 1913, Jaspers asked Husserl what phenomenology was and what it signified philosophically, Husserl replied: "You employ the method excellently. Just proceed as before. You do not at all need to know what it is. That is really a difficult matter." PE I, xvii.

[8] See APT 303, n. 1.   [9] PFT 210.

5

strongly to the exclusiveness of the various schools of psychiatry.

In 1913, with recommendations from Max Weber, the Heidelberg sociologist, and Oswald Külpe, formerly leader of the school of imageless thought, now settled in Munich, he received a teaching appointment as a psychologist within the Heidelberg philosophical faculty under Wilhelm Windelband. Gradually his interest in the understanding of various points of view led to a series of lectures that reached fruition in the *Psychologie der Weltanschauungen* which appeared in print shortly after the First World War. In this youthful work, glowing with enthusiasm, but hastily written, carelessly revised, and not completely thought out, appeared what he later came to regard as the first twentieth-century work in *Existenzphilosophie,* and the basis of his future thinking.[10] Here, in connection with the various typical world-views, appear discussions of extreme (or "ultimate") situations, freedom, Existenz, nihilism, protective shells, love, mysticism, the demonic, and the like.

It is not surprising that neither Windelband, who died in 1915, nor Rickert, who succeeded him, were sympathetic to so unorthodox a standpoint—especially when it was advocated by a medical man with no formal training in philosophy. Jaspers, however, who had set his hopes for philosophy on the sort of frank and uninhibited communication that we find in the Platonic dialogues, and who regarded deceitful evasion of fundamental issues as shameless and unpardonable betrayal of the truth, irritated his colleagues by insisting that scientific philosophy was impossible, and that no philosophical propositions could ever be universal and necessary. And as though this weren't enough, he undiplomatically drove his point home by telling Rickert that "his theses were by no means compelling for everyone, least of all his 'value system.' "[11] After the death in 1920 of the celebrated sociologist, Max Weber, a friend whom Jaspers

[10] PFT 221.   [11] PFT 224.

regarded as a profound thinker and "the greatest German of our age,"[12] the breach was finalized when, in connection with a eulogy which Jaspers had given at the behest of the student body, Rickert described Weber as his own disciple, belittled his accomplishments, and denied that he was in any sense a philosopher. When Jaspers was finally made a full professor at Heidelberg (after turning down offers from Greifswald and Kiel), it was at the insistence of the appointment committee and the general faculty, and in spite of the efforts of Rickert and the other professionals to block his advancement.

During the next decade Jaspers was too busy developing his philosophy to publish even a minimal number of books and articles, and people were inclined to believe that, having arrived at his academic goal, he had chosen to enjoy the easy indolence of the frail and socially irresponsible intellectual.[13] Though the students found him most stimulating and came to him in large numbers, his professional rivals treated him as an interloper. As he wrote in 1957: "While Rickert in his lectures delighted—and sometimes angered—the students by attacking me, I taught as if the other academic philosophers did not exist. I never assailed my colleagues. I felt I was on the right track, on the whole, even though beset by doubts."[14]

In December 1931 the situation changed radically. *Die geistige Situation der Zeit* (subsequently published in English as *Man in the Modern Age*) appeared as the one-thousandth volume in the Göschen series of paperbacks. And almost simultaneously *Philosophie*, his *magnum opus*,[15] became available under the dateline of 1932. This latter book consisted of three substantial volumes, each of which pre-

[12] MWT 189.
[13] From 1923 to 1931 Jaspers published nothing at all. See WW 181.
[14] PFT 231-32.
[15] In an afterword added to the third edition of his *Philosophie*, written almost a quarter of a century after the first edition had appeared, he described this work as "his favorite among all his writings" (*das liebste meiner Bücher*). PE I (3d ed., 1955), p. xv.

sented one of the main methods which Jaspers believed to have been employed by philosophers from the very beginning. The first volume, entitled *Philosophische Weltorientierung,* by demarcating the limits of science, provides awareness of the sharp contrast between the objective knowledge which is universal and necessary and the indemonstrable convictions that constitute philosophical faith. The second, *Existenzerhellung,* elucidates the potentialities of man, and appeals to him to exercise his freedom in actualizing them. *Metaphysik,* the third volume, tells of attitudes and of intellectual procedures, both negative and positive, which converge upon God, or, as he would say, upon "Transcendence." Shortly thereafter, Jaspers began to overshadow his colleagues at Heidelberg, and the intellectual climate became charged with an awareness of a new direction in philosophy. People spoke of "Existenz" rather than the "soul," and Jaspers' students began to hear of the modes of the encompassing (*die Weisen des Umgreifenden*) soon to be presented to the public in the Groningen lectures of 1935. *Existenzphilosophie* had come of age.

Soon the Nazi terror erupted, and for twelve years the threat of the concentration camp was personified by the omnipresent secret police. In 1933 Jaspers was excluded from all administrative duties at the University, though permitted to continue to lecture to his large classes; in 1937 he was denied the right to teach, though allowed to draw a modest pension.[16] When, a year later, he was forbidden to publish, he had to pursue his scholarly task alone, with little hope of ever finding an audience. That during this awful time he was able to revise his *Psychopathologie,* prepare the first one-thousand page volume of his projected three-volume *Logik,* and write an equally lengthy account of certain of the great philosophers (in addition to elaborate preparations for further volumes to come) shows what can be achieved even under intolerable circumstances.

[16] PFT 267.

As the disastrous war continued, difficulties multiplied. "What I planned in 1941," he writes, "has only been accomplished in part. The years that followed . . . sapped my ability to work and finally made work impossible. After 1945 the problems of the day supervened. The philosophical work remained in the background."[17] Actually it was touch and go for this uncompromising professor and his Jewish wife. As he tells us laconically in his *Memoir*: "Our deportation [to an extermination camp], as we learned from the police by way of the customary indiscretions, was scheduled for April 14, 1945; other transports had left in the preceding weeks. On April 1, Heidelberg was occupied by the Americans."[18]

Though offered the rectorship of the University and asked to be Minister of Education, his poor health stood in the way, and he resumed teaching and writing. In 1946 appeared *Die Schuldfrage* (translated by E. B. Ashton as *The Question of German Guilt*); in 1947, *Von der Wahrheit* (*On Truth*, still untranslated) which he had written during the Nazi era; and in 1948, as though to signalize his move to Switzerland, *Der philosophische Glaube* (translated by Ralph Manheim as *The Perennial Scope of Philosophy*), six guest-lectures presented at the University of Basel. In 1957 the first huge volume of his *Die grossen Philosophen* (appearing in Manheim's translation as the first two volumes of *The Great Philosophers*) showed him to be a superb historian of philosophy.

Things finally turned out well for this semi-invalid who escaped death from illness in his thirties to be rejected as incompetent and ostracized by his colleagues in his forties, condemned to oblivion by the Nazis in his fifties, and, with his wife, selected for routine extermination in his sixties. According to a recent reckoning that appeared in 1963, in a *Festschrift* published in honor of his eightieth birthday, 120,000 copies of the book on the atom bomb (1958), including translations into Italian, French, and English were

---

[17] UPT 158.   [18] PFT 266.

9

sold. Altogether the German editions of his works have sold nearly one million copies. Translations have appeared in 160 editions and in no less than sixteen languages.[19] In 1966 appeared his critical study of the present German state (*Wohin treibt die Bundesrepublik?*) followed by the above-mentioned lengthy reply to his critics.[20] Probably much will appear posthumously. If his early years remind us of the career of William James, his later years may well suggest the last decades in the life of John Dewey. Existentialism, like instrumentalism, is a revolt against the sterile academic philosophies that are indifferent to the affairs of life, and an affirmation of the power of man freely to transform himself and create a better world.

[19] WW 13-14.

[20] *Antwort zur Kritik meiner Schrift: Wohin treibt die Bundesrepublik?* (Munich: R. Piper, 1967), 233 pp.

chapter one

Introduction: Disputed Topics

Heirs to the tradition deriving from Locke and his enlightened followers tend to be antipathetic to the varieties of philosophy that have appeared on the Continent—whether idealistic, materialistic, or existentialistic. Ideologically the English Channel is, as it were, wider than the Atlantic Ocean, and one might even say that the same climate of opinion that unites the Americans with the English alienates both from the turbulent atmosphere of Continental thought. British and American followers of Wittgenstein and Austin, for instance, who are sufficiently ethnocentric to find it natural, as one English writer does, to identify "modern philosophy" with "that present-day version of our traditional empiricism which is known as linguistic analysis"[1] have remarkably little in common with the exponents of *Existenzphilosophie*[2] who believe with Karl Jaspers that "the contemporary philosophical situation is determined by the fact that two philosophers, Kierkegaard and Nietzsche . . . have continually grown in significance . . . [and] stand today unquestioned as the authentically great thinkers of their age."[3] Intellectual leaders but a few miles apart live in quite different worlds and "do philosophy" or philosophize, as the case may be, with astonishing indifference to each other. This is acknowledged at once by the above-quoted empiricist when she

[1] "Metaphysics and Ethics," in *The Nature of Metaphysics*, ed. D. F. Pears (London: Macmillan, 1957), p. 99.

[2] However many thinkers may have sought to preempt this term, I have chosen to reserve it for Jaspers' philosophy, as does W. Kaufmann in his *Existentialism from Dostoevsky to Sartre* (New York: Meridian, 1956), pp. 22, 131. While Jaspers, like Heidegger, sometimes denies that he is an "existentialist," the little book in which, just before the outbreak of war, he presented his own view was called *Existenzphilosophie* (Berlin: Gruyter, 1938).

[3] VET 23-24.

turns her attention to Sartre. "The 'world' of Ryle's *The Concept of Mind*," Iris Murdock writes, "is the world in which people play cricket, cook cakes, make simple decisions, remember their childhood and go to the circus; not the Existentialist world in which they commit sins, fall in love, say prayers or join the Communist Party."[4]

Gaining acquaintance with the world of the existentialists requires considerable orientation, especially on the part of representatives of other standpoints who must proceed *ab extra*. However sympathetic such readers may be, still the insights that they encounter first are bound to seem strained and far-fetched until they can be placed within the mental context that constitutes their proper setting. Meanwhile this enveloping whole, being composed of these insights in addition to a great many still to come, is not initially available at all. This difficulty, known on the Continent as the "hermeneutic circle,"[5] is, of course, unavoidable. The reader can only hope, by gaining partial insights and patiently bringing them together, gradually to constitute the necessary whole.

If acquisition of the context required to make existentialism at least tentatively thinkable is difficult and slow, momentary exclusion, somewhat after the manner of Descartes, of disturbing preconceptions can be comparatively easy. One can for a time, in other words, experimentally call into question, or "bracket out"[6] some of the familiar views that obscure and distort the existentialist outlook. Such a move in the direction of sympathetic understanding would seem to be especially necessary when one is confronted by an original thinker who, like Socrates, requires a radical questioning of entrenched beliefs. Naturally *Existenzphilosophie* makes no sense when taken together with the very doc-

---

[4] *Sartre: Romantic Rationalist* (New Haven: Yale University Press, 1959), p. 42.

[5] Richard Palmer, *Hermeneutics* (Evanston, Ill.: Northwestern University Press, 1969), p. 118.

[6] See, for example, Herbert Spiegelberg, *The Phenomenological Movement* (The Hague, Holland: Martinus Nijhoff, 1960), p. 135.

trines which it denies, including, as it happens, several currently fashionable views which, through the medium of textbooks, anthologies, college outline series, and the like, have come to be taken for granted by an entire generation of students. It must be emphasized, however, that something less than refutation is here intended. The philosophies which Jaspers rejects are of course not houses of cards which collapse at a touch, and one cannot in a single chapter—in part for reasons which this chapter offers—demonstrate the falsity of half a dozen widely accepted views. In this introduction it must suffice to point out that none of the views here in question are sacrosanct, that all of them can meaningfully be criticized, that the existentialists who contest them have their reasons for doing so, and that, in contesting them they are, as a rule, in excellent company. To accomplish this much is, I believe, considerably to facilitate the understanding of Jaspers' philosophy.

Philosophy and Life

That philosophy should deal with life's problems is of course a very old-fashioned doctrine, and the reasons why ambitious academicians are chary of it are now generally known. Philosophy can only measure up to rational cognitive standards, and the techniques used in "doing philosophy" can only be reliable and teachable so long as philosophy is assigned to some limited field within which confirmation and disconfirmation are possible.

At the same time, philosophy's past cannot be ignored. "We find in some of the earliest philosophers, . . ." as Walter Kaufmann reminds us, "a striking unity of life and thought. . . . In the Socratic schools and in Stoicism a little later, philosophy is above all a way of life."[7] The same, of course, could be said of the Epicureans. And for nearly two millennia Christian thinkers have assumed the relevance of philosophy to far-reaching human issues.

Even in Anglo-American countries today one may note a

[7] *Existentialism from Dostoevsky to Sartre*, p. 12.

general reluctance to admit that philosophy has become effete. Many of the introductory textbooks in the field receive such honorific titles as *The Enduring Questions* (Rader), *The Things that Matter Most* (Flewelling), *Living Issues in Philosophy* (Titus), and *Philosophies Men Live By* (Davidson), or conceal behind as uninformative a title as *A Modern Introduction to Philosophy* a large number of classic pronouncements on such traditional topics as freedom, the mind or soul, God, and *a priori* knowledge (Edwards and Pap). The big questions are now as importunate as ever.

Jaspers does not believe that today's philosophers can meaningfully continue in the pre-Kantian manner: "To answer the question of the nature of ultimate reality by providing a picture or conceptual construct of the world in its entirety is, and has always been, a mistake,"[8] he says. But whatever our methodological innovations, philosophy need not relinquish its concern with the traditional problems, turning them over for consideration to preachers of innumerable faiths, self-appointed sages and seers, and those unscrupulous representatives of exotic cults who prey upon the poor in spirit. Since the "death of God,"[9] which the masses are now belatedly discovering,[10] philosophy alone is left to provide a suitable foundation for the lives of "the great mass of denominationally nonbelieving youth."[11] The faith for which philosophy's martyrs (including Socrates, Boethius, Bruno) were willing to die is not outmoded. Jaspers would still subscribe, with minor modifications at most, to the enthusiastic accolade which as a young man he placed near the beginning of his first philosophical treatise:

> Philosophy has always been more than universal contemplation: it has provided impulses, erected tables of

[8] NET 287.

[9] Friedrich Nietzsche, *Thus Spoke Zarathustra* (1883). In Walter Kaufmann, *The Portable Nietzsche* (New York: Viking, 1954), p. 124.

[10] See "Toward a Hidden God" (Cover Story), *Time*, April 8, 1966, pp. 82-87.

[11] PFT 293.

values, given human life its meaning and goal, offered man
a world within which he could feel secure, and, in a word,
furnished a weltanschauung. . . . Philosophers have not
been idle and irresponsible observers, but movers and re-
formers of the world.[12]

Philosophy is not the property of any single group; it is "for
everyman,"[13] and "philosophers are, as it were, only the
creators and keepers of the archives. . . ."[14] "There is no
escape from philosophy. The question is only whether a
philosophy is conscious or not, whether it is good or bad,
muddled or clear. Anyone who rejects philosophy is himself
unconsciously practising a philosophy."[15] And finally, whoever I may be, philosophy concerns me profoundly, for it
enters into my very being: it constitutes "the truth which I
not only think about, but live with, which I not merely know
but am convinced of and actualize; the truth which, far
from being a mere possibility for thought, is reconfirmed
whenever it is actualized."[16]

The Pre-eminence of the Contemporary

The present, for obvious psychological reasons, tends to
assume precedence over the past. "Every moment," says
Hegel, meaning every present outlook, "being a moment of
the essential process of reality, must [logically] arrive at the
stage where it comes to look upon itself as the sole repre-
sentative of the essential process."[17] And Hegel himself
appears to have regarded his own system as the completion
of all that went before. William James remarked that when
pragmatism triumphed, old-fashioned philosophers (whom
he called those of the "ultra-rationalistic type") would be
"frozen out."[18] Husserl was downright contemptuous of the

---

[12] PY 2.   [13] Title of KST.   [14] KST 120.
[15] EPT 12.   [16] PE II, 114.
[17] Quoted and translated by J. Loewenberg in *Hegel's Phenomenology: Dialogues on the Life of Mind* (La Salle, Ill.: Open Court, 1965),
pp. 153-54.
[18] "What Pragmatism Means," *Essays in Pragmatism*, ed. Alburey
Castell (New York: Hafner, 1948), p. 145.

15

unscientific essays of all pre-phenomenological thinkers, and frank to say that prior to the revolution which he himself inaugurated philosophy had accomplished nothing.[19] When the *Wiener Kreis*, ignoring pragmatism as well as Husserl's phenomenology, promoted a revolution of their own, they plumed themselves upon having "the tools to solve those problems that in earlier times [had] been the subject of guess-work only."[20] And P. F. Strawson would seem to express a similar attitude on the part of his colleagues when he writes: "The gains and advances made [by English philosophers] in the dozen years which followed the war were probably as great as any which have been made in an equivalent period in the history of the subject. A new level of refinement and accuracy in conceptual awareness has been reached."[21] This self-congratulatory pride in present achievement has been considerably heightened by increased professional-ization, requiring, as it does, that philosophic problems be tackled by knowledgeable and unbiased experts, skilled in the use of rigorous methods, and ready to submit their judgments to the criticism of their peers.[22]

Claims such as these have seldom, if ever, stood the test of history. The idealists who aroused James's indignation were never quite "frozen out," while the phenomenology of Husserl (never prominent on the American scene) is best known to most of us through the existentialism of Heideg-ger and Sartre. The logical empiricism of the *Wiener Kreis*, having, as they say, "run its course" (or "spent its force"), has been consigned to its place in the recent past (*De mortuis nil nisi bonum!*). And, somewhat oddly, the suc-cess of linguistic analysis in dealing with its critics seems

[19] See Quentin Lauer's Introduction to E. Husserl, *Phenomenology and the Crisis of Philosophy*, trans. Quentin Lauer (New York: Har-per and Row, 1965), pp. 4, 34.

[20] Hans Reichenbach, *The Rise of Scientific Philosophy* (Berkeley: University of California Press, 1951), p. vii.

[21] As quoted in Ved Mehta, "Onward and Upward with the Arts," *The New Yorker*, December 9, 1961, p. 126.

[22] See G. J. Warnock, *English Philosophy Since 1900* (New York: Oxford University Press, 1966), chap. xiii.

to derive in large part from a growing disunity which no longer allows it to present a clear target. It appears that, as Ved Mehta says, "the Oxford school is breaking up. . . . There isn't going to be an orthodoxy much longer. . . ."[23]

Jaspers' attitude toward this situation can be summarized as follows. The overbearing confidence of philosophy's leaders is not surprising, for everyone must have some view or other, and to *have* a view is to be convinced that that view is true. But since there are many views, the probability of the truth of any given view is minimal. There is, as Wilhelm Dilthey saw, an "antinomy between the claim of every philosophical Weltanschauung to universal validity, and the historical consciousness of the variety of such Weltanschauugen."[24] Or, in Jaspers' words: "While one must invariably *have* a standpoint if he is to think at all, one can never accept the objective validity which every standpoint claims."[25] It is *science* rather than philosophy that offers "compellingly certain and universally recognized insights."[26] To those who find such relativistic fallibilism incompatible with any sustaining faith or firm commitment, Jaspers says: "Humans do not find it impossible but only infinitely difficult psychologically . . . to carry out their own beliefs and at the same time to accept as valid for others what is invalid for them."[27]

Confidence in the supremacy of the present derives largely from pressing an indefensible analogy. That science has made steady progress and that the science of today sublates and surpasses that of all previous times is undeniable. But in philosophy it is typical that "the new is not encompassed in what went before. The successor often relinquishes the essence of the earlier thought, sometimes he no longer even understands it."[28] In fact, the history of philosophy is more like that of art than of science. As in art, certain lines of development, certain periods and schools are discernible.

[23] "Onward and Upward with the Arts," p. 158. Cf. pp. 72, 123.
[24] Werner Brock, *An Introduction to Contemporary German Philosophy* (Cambridge: Cambridge University Press, 1935), p. 25.
[25] PE II, 124.   [26] EPT 7.   [27] VW 974.
[28] EPT 140.

17

"For example: from Socrates to Plato and Aristotle, from Kant to Hegel, from Locke to Hume." Furthermore, "the history of philosophy resembles the history of art in that its supreme works are irreplaceable and unique."[29] Like art it goes through periods of decadence.[30] And success in philosophy depends less upon rigorous training than upon talent.

If the progress of science suggests a staircase, the procession of philosophies resembles a chain of hills and valleys. "We are far more advanced than Hippocrates, the Greek physician. But we are scarcely entitled to say that we have progressed beyond Plato. We have advanced beyond his materials, beyond the scientific findings of which he made use. In philosophy itself we have scarcely regained his level."[31]

Philosophy, unlike religion, has no institutional embodiment, and no one should have the effrontery to ask to be known as a philosopher. Rather, "the reality of philosophy is the great philosophers themselves. What we call their doctrine permeated their lives and comes to life again in those who hear what they have to say."[32] They "encourage us and make us humble. [They] want no disciples, but men who are themselves."[33] "Wherever men engage in philosophical thinking, an acceptance of the great philosophers and their works—similar to the canon of the Holy Scriptures—takes shape. . . . It is in their company . . . that we can attain to what we ourselves are capable of being."[34] "It is only through these men that we can enter into the core of philosophy. . . . They are like eternal contemporaries."[35]

The Philosophical Unavailability of Clarity

"Our discussion will be adequate," says Aristotle, "if it has as much clearness as the subject matter admits of. . . . It is the mark of an educated man to look for precision in each class of things just so far as the nature of the subject

[29] *Ibid.* [30] EPT 141. [31] EPT 8.
[32] GPT I, xi. [33] GPT I, x. [34] GPT I, ix.
[35] GPT I, viii.

18

admits. . . ."[36] Nevertheless, modern thinkers have repeatedly singled out clarity (sometimes adding distinctness) as an indispensable criterion of truth or significance. During the prewar years, instrumentalists, operationists, and logical positivists championed a kind of conceptual clarification suggestive of Hume's empiristic skepticism and Peirce's early "pragmaticism." And when existentialists entered the picture after the war, English philosophers began to dismiss them with such condescending comments as: "The thing wrong with the Existentialists . . . is that they haven't had their noses rubbed in the necessity of saying exactly what they mean."[37]

As though one *could* always say exactly what he meant! "Clarity," unfortunately, badly needs to be clarified. It is an unusually obscure term, and, in the opinion of some authorities, impossible to define. Originally metaphorical, it relates first of all to the well-illuminated, unclouded, transparent, pellucid, brilliant, lustrous, and shining.[38] Thus conceived, it quite naturally suggests the "illumination" or "elucidation" which Jaspers strives for throughout his lengthy *Existenzerhellung*. But this is not what is meant in English-speaking countries.

Clarity as understood by Hume, Peirce, and their followers, i.e., a clarity achieved through precise definition, or a formal system of logical signs,[39] is, says Jaspers, a scientific rather than a philosophical ideal. It is to be found in phenomena and the logical and mathematical tools used in dealing with phenomena, but it is not a possible characteristic of the cognitive vehicles by which we approach the transcendent. Jaspers' position on this matter derives directly from the latter part of Kant's first critique. Just as Berkeley abandons "ideas" for "notions" when he passes from science to theology, so Jaspers emulates Kant in dismissing all "concepts of the understanding" in favor of the "ideas of rea-

---

[36] *Nicomachean Ethics*, Bk. I, chap. iii.
[37] Ved Mehta, p. 106.
[38] See my *Philosophical Theory and Psychological Fact* (Tucson, Ariz.: University of Arizona Press, 1961), pp. 122-31.
[39] VW 463.

son" when he passes from scientific knowledge of empirical objects to the "nonknowledge" of philosophical faith in the noumenal, the psychical, and the divine.

To begin with the noumenal, it is obvious that if there are things existing wholly by themselves and outside of the mind (e.g., the earth before life appeared on it, inexperienceable electrons, material substances underlying the qualities that we can discover), we cannot conceive of them clearly. As Hume was quick to see: "Nature has kept us at a great distance from all her secrets, and has afforded us only the knowledge of a few superficial qualities of objects, while she conceals from us those powers and principles on which the influence of these objects entirely depends."[40] Or, in Kantian terms, "ideas of reason" are inevitably vague and indefinite. As A. C. Ewing explains, to pass beyond the appearances of sense is to exchange "determinate knowledge" for "indeterminate thought":

> We do not know anything about things-in-themselves except that they exist, but we can do what might be described as thinking them in a sort of way. . . . Again, we have no knowledge of them according to the categories but we can and must use the categories in thinking of them, however indeterminate and formal this use must inevitably be. Vague ideas are undesirable and unphilosophical where we can have clearer and more definite ones, but in some cases indeterminate ideas may be the best we have.[41]

As Kant insisted, clarity appears only within the limits of the scientifically knowable. We can have only the most vague and indefinite awareness of " 'the thing in itself,' the intelligible or noumenal world. Our understanding does not tell us whether it is or even whether it is possible. We can con-

---

[40] *Inquiry Concerning Human Understanding* (New York: Liberal Arts Press, 1955), p. 47.

[41] *A Short Commentary on Kant's Critique of Pure Reason* (Chicago, Ill.: University of Chicago Press, 1950), p. 188.

ceive of the boundary, but not pass beyond it. . . . As thought we are confined to consciousness as such."[42]

This applies *a fortiori* to judgments concerning the mind, soul, or spirit. Descartes, in his passion for mathematical clarity, "overlooked the fact that there is a certainty which in no way implies clarity and distinctness. A magnificent example of this is the foundation of his own philosophy. His *cogito ergo sum* is a certainty, but its content is vague and both its principle and its object are utterly devoid of clarity and distinctness."[43] The self which Hume repeatedly alludes to but claims to be unable to discover, the pure ego or Thinker which, according to William James, tends to evaporate to the estate of pure diaphaneity, the transcendental unity of apperception which, in the Kantian scheme of things is presupposed by but not observable in all experience—this inner nucleus, whatever it may be called, is not given, and not clearly describable. We may know *that* it is, but not *what* it is, and any attempt to conceive it clearly is futile. When I talk about my *self*, I quite literally do not (in the strict sense of the word) know what I am talking about. Jaspers' position, as he suggests in his youthful work on weltanschauungen,[44] is virtually that of Socrates who, when discussing immortality with his disciples immediately prior to his execution, exchanged literal for vague and mythical language, on the ground that, as he expresses it: "A man of sense ought not to say . . . that the description which I have given of the soul and her mansions is exactly true. But I do say that, inasmuch as the soul is shown to be immortal, he may venture to think . . . that something of the kind is true."[45]

When the Philo of Hume's dialogues remarks that since "our ideas reach no farther than our experience: We have no

---

[42] GPT I, 280.   [43] DPT 101.
[44] PY 385.
[45] Plato, "Phaedo," in *The Dialogues of Plato*, trans. B. Jowett (2 vols.; New York: Random House, 1937), I, 498.

experience of divine attributes and operations,"[46] he states very well the upshot of Jaspers' negative theology. God is not a scientific concept but a religious idea. It is no longer possible to believe, as Spinoza once did, that "the idea of God which is in us is adequate and perfect."[47] God differs so markedly from everything finite that we have no reason to attribute to Him any of the finite predicates which the human intellect can entertain. Things in the world are directly accessible. "But the one God is distant, the wholly other, absolutely hidden. Hence it is not only easy, but for the understanding and sensuous experience almost mandatory to deny Him. He cannot be inferred from any particular appearance or perceived in any specific object. Everything points to Him and derives from Him, but even this is incomprehensible."[48] "Even if there could be a direct experience of the one God, this would be incommunicable. . . ."[49] In the end, "the field is held by the negative theology that tells us what God is not —to wit, He is not something that stands in finite form before the eyes or the mind."[50] What cannot be known, however, is present to me through faith: "Here cognition ceases, but not thought. By technically applying my knowledge I can act outwardly, but nonknowledge makes possible an inner action by which I transform myself."[51] And this inner transformation is all-important: "Only transcendence can make this questionable life good, the world beautiful, and existence itself a fulfilment."[52]

The Role of Demonstration in Philosophy

It is commonly claimed that philosophers, *qua* philosophers, rest their contentions upon logical inferences from unquestionable facts. Whatever they think and say is subject to rigid standards vouched for by the most rational of methods.

[46] Hume, "Dialogues Concerning Natural Religion," in *Hume: Selections*, ed. Charles W. Hendel, Jr. (New York: Scribners, 1927), p. 302.
[47] *Ethics*, Bk. V, Prop. XVIII.   [48] VW 1049-50.
[49] VW 1051.   [50] PHT 33.   [51] EPT 127.
[52] EPT 126.

"Metaphysicians," says B.A.O. Williams, "do not just assert their positions. They attempt to support them by argument, and to give proofs for their conclusions." It is this that "chiefly distinguishes the philosophical metaphysician from the mystic, the moralist, and others. . . ."[53] In similar spirit, a currently popular textbook tells us that the philosopher normally asks in connection with any statement relating to his field: "What are the grounds for believing it? . . . Do we have good grounds for believing it?"[54]

It is odd that philosophers should lay this flattering unction to their souls, for it is sheer bluff. Neither in daily life, in science, nor in philosophy can the most crucial matters be made to rest exclusively upon proof. At the level of everyday existence we simply assume, and could never prove, that members of our own families are not automata and that they care for us, that—Descartes and the extreme behaviorists to the contrary—our domestic animals are conscious of our presence and capable of returning our affections, that, within certain limits, we can trust our memories, and so on. All of us are, as James said of his students, "chock-full of some faith or other. . . ."[55] As Locke was quick to see: "He that, in the ordinary affairs of life, would admit of nothing but direct plain demonstration, would be sure of nothing in this world but of perishing quickly."[56]

Scientific thought, to be sure, makes use of logical principles, but it is not bound by them. Frequently, as everyone recognizes, the scientist performs a so-called inductive leap to unsupported hypotheses, fallaciously affirms the consequent when arguing from prediction, and frankly rests his case upon unproved but necessary presuppositions. What cannot be proved (the maxim of parsimony, limited variety, et

---

[53] "Metaphysical Arguments," in *Metaphysics*, ed. Charles A. Balis (New York: Macmillan, 1965), p. 108.

[54] Elmer Sprague, Paul W. Taylor, et al., eds., *Knowledge and Value* (New York: Harcourt Brace, 1959), p. 303.

[55] *Essays in Pragmatism*, p. 94.

[56] *An Essay Concerning Human Understanding* (New York: Everyman, 1948), p. 307.

cetera) must be postulated, or, as Reichenbach would have it, "posited." In Jaspers' terms: "A [scientific] truth which I can prove . . . depends on finite premises and methods. . . ."[57] Although it is "universally valid, it remains relative to method and assumptions. . . ."[58] It is objective but not absolute.

The unavailability of strict proof is even more obvious when we continue in the direction of increasing generality. A world-view can no more afford to rest its case upon learned argument than can a revealed religion. Viewed scientifically, a metaphysical system is, as Stephen Pepper has urged for years, simply a "world hypothesis," the truth of which can never be proved.

In a word, whether we proceed at the level of common sense, of science, or of speculative philosophy, we cannot hope to rest more than a fraction of our beliefs upon any defensible sort of demonstration. In Humian language, knowledge of relations of ideas provides no access to matters of fact and existence. Logic stops short before reality: "Highly developed insight into the logical connections of the meanings of statements . . . still finds that logical rigor invariably ceases at the point at which the thing itself (*die Sache selbst*) appears. Truth lies in that which for logical analysis is always contained in the presuppositions. . . ."[59]

Jaspers' position, then, is at this point similar to that taken by F. Waismann in his well-known article, "How I See Philosophy."[60] "Proof" and "refutation" are "dying words in philosophy,"[61] says Waismann. While it cannot be proved that there are no proofs in philosophy, still it is a revealing exercise "to write down lists of propositions 'proved' by Plato or Kant."[62] Experience leads to a "somewhat shocking conclusion: that the thing cannot be done. No philosopher has ever proved anything. The whole claim is spuri-

[57] PHT 4.   [58] EPT 162.   [59] VW 605.
[60] *Contemporary British Philosophy: Third Series*, ed. H. D. Lewis (New York: Macmillan, 1956), p. 471.
[61] *Ibid.*, p. 447.   [62] *Ibid.*, p. 448.

ous. . . . Philosophic arguments are not deductive; therefore they are not rigorous; and therefore they don't prove anything."[63]

Since logic, in spite of its obvious incapacities, arouses immense expectations, it presents an opportunity for an appalling amount of intellectual chicanery, as the ancient sophists were quick to discover.[64] "Logical argument, laying claim to compelling certainty, appears to provide material truth. Formal argument is an accommodating instrument: ever since the sophists men have been aware that they can always find grounds by which to prove or disprove anything at all."[65] Socrates' maieutic method and intuition of essence (*Wesensschau*)[66] were calculated to cope with an otherwise insufferable situation. Using the logical methods available at the time, "philosophers generally contradicted each other and based mutually exclusive conclusions upon equally pertinent evidence. . . . Following after Zeno the Eleatic they developed eristic. . . . Formal logic was created. The mere manipulation of concepts took the place of insight, and formal calculation replaced knowledge."[67] Logic proves that nothing—and everything—can be proved by logic. "If one is unwilling to look [beyond logic] to intuition for his grounds, then his logic can only deny. . . . This continues until nothing remains but a negatively defined concept. . . ."[68]

This is not to say that argument is futile. "To philosophize is to think,"[69] and "In all thinking (*Denken*) we argue. . . ."[70] This is the form that thought naturally assumes. But the

---

[63] *Ibid.*, p. 471. While the longer statement from which these excerpts are taken seems to leave no doubt as to where Waismann stands on this point, we do find him slipping into the old way of thinking when, on p. 68 of *Principles of Linguistic Philosophy* (New York: St. Martin's Press, 1965) he tells us that "whoever will maintain that a particular proposition is a synthetic a priori judgment has to demonstrate in a precise way that it cannot be deduced from mere conventions as to the use of language." Of course we cannot require impossibilities even of those with whom we most strongly disagree.

[64] PY 213. [65] VW 473. [66] PY 214.
[67] PY 213-14. [68] *Ibid.* [69] GPT II, 56.
[70] VW 569.

limitations of logical argument should be kept constantly in mind:

1. As Hegel and his followers have insisted, in the absence of a suitable "universe of discourse" or "climate of opinion" —here Jaspers would prefer to speak of a Kantian "idea"— no train of thought can be logically compelling. "In every successful conquest of truth, the argument proceeds within an encompassing context which accounts for its truth and indicates its limitations. Apart from such a context the argument is arbitrary and interminable."[71]

2. In logical arguments it is the form rather than the content which yields cognitive security. That is why logic provides validity rather than truth. "Logical argument as compelling certainty [merely] simulates material truth."[72] Without intuition logical concepts are empty. "The give-and-take between vital intuition and fixating, enervating, stultifying thought shows the rationally inclined person that he must constantly return to the fuller, more dynamic, vibrant, and unconceptualized intuition. When he fails to do this, his awareness of things becomes limited and inflexible, and, caught up in rigid concepts, it dies."[73]

3. Questions of right and wrong are not to be settled by argument. "I can only argue against a law with a new law. . . . Such argumentation concerning legal generalities is intrinsically arbitrary. It has neither direction nor content apart from present Existenz."[74]

4. Furthermore, argument relates only to things in the world. "All confirmation and disconfirmation, proof and categorial fixation through rational means occur in the world and are irrelevant to Existenz."[75] Neither do logical arguments concern Providence or the world as a whole. It is foolish to believe in the absolute power of proof in all things, "as

[71] *Ibid.*   [72] VW 473.   [73] PY 212.
[74] PE II, 332.   [75] PE II, 21. Cf. p. 5.

though either religious mysteries or political conflicts could be settled by disputations!"[76]

5. The frequent futility of actual philosophic disputes is signalized by their interminability. Since every philosophic question is hopelessly intricate, such debates are never concluded on any rational basis, but simply terminated when they threaten to lead to the hopeless tedium of "endless reflection." In *Reason and Existenz* Jaspers points out the dangers of "reasoning without restraint," which he characterizes as "boundless," "empty," "unending," and "endless."[77] Reflection can lead to "complete ruin" when it is undertaken for the sake of amusement, or self-justification (*Rechthabenwollen*). "Reflection cannot exhaust or stop itself. It is faithless since it hinders every decision. It is never finished and, in the end, can become 'dialectical twaddle': in this respect [Kierkegaard] called it the poison of reflection. ... Anything can mean something else for reflection."[78]

Rational argument is indispensable but treacherous. Everything depends upon the user and his intentions. As Plato says, the crucial distinction is not that between supporting a view with logical argument and failing to do so; it is between serious and responsible reasoning carried on with a view to the truth, and frivolous argument undertaken for philosophically extraneous purposes. Surely he had in mind emotional and intellectual maturity rather than mere chronological age when he advised against introducing students to dialectic during adolescence when, like puppy dogs, they care only for amusement, and added that "when a man begins to get older, he will no longer be guilty of such insanity [but] will imitate the dialectician who is seeking for

[76] GPT II, 149.

[77] VET 31, 127-28. In the original the terms used are *"Räsonnieren ohne Bindung," "grenzenlos," "leer," "unendlich,"* and *"endlos."* Pp. 11f, 93.

[78] VET 31.

27

truth, and not the eristic, who is contradicting for the sake of amusement. . . ."[79]

The game of words which sophists enjoy becomes serious when used as an instrument in a social or political struggle. Ceasing to be a mere distraction it becomes a contest aiming at self-aggrandizement at the expense of all competitors. "The mere will to live," as we were told in 1947, "uses all fundamental principles capriciously and almost interchangeably as arguments that serve simply to promote the purposes of the moment. It does not look to them for truth but for sophistical weapons."[80] Where philosophical and psychological "schools" develop, the struggle against philosophical heterodoxy is often accompanied by "the fury, the partiality, and the breaking through all arguments and breaking off of all communication and of all attempts to explain what the other view really means when the validity of one's own position is threatened. Unconsciously the truth is identified with one's own interests."[81] When position, status, role, and the means to the good life are at stake, the will to be right overpowers the will to truth.

Fortunately, many of our traditional "proofs" serve well in some other capacity, and many of our most basic beliefs do not require any proof at all. What purports to be a philosopher's proof may actually be simply the verbal embodiment of a belief. "As Descartes himself expressly states," for instance, "the *cogito ergo sum* is not an inference; for an inference would presuppose other truths from which the *sum* followed, whereas this thought itself is represented as the source. . . . The *ergo* is employed only as an analogy to the syllogism."[82] Anyone who regards this Cartesian insight as an argument which derives its cogency from traditional logic may well ask himself which one of the many logical forms of thought (syllogism, immediate inference, et cetera) it exemplifies. Again, when removed from its devotional context, what is commonly spoken of as Anselm's ontological

[79] *The Republic*, trans. Jowett, Bk. VII.
[80] VW 517.   [81] VW 497.   [82] DPT 67.

argument "can be mistaken for a logical operation by which the existence of an object . . . is 'proved.' . . . Seen in this light Anselm's idea may appear [as it did to Kant] to be a logical trick. . . ."[83] But since Anselm's God is "*a being greater than everything that can be conceived*,"[84] He cannot be an object of judgment and cannot be dealt with logically like a thing within the world. The *ens realissimum*, being inconceivable and ineffable, is unarguable.

Many of our other tenets require no proof because it is impossible for us to doubt them. As Hume's "natural belief," Santayana's "animal faith," and James's "will to believe," as well as Broad's strictures on "silly theories," and Moore's defense of common sense suggest, no one in his senses can fail to allow his beliefs to exceed the cognitive grounds on which they may be said to rest. No proofs are required to rescue us from ultimate skepticism, but only, as Hume saw, a relaxation of philosophic tension. "Something innate and simply *given* to man," viz., the "brute empirical existence of our being,"[85] stands between us and the conclusions of nihilism. When belief is inevitable, proofs are superfluous. How philosophers proceed and have proceeded in the absence of proof will gradually appear as we continue.

Current Overemphasis on the Explicit, Sensible, and Tangible

Much misunderstanding may be presumed to come from Jaspers' tendency to concern himself with background rather than foreground, and with the peripheral rather than the central, i.e., with those ingredients in human experience that could be described as obscure, impalpable, ineffable, imponderable, immaterial, and diaphanous. This emphasis, of course, is not a matter of overlooking the essential, and it is not anomalous. It appears to have been anticipated by Moses' insistence that nothing as determinate as a graven image could be used to represent Yahweh, and Berkeley's

---

[83] GP II, 95.   [84] GP II, 97.   [85] PY 290.

29

awareness that only "notions," and not the relatively distinct images which he called "ideas," could signify the Supreme Being. Kant, as we have seen, preserved a place for metaphysical pursuits by showing that the comparatively clear concepts of the understanding must in the end be supplemented by indistinct and indeterminate "ideas of reason." A century later emphasis upon the impalpable seemed, if anything, to increase. Von Ehrenfels provided impetus for gestalt psychology when he showed the importance of the previously neglected *"Gestaltqualitäten"* which he believed to supervene upon the qualities of sense, and Woodworth in America, simultaneously with Külpe at the Würzburg school of "imageless thought," demonstrated the indispensability of impalpable meanings within all mental contents. Brentano's concern with intentionality helped prepare the way for the phenomenological approach which influenced Jaspers directly. A similar trend appears in James's "radical empiricism," with its abandonment of a crude sensationalism in favor of a frank recognition of whatever entities—be they relations, meanings, values, or what not—are in fact experienced, and the emphasis of R. G. Collingwood on the "absolute presuppositions" which, though normally taken for granted, tend to lurk in the background of the sciences of every era. Likewise Whitehead stressed the importance of turning from the explicit doctrines which in a given epoch are acknowledged and defended to those fundamental assumptions which are unconsciously presupposed. These assumptions which everyone makes and no one acknowledges, he says, "appear so obvious that people do not know what they are assuming, because no other way of putting things has ever occurred to them."[86]

In similar vein Jaspers emphasizes that the definite methods and results of science are supported by ideas that are vague and amorphous. "The concrete work of the scientist," he says, "is guided by his conscious or unconscious phi-

[86] *Science and the Modern World* (New York: New American Library, 1948), pp. 49-50.

losophy, and this philosophy cannot be the object of scientific method." Scientific "ideas" (the maxim of parsimony, the uniformity of nature, et cetera) are never scientifically investigable and verifiable, and scientific goals are never rationally justifiable.[87] It is in line with this trend that he regards feelings and emotions as cognitive vehicles, elevates "non-knowledge," or philosophical faith, above knowledge, is more intent upon the encompassing whole than upon the things encompassed, and makes central the concept of Existenz. This concern with the intangible and implicit will be illustrated many times as we proceed.

Feelings as Cognitive

Like the phenomenologists, by whom they have been strongly influenced, existentially inclined philosophers can see no reason to deny that feelings perform cognitive functions. Recognizing with Hume that "every impression, external and internal, passions, affections, sensations, pains and pleasures are originally on the same footing,"[88] they ignore the popular dogma according to which objectivity in cognition requires exclusion of feelings, and are at one with the claim of James's "radical empiricism" that "if there be such things as feelings at all, then so surely as relations between objects exist *in rerum natura*, so surely . . . do feelings exist to which these relations are known."[89] Except for certain specific scientific purposes, senseless feeling need not be abandoned in favor of unfeeling sensation.

This view is familiar to German thinkers. In Hegel's *Phenomenology*, as J. Loewenberg points out, "knowledge

[87] EPT 158.

[88] *A Treatise of Human Nature* (New York: Dutton, 1926), I, 184-85. Accordingly Hume finds it natural to hold that we owe the idea of necessary connection to our ability to "*feel* a new sentiment or impression, to wit, a customary connection in the thought or imagination between one object and its usual attendant. . . ." (Inquiry, p. 89. Italics mine.) Cf. *Philosophical Theory and Psychological Fact*, pp. 27-29.

[89] *Psychology: Briefer Course* (New York: Holt, 1892), p. 162.

and experience are held to be virtually interchangeable, awareness or feeling of anything having a cognitive import."[90] Max Scheler based his claim to knowledge of values upon phenomenologically conceived "intentional feelings,"[91] and, as Calvin Schrag tells us, "Heidegger, like Kierkegaard, analyzes mood (*Stimmung*) as an intentional or revealing phenomenon. . . . Anxiety discloses my freedom. . . . Boredom and melancholy disclose various threats in my world-orientation. . . ."[92] When Jaspers tells us that "even despair, by the very fact that it is possible in the world, points beyond the world," and that "in ultimate situations [e.g. death, chance, guilt, struggle, et cetera] man either perceives nothingness or senses true being,"[93] when he tells us flatly that love is clearsighted enough to "enjoy a revelation of what *is*,"[94] he is not writing as a poet or advocating a return to a precognitive level of awareness, but seeking to exploit the highest cognitive possibilities of man's affective life.

Scientific Knowledge and Philosophic Nonknowledge

Jaspers is as distrustful of scientism, or what he calls "scientific superstition" (*Wissenschaftsaberglaube*), as he is confident of science. "It is incumbent upon us," he says, "really to know how much we can know, if we are to attain to true nonknowledge."[95] In passages reminiscent of the age of faith he contrasts scientific knowledge with philosophic vision: "Faith," he says, "is a different thing from knowledge. Giordano Bruno believed and Galileo knew. . . . On the one hand we have a truth that suffers by retraction, and on the other a truth which retraction leaves intact. . . . A truth by which I live stands only if I become identical with

[90] *Hegel's Phenomenology* (La Salle, Ill.: Open Court, 1965), p. 25.
[91] *Formalismus in der Ethik* (Halle: Max Miemeyer, 1927), pp. 260ff.
[92] *Existence and Freedom* (Evanston, Ill.: Northwestern University Press, 1961), p. 21.
[93] EPT 23.   [94] PE II, 277. Cf. VW 987-1021.
[95] PE II, 262.

it. . . . A truth which I can prove, stands without me; . . . it depends on finite premises and methods of attaining knowledge of the finite. It would be unfitting to die for a truth that is susceptible to proof."[96]

The objects with which we are everywhere confronted are affairs of the special sciences rather than of philosophy. As Heidegger expresses it, philosophy is concerned with being rather than things-in-being.[97] To identify the universe with, for instance, water, soul, or matter, is to refer to objects within the world as science does, instead of dealing with being *per se*. Being is no more an object (as realism would have it) than it is a subject (as idealism suggests). It includes both. Jaspers, like Faust, is obsessed with "the All-enfolding, the All-upholding" (*der Allumfasser, der Allerhalter*)[98] that, never being objectified through categorization and location within space and time, lies beyond our limited horizons. "This being of which we are in search we call the encompassing. It is not the horizon within which our knowledge remains, but that which under no circumstances can be viewed as a horizon. It is that from which the horizons always emerge."[99]

Beyond our horizon lies "transcendence" or God, which, together with the world, constitutes "the encompassing that is being itself." The world is too great to be known; to us it is simply an "idea." And transcendence is hidden. It is, as St. Paul said, seen through a glass darkly. It cannot be studied scientifically and cannot, properly speaking be "known." Here "negative theology" has the last word. But unknowability is not unavailability, and where knowledge and thought are, as it were, sublated, "nonknowledge" begins.

[96] PHT 4.

[97] Gerhard Knauss emphasizes that Jaspers and Heidegger share this insight. See "The Concept of the Encompassing in Jaspers' Philosophy" in PX 146.

[98] *Faust*, trans. Bayard Taylor, Part I, Scene 16. Jaspers speaks of Goethe as one of the "irreplaceable companions of my life" (PX 844).

[99] EX 13-14.

It is "in the cessation of the capacity for thought that the being of transcendence can be felt."[100]

Terms designating the kind of awareness enjoyed when thought is transformed and we pass beyond knowledge are numerous. We may, for example, be said to "track down," "search for," "hear or learn of," "feel," "allude to," "experience," "ponder deeply upon," "brood over," "bring home to our minds," "be aware of," "thoughtfully intuit," "refer to," or "reveal"[101] what cannot be either perceived or conceived. Science provides us with a paradigm of clear thought and accurate knowledge. But philosophy is not science, and any attempt on the part of the philosopher to imitate the scientist will simply confound the former and confuse the latter. "We must learn to know what we know, and what we do not know; how, and in what sense, and within what limits, we know anything; by what means this knowledge has been obtained, and upon what it is founded."[102] Only then can we surpass the determinate knowledge of science. Nothing could concern us more, for "only transcendence can make this questionable life good, the world beautiful, and existence itself a fulfilment."[103]

The Elucidation of Existenz

Whether writing as a philosopher or as a psychiatrist, Jaspers repeatedly speaks of a basic core in man which lies beyond all that the social sciences can discover, viz., what is called the soul, mind, spirit, ego, psyche, or innermost self. Personalism aside, this core has consistently proved more

---

[100] PE II, 263.

[101] In the same order the German terms are: *spüren* (PE II, 258), *nachspüren* (*Ibid.*, p. 285), *vernehmen* (VW 1033), *fühlen* (PE II, 263), *berühren* (SG 139), *erfahren* (PE III, 7), *ergrübeln* (PE III, 17), *hingrübeln* (PE III, 67), *vergegenwärtigen* (AP 632), *innewerden* (VW 1032), *denkende Schauen* (VW 1032), *verweisen* (PE II, 263), *offenbaren* (VW 1033). This list is, of course, intended merely as a sample.

[102] Quoted by Werner Brock in *Contemporary German Philosophy*, p. 96.

[103] EPT 126.

embarrassing than instructive to modern philosophers. We are perplexed by its conspicuous absence in the world of objective idealism and by its intrusive presence in the thought of subjective empiricism.

From the time of Kierkegaard on, it has been objected that the individual is "swallowed up" in the idealist's absolute. If we take Blanshard as an outstanding and exemplary exponent, we can easily see what is meant, for the chief conclusion of the first volume of his investigation of "the nature of thought" is that "there are no particulars," or, in other words, that "the only true particular is the absolute."[104] In the end, "the individual revealed . . . nothing but a synthesis of characters and relations which were themselves universals in the traditional sense."[105] "The particular, like the individual thing, turned out to be an aggregate of specific universals."[106] This is hard for anyone to believe about *himself*,[107] and we cannot but sympathize with the younger Bradley's reluctance to accept the view that "the world of real existence is a 'spectral woof of abstractions, or unearthly ballet of bloodless categories.' "[108] At the very least, we are inclined to say, as Ewing, following Broad, said in another connection, that in such cases, "the fact that we could not give a satisfactory statement of what else there was . . . would not prove that there was nothing else. . . ."[109] What, after all, is the absolute to an existing individual like myself?

To the orthodox empiricists, this self has been something of an enigma. Hume, who said explicitly that "the idea, or rather impression of ourselves is always intimately present

---

[104] Brand Blanshard, *The Nature of Thought* (London: Allen and Unwin, 1939), I, 631, 639.

[105] *Op.cit.*, p. 652.

[106] *Ibid.*

[107] *Ibid.* Blanshard is *not* referring to things to the exclusion of human beings. On this same page he uses "individual men" as an example.

[108] *Ibid.*, p. 632.

[109] *Idealism: A Critical Survey* (New York: Humanities Press, 1933), p. 155.

with us,"[110] nevertheless found as did Kant, shortly thereafter, that the self is somehow not observable as are things within the world.[111] James, speaking for the introspectionists of his time, carefully explained that although the total self, "being as it were duplex, partly known and partly knower, partly object and partly subject, must have two aspects": the "me" and the "I," or the "empirical ego" and the "pure ego,"[112] still scientific psychologists must confine their inquiries to the former, leaving the latter to the metaphysicians. Behaviorists generally study psychology without the psyche, and often—in limiting themselves to the observation of stimulus and response—without the organism. Those who envisage the eventual reduction of psychology to neurology (together, presumably with endocrinology and the like) carefully consign all "personal" questions to the extrascientific portion of their lives. Always something escapes scientific scrutiny, especially that from which the science received its name. It is with this—with what has long been roughly designated as the psyche—the soul, mind, spirit, or anima—that Jaspers is chiefly concerned.

"What in mythical terminology are called the soul and God, and in philosophical language Existenz and transcendence, . . . do not have the same mode of being as the things in the world . . . but they can have some other. Although they are not known, they are not nothing, and our failure to come to cognitive grips with them does not imply that they are not thought of."[113] In this revealing statement, which appears at the beginning of the *Existenzerhellung*, Jaspers expresses his intention to deal with the soul as well as with God, elucidating indirectly what is too intimate and intangible to be described in straightforward fashion.

The word "Existenz," as here employed, is not new. Schelling, to whom Jaspers has devoted an entire book, spoke of his philosophy as *"Existentialphilosophie,"*[114] and contrasted "the negative [which he took to be] a science of

---

[110] *Treatise*, II, 41. [111] *Ibid.*, I, 238-39. [112] *Op.cit.*, p. 176.
[113] PE II, 1. [114] SG 98.

essence," with "the positive, a science of Existenz. The former [he said] has the ideal in view; the latter, the real."[115] The term, however, was transmitted through one of Schelling's auditors: the years of World War I brought Jaspers "an illumination by Kierkegaard. To him [he says] I owe the concept of 'Existenz,' which ever since 1916 has governed my understanding of what until then I had been restlessly striving for."[116]

As the *Existenzerhellung* shows, one can illuminate, if not clarify, this innermost self which constitutes the *fons et origo* of the moral life—this "actuality of self-being"[117] that presupposes honesty[118] and consists, above all, in freedom;[119] this unconditionality[120] that relates to "a life of high rank,"[121] and is realized only so long as I am authentic.[122] This, of course, is central to Jaspers' philosophizing.

[115] *Ibid.*
[116] PFT 301.
[117] AP 11.
[118] NET 202.
[119] PO 116.
[120] PE II, 377.
[121] NET 191.
[122] PE II, 377.

chapter two

Science and Philosophy

With the familiar twentieth century "revolution in philosophy" Karl Jaspers has had nothing to do: without involvement, rebellion is impossible. From his youth on he
found academic orthodoxies incredible and irrelevant to the
human situation. The teachers of philosophy seemed to him
to be "personally pretentious and dogmatic,"[1] while their
teaching struck him as "not really philosophy: for all its
scientific pretensions it was always threshing out things not
vital to the basic questions of our existence [Dasein]."[2]
Later on, as a full professor, while recognizing that to be in
any sense effective "we must proceed in conjunction with
the apparatus and strive for rescue even while we are enmeshed in it,"[3] he continued to find "the philosophy of the
schools . . . discursive, disintegrated and disintegrating."[4]
As taught today it would appear to be scarcely worth learning: "The mass of sham philosophical knowledge taught
in the schools originates in the hypostatization of entities
that have served for a time as the signpost of philosophy.
Such hypostatized entities are nothing but the *capita
mortua . . .* of the great metaphysical systems."[5] There is, of
course, no harm in preserving *capita mortua*, and downright "falsification begins only with the founding of schools
in the name of distinct philosophies, each of which purports
to be a science capable of imparting the truth."[6] Jaspers
was not alone in his disappointment:

> The young people of those days [he says] must have been
> cruelly disenchanted: this was not what they had ex-
> pected from philosophy. Love of the sort of philosophy
> that supplies a basis for life comports badly with a scien-

[1] PFT 197-98.   [2] PFT 228.   [3] GET 152.
[4] GET 155.   [5] EPT 161.   [6] PE I, 289.

tific philosophy that—however impressive it may be as training, due to the methodological rigor and painstaking, laborious thought required—was too innocent, too unpretentious, too blind to actuality. Deep concern with actuality repudiated trite conceptualizations that, however systematic, were merely playful, and proofs that in spite of their huge outlay, really proved nothing. Many proceeded in the direction tacitly indicated by the judgment which philosophy passed upon itself when it measured its rank by the standards of the empirical sciences. Such students simply gave up philosophy and went into science—perhaps believing all the while in some other not as yet explicitly acknowledged philosophy."[7]

Repeatedly Jaspers tells us of the enthusiasm with which he and many of his fellow students turned to science for the sake of its direct and accurate knowledge of reality. "Here the will to know could be satisfied; what astonishing, terrifying, and again hopeful facts of nature, of human existence, of society, and of historical events!"[8] Science eschews nonsense, provides reliable knowledge of the world, and, though fallible, employs a method that is self-corrective. But what is science and what is philosophy, and what may we expect from the impact of the one upon the other?

What Philosophy Owes to Science

To abandon all metaphysics on the ground that science is the only acceptable path to knowledge (as "scientism" would have it) or to continue to develop metaphysics in the grand manner in independence of science would be equally futile. What is needed is a view of the relation between philosophy and science that does not eliminate one of the two or assimilate it to the other, depreciate one to the advantage of the other, or overlook the dependence of each upon the other. Above all, philosophy cannot afford to ignore science: "Any philosopher who is not trained in a scientific discipline

[7] EX 3-4.   [8] Ibid.

and who fails to keep his scientific interests constantly alive will inevitably bungle and stumble. . . . Unless an idea is submitted to the coldly dispassionate test of scientific inquiry, it is rapidly consumed in the fire of emotions and passions, or else it withers into dry and narrow fanaticism."[9]

Turning from a negative to a positive outlook we may note a number of ways in which science contributes to philosophy. In the first place, knowledge of science is the only reliable preventive against the spurious claims of pseudo-science. He who has done serious work in at least one science, and through direct personal experience learned what scientific method is and how to discriminate between the scientific outlook and scientific superstition (*Wissenschafts-aberglaube*) knows how to deal with the *ex cathedra* pronouncements of self-appointed exponents of the scientific verities. "A modern form of superstition for example," which could deceive all but the very elect, "is psychoanalysis taken as a philosophy, and the pseudo-medicine that makes man's freedom a supposed object of scientific research."[10] More generally speaking, it is the essence of "scientific superstition" to identify being per se with what is physically present in space and time: the average man who "wishes to have, taste, see, and know what he believes in . . . tends toward superstition—most strikingly toward the scientific superstition that seeks to find and possess absolute being in the objects of scientific knowledge."[11] Scientific training immunizes one to many spurious authoritarian claims.

In the second place, the classic question about the difference between knowledge and belief which inspired Plato's "myth of the cave" and has haunted us ever since has received its definitive answer from modern science. Since the seventeenth century we have acquired the ability to say what we know, how we know it, and why the limits of our knowledge are where they are. "Scientism" is not so much mistaken in limiting knowledge to science as in failing to discover the extent and importance of the area disclosed by non-

---

[9] EPT 159.   [10] PHT 65-66.   [11] VW 806.

knowledge—i.e. by modes of awareness such as opinion and belief, which lack the precision and comparative certainty which science offers.[12]

In the third place, philosophy, insofar as it is to assist man in orienting himself within the world, must rely on science for its facts, the facts of common sense being insufficient. Existentialists can never believe, as some seemingly do, that philosophical statements are too empty of content or too trivial to relate to matters of fact. Effective thinking about the human condition depends upon knowing more than the implications of our definitions, various truisms such as that man has eyes, ears, and a brain, or a few select facts concerning the language we use. Nothing human need be alien to us, and nothing at all should be disqualified in advance.

Finally, we must know enough about science to recognize its limits if we are to respect certain extrascientific modes of awareness. When Kant characterized "the territory of pure [scientific] understanding" as "an island enclosed by nature itself within unalterable limits," he was only incidentally concerned to show that this "land of truth" is "surrounded by a wide and stormy ocean, the native home of illusion. . . ."[13] For, as every tyro knows, he was above all intent upon setting limits to knowledge in order to make room for faith, or—to put it otherwise—upon restraining the concepts of the understanding in favor of the ideas through which reason begets and directs moral conviction and religious belief. To this topic we shall return in Chapter VII.

The Nature of Science

Jaspers has repeatedly characterized science in nearly identical terms.[14] From the very beginning among the pre-

[12] On any view we are faced with the troublesome paradox that while *certainty* appears to be one of the differentiae of knowledge, still the conclusions of scientific induction are not certain but merely probable. See C. I. Lewis' *An Analysis of Knowledge and Valuation* (La Salle, Ill.: Open Court, 1946), pp. 27-29.

[13] *Critique of Pure Reason*, trans. Norman Kemp Smith (New York: St. Martin's Press, 1965), p. 257.

[14] VU 83ff.; EPT 150ff.; PO 95-103. Cf. NET 176-84.

Socratics, all science has been *methodical, compellingly certain,* and *universally valid.* To say that science can be characterized as *methodical* does not, of course, mean that there is such a thing as *the* scientific method, for each of the many sciences may be said to employ many methods (Gordon Allport, for example, found that the psychology of personality alone employed upward of 52 specific methods).[15] But concern with method is fundamental: "My knowledge is truly scientific only when I am sufficiently cognizant of *the method* by which it was gained to be able to point out the grounds upon which it rests and fix the limits beyond which it is inapplicable."[16]

More striking still is the *compelling certainty* of scientific findings. "How grand," as Nietzsche remarked, "to discover something that is calculable and determinate! There are laws whose truth remains beyond the reach of any individual." We do not merely "think," we *know* that water contains hydrogen and oxygen. "It is a source of deep and abiding satisfaction that scientific findings are indefeasible. . . ."[17] While we might be said to be free to accept the end-results of science, we are surely not free to impugn them.

This whole-hearted endorsement of scientific results on the part of an existential thinker is, however, not intended to deny certain facts which every student of the subject takes for granted, or to introduce a qualification to Jaspers' usual interpretationism. Naturally, at any given time, many matters at the frontiers of science are highly problematic. And inductive reasoning from limited samples does of course yield probability rather than certainty. He follows Nietzsche[18] in holding that "scientific knowledge can be included in the general proposition: All knowledge is interpretation. . . . For we possess being only in its interpretations. To speak of it is to interpret it. . . ."[19] And there is no need to deny

15 See *Personality: A Psychological Interpretation* (New York: Holt, 1937), chap. xiv.
16 VU 83.   17 NET 172.   18 NET Bk. II, chap. v.
19 EPT 77.

that a scientific conclusion inevitably "remains relative to methods and assumptions."[20] The results of a psychophysical measurement of the difference threshold, for instance, depends in large part upon the method used to arrive at it. And as he says in his book to psychopathologists: "Presuppositions are a necessary part of understanding. . . . Without [them] we cannot comprehend the essence of anything."[21] But when all this is granted, there remains a striking contrast between the factuality and reliability of scientific results and the uncertainty and debatability of philosophic conclusions. The law of falling bodies is a well-known scientific fact, not open to debate. The law of excluded middle—to choose the philosophic principle which is perhaps least open to question —is problematic, and on the organicist's view it is merely an approximation that "cannot be accepted without reservation."[22]

In the third place, scientific knowledge, as Kant recognized, possesses universal validity (*Allgemeingültigkeit*). Once true, always true; what science vouches for is always and everywhere valid. It is as easy for Orientals to assimilate Occidental science as it is difficult for them to assimilate Occidental religion. In a word, scientific knowledge, unlike religious faith (we need only think of gods who, like Zeus and Dionysus, are everywhere dead) is valid in every culture independently of all conceivable changes in conditions and circumstances. It is not merely true for me, or for my people or my era; it is true objectively for all men and for all eternity. In addition to the above, Jaspers holds that modern science possesses the following traits to a high degree:

1. Within the world of objects it is all-inclusive. While it has no concern with the "ultimate reality" of the metaphysician and cannot evaluate or prescribe ends without renouncing its objectivity,[23] it can properly undertake to study

---

[20] EPT 162.   [21] APT 21.
[22] Brand Blanshard, *The Nature of Thought* (London: Allen & Unwin, 1939), II, 329.
[23] This point, I believe, need not be argued here. Jaspers commonly

all that appears and can appear to human beings. Science signifies "the idea [in the Kantian sense] of a compelling and universally valid cognitive activity that, using certain specific methods, is directed upon everything that we find to be real, objective, and thinkable."[24]

2. Inspired by a belief in progress, it presses constantly onward, and, as a result, is and must always remain unfinished. On the one hand it enjoys the boundlessness of its domain; on the other, it is burdened by the infinite distance and inaccessibility of its end.

3. Having sprung from a pious love of nature based upon Christianity, it can be indifferent to nothing. Every fact is important and, in the end, all facts must be taken into account. "Everywhere the will to approach and grasp the realities of the world securely derives from the delight we take in them."[25]

4. While the unity of science is an ideal rather than an achievement, the scientist constantly strives for the eventual organic unification of all scientific knowledge, and is impressed by the kinship of the various sciences. All are methodical, employ categories and other abstract concepts, and provide reliable knowledge. They often relate closely to each other and serve each other's purposes. And all pursue the universally valid and necessary.

5. The radicalness of scientific doubt is unparalleled. Thinking that transgresses sense-appearances, but hopes in the end to save them, begun by the ancients in the field of

---

attributes to Max Weber the view, found in MWT 241, that "no empirical investigation can provide a foundation on which to determine what has value and what I ought to do." With this we may compare the—surely exaggerated—conclusion of Iris Murdock, that "this argument . . . to the effect that we cannot derive values from facts is the most important argument in modern moral philosophy—indeed it is almost the whole of modern moral philosophy." "Metaphysics and Ethics," in *The Nature of Metaphysics*, ed. D. F. Pears (London: Macmillan, 1962), p. 106.

[24] PO 97.   [25] *Ibid.*

astronomy, has culminated within modern physics "in a trafficking with the unrepresentable through mathematical means that are unintuitable."[26] Readiness to call established doctrine into question makes possible the investigation of even the most paradoxical new hypotheses. Time and again tacitly held and unacknowledged presuppositions are discovered, tested, and replaced by other presuppositions.

6. While it may seem that the use of certain categories, such as endlessness or causality, is typical of modern science, it is more accurate to stress the inclusiveness of our concern with categories and methods. "Whatever appears possible in mathematics, physics, biology, hermeneutics, or speculation is attempted and every object is grasped. The result is a limitless increase in our world of categories."[27]

7. Finally, in our era, science has given rise, among its devotees, to a new attitude best described, perhaps, as scientificalness (*Wissenschaftlichkeit*, or *die wissenschaftliche Haltung*). It is only realized occasionally, and often the few scientists who attain to it do so only in their own special fields. What is involved is a readiness rationally and freely to question, discuss, investigate, test, and criticize everything conceivable. It distinguishes between what is and what is not logically compelling, looks beyond findings and principles, and wishes to know the method through which each item of knowledge was obtained, in order the better to judge of its meaning and the limits of its applicability. It is not doctrinaire, avoids dogmatic finality, and, with a view to preserving flexibility and receptiveness, shies away from sects, cults, creeds, articles of faith, and societies of like-minded enthusiasts. It strives for the clarity of the precise and determinate as opposed to the vague approximations of what everyone says. Today this attitude is the source of veracity, and to neglect it is to invite dishonesty and false enlightenment. It sees through the "life-lie" (Ibsen), and has the courage of the *sapere aude*.

[26] VU 86.   [27] VU 87.

Scientific and Philosophical World-Orientation

A survey of the 2,500 year history of philosophy shows it to have been engaged in three tasks, to each of which Jaspers has devoted a separate volume of his *Philosophie*: world-orientation, elucidation of Existenz, and metaphysics. World-orientation, with which the present chapter is primarily concerned, began as an attempt on the part of man to learn something of his place in nature, and thereby to prepare himself for suitable adaptation to his environment. Scientific world-orientation, proceeding at the level of the Kantian understanding (*Verstand*), has sought to come to terms with the common world of public objects—ideal objects like the Pythagorean theorem and the law of gravity, and real objects like the earth and the Rosetta stone. Such objects are readily available to clear cognition and capable of being directly and accurately communicated.

Philosophical world-orientation, however, is another matter. Its aim is not to round out a self-sufficient and self-explanatory natural world, but to show in detail how the limits of scientific knowledge make such an intention forever untenable, and to point the way to a truth that does not depend upon science. "In philosophical world-orientation a consciousness of these limits is sought. . . . [They] are relevant to possible Existenz. . . . They show that the world in itself is not a self-sufficient being—to know the world is not to know all."[28]

Philosophical world-orientation discloses two all-important limits of science. First of all, science in the pursuit of universally valid truth must abstract from the subjective, which it regards as a source of error. Wishing to avoid feelings and desires, perspectival distortions, capricious evaluations, arbitrary standpoints and the like, it omits these things from view, and relegates them to the social sciences. Naturally they remain as objects of empirical investigation, but as such they are robbed of their inner being and egregiously

[28] PE I, 88.

falsified. To these matters we shall return in the next chapter.

In the second place, philosophical world-orientation encounters another set of limits "which in its pure objectivity is found to be such that its intentions can never be completely carried out. I attain to coercive insight, but the coerciveness is not absolute; I master endlessness, but find that it is still not completely under my domination; I arrive at unities, but never the unity of the world."[29] To these difficulties we now turn.

The Relativity of the Coercive

Knowledge is scientific in the eulogistic sense when it is composed of judgments which are bound to be accepted by all who understand them. Of such judgments there are three main varieties: the *logico-mathematical*, the *empirical*, and the *phenomenological*.[30] Logico-mathematical systems, when properly developed, are indeed indefeasible. But they can never be more reliable than the first principles upon which they rest. If these latter are arbitrarily selected postulates (as in non-Euclidean geometry), then the whole affair is a game whose validity (or "mathematical truth") is irrelevant to the question of its physical truth. But if, on the other hand, the basic assumptions were selected because they were seen to be true prior to the logical derivation, then truth derives from some extralogical source. In other words, if the method is postulational, it provides validity rather than

[29] PE I, 87. Statements about endlessness in science seem to be especially subject to misunderstanding. It is, of course, equally true to say that there is no limit to the task of science, meaning that an exhaustive scientific study of the universe, present, past, and future, could never be concluded, and to insist upon the limits of science, meaning that religion, philosophy, and the human studies provide questions with which science cannot deal. Furthermore, since science does (as will appear) come to terms with the infinite, but continues to be plagued by it, one can equally well say that one does (PE I, 87) or does not (PE I, 166) master endlessness. A road infinite in length would, of course, be limited by its sides.

[30] PE I, 89-93.

truth. But if the logical starting point is self-evident, then we must look beyond logic for the source of this evidence. As Hume saw, relations of ideas taken wholly by themselves can never yield knowledge of matters of fact and existence. Thoughts without content are empty.

The empirical sciences, of course, look to the things and processes of nature for data that are compellingly evident. It is not what we think but what we *find* that counts. Findings that we are forced to accept are of course what we call "facts." Facts, however, as any follower of Kant knows, can be extremely puzzling, for the difference between the factual and the factitious is not itself a matter of fact. Only the inexperienced believe that facts are simply "there," to be had for the asking. We cannot afford to ignore "the distinction between true sense-perceptions and errors of sense, the degree of accuracy of measurement, the meaning of testimony and of documents, the alteration of observed objects by the conditions of observation."[31] It is proverbial that "every fact is already a theory."[32]

Theories lend intelligibility to our discoveries but are interpretive and often ambiguous. When, however, we turn from theory and attend to so-called brute facts, we find that these, as prime examples of unintelligibility, fall outside of science. "Scientific research always ends in materials that, being opaque, constitute a limit to the understanding. . . . The compelling is by no means the whole of actuality."[33] Brute facts are simply incapable of being explained, unless, of course, our concept of explanation has been carefully tailored to their measure. That there are as many chemical elements as there are, and that a wave length of 580 millimicrons gives rise to the sensation of yellow are things that just are "so."

The "intuition of essence" that derives from the *phenomenological* approach of Brentano and Husserl is equally co-

---

[31] PE I, 90. On this point Nietzsche's influence may have been as decisive as Kant's. See NET 184-200, and Bk. II, chap. v.
[32] PE I, 90.   [33] PE I, 91.

ercive. If one does actually intuit a certain value, or discover a relation, or directly apprehend a gestalt, then these things really are given and there is literally no sense in denying them. The question of what we actually do observe is prior to the further question of how such observation is possible, and the answer to the second question must not be allowed to prejudice the answer to the first. Here again, Jaspers is concerned to point out that, *qua* scientists, we encounter boundaries. Suppose that, like Max Scheler, we have made a thorough phenomenological investigation of the world of value, and are convinced that we know the object of our investigation directly and without intermediaries. Two boundaries appear at once. In the first place, however coercive our findings may be, findings as such are prejudgmental, and, strictly speaking, neither true nor false. If results are to be scientific, then they must be vouched for and presented to the public. But the attempt to communicate the immediate is hazardous. Apart from the fact that we may lie or "engage in foolish talk or simply say words instead of telling what it is that we have seen, we can never be sure that others will view it precisely as we do."[34] There is a sense in which, as Schlick used to say, content cannot be communicated. We can never be confident of saying what we mean or meaning what we say. No one can convey the beauty of Beethoven's *An die Hoffnung* to a musical dullard, describe the wonders of stereoscopic vision to a cyclopean perceiver, or enable a man with only blue-yellow vision to imagine a patch of red.

In the second place, the compellingness of phenomenological awareness does not reach as far as the *organization* of the given. Whether or not Scheler was correct in believing that he could immediately intuit value-qualities (much as G. E. Moore seemed to say that *he* could), the immediacy of his intuition can hardly provide a guarantee of the four levels at which he placed what he intuited. By the same token, immediate awareness of color does not vouch for

[34] PE I, 92.

either the color circle, the color triangle, or the color spindle. In the sense in which the immediate may be characterized as "certain," it can hardly be regarded as knowledge, and when knowledge of it is finally obtained, it is no longer either immediate or certain.[35]

The Endless and the Unending

As Pascal and Kant in their different ways brought out, the unbounded hems us in on all sides, for, like an immense desert, it is the most impassable of all bounds. In space we are limited, at one extreme, by the infinitesimal, and, at the other, by the infinite. In time, the objects we investigate follow upon an opaque and endless past and proceed toward an impenetrable and interminable future. Thus the world that we can observe and know is, both spatially and temporally, but a tiny segment of an indescribably lengthy continuum. It is within these limits that science operates.

Furthermore science, in its search for reliable generalizations, has no satisfactory way of dealing with the huge number of instances from which it must choose its samples. We cannot, for instance, observe all falling bodies in order to generalize about them, and the number of instances that we do observe is vanishingly small in comparison with the number of instances (past and future as well as present) which escape observation. Our difficulties increase when we note that aggregates that are not literally endless are still endless for all practical purposes whenever they are too numerous to be exhaustively examined by beings like ourselves with limited funds and brief life-spans. Thus the fourteen or so billion cells in the cerebral cortex are practically if not theoretically incapable of being investigated in their entirety. While a machine may be known *in toto*, the human body may not—a consideration that favors the success of the mechanical as compared to the medical sciences. The

[35] See my *Philosophical Theory and Psychological Fact* (Tucson, Ariz.: University of Arizona Press, 1961), chap. ii.

point is not that science neglects to deal with these problems, but rather that the ways in which it *does* deal with them are never entirely satisfactory. In generalizing on the basis of a few instances the knowledgeable scientist is obsessed by Hume's skeptical questions as well as Peirce's belief that there is real chance in the universe, and that the "habits" of nature may change. To face squarely the problems raised by endlessness is to feel insecure and shaken. While it is true enough that "the cognitive conquest of endlessness has been theoretically achieved,"[36] it is also undeniable that always "an endlessness that has not been methodically mastered remains before us as a limit."[37]

Sometimes the problems involved are direct, obvious, inescapable, and urgent. The psychiatrist in writing case histories (the problem is certainly "writ large" for the author of a world history) cannot be objective in the sense of simply stating the facts of the case, for there are too many of them. Again, in preparing such a book as the *General Psychopathology*, the author is confronted by a practically unlimited literature, for the heritage from the past is vast and journals and books appear faster than one can read them. "In describing a given field of knowledge, one must know the literature referring to it, but too exacting a thoroughness in this comprehensive occupation may go on forever. . . . This activity will grow endless once we fail to recognize certain areas of agreement. . . ."[38] Of course the same difficulty applies to the choice of hypotheses. Since, as Henri Poincaré points out,[39] the number of hypotheses that could account for any given fact or set of facts is theoretically infinite, and since, once a theory is accepted, it will require various other *ad hoc* hypotheses to support it,[40] there is no end to theory-making, and no way of showing (as those innocent of sci-

[36] PE I, 97.   [37] PE I, 98.   [38] APT 33-34.
[39] *Science and Hypothesis* (New York: Dover, 1952), chaps. ix and x.
[40] APT 33.

ence sometimes urge) that any specific theory is the only one that can account for all the facts.

Jaspers goes on to distinguish such "endlessness" (*Endlosigkeit*) as that described above from the "unendingness" (*Unendlichkeit*) which we encounter in the social sciences and the humanities (i.e. the "*Geisteswissenschaften*"), somewhat to the disparagement of the former, which is seen to resemble the "bad" or "empty" (as opposed to the "replete") infinite of Schiller and Hegel.[41] While this distinction is of great importance in other contexts, it is here necessary merely to note the difference between the quantitative endlessness of induction by simple enumeration—the simple "again and again and again" of the natural sciences—and the unendingness of a Leibnizian monad which, like a spherical mirror, reflects and thus represents the entire universe, or a Whiteheadian "actual entity" which "in a sense . . . pervades the whole world."[42] The person, constituted as he is by his relations to all that surrounds him is not infinite in the same way as is a series of natural events. Scientific thought must draw back before the unending, and philosophic thought transgresses the line only by means of indistinct imageless thoughts that point the way we should go without disclosing the objective.

[41] See, for example, Walter Kaufmann's *Hegel* (Garden City, New York: Doubleday, 1965), pp. 53-54. This would seem to relate to the distinction which Stephen Pepper makes between "multiplicative corroboration" and "structural corroboration" in *World Hypotheses* (Berkeley: University of California Press, 1942), pp. 47ff. The difference emerges clearly when Jaspers contrasts the *endless* correctnesses which science accumulates with the *unending* complexity of an organized whole in which, as Goethe's Faust expresses it, "each the whole its substance gives." "While correctnesses remain *endless* and leaves us empty," says Jaspers, "we are satisfied by the way in which the unending connections within a whole develop and are completed before our eyes" (VW, 612). The former is an endless but insignificant and tedious repetition of similar entities, the latter is an inexhaustible complexity of dissimilar entities which mutually qualify and influence each other, as do, for example, the members of a planetary system, a family, or a society.

[42] *Process and Reality* (New York: Humanities Press, 1955), p. 42.

Evidences of Pluralism

It is natural to suppose that the world is a unity, and primitive animism as well as modern science has taken it to be such. And yet unity always turns out to be a unity *within* the world rather than the unity *of* the world. Descartes had some awareness of this but was too easily satisfied. Since the material world alone follows mechanical laws, he could see no feasible alternative to placing everything nonmaterial and nonmechanical (i.e. whatever does not clearly possess "simple location" within the spatio-temporal continuum) in another realm. The notorious difficulties of Descartes's successors in showing how these two realms could relate causally to each other, and the patent unsuitability of the solutions that have since been offered brings out the point that Jaspers wishes to emphasize: the realm of matter is so different from the realm of spirit, substantially as well as functionally, that much ingenuity is required to avoid the absurd conclusion that the two realms are as separate as they are distinct. This becomes more puzzling when it is seen that, as Spinoza soon pointed out, Descartes's theological commitments require another substance and hence a trialistic universe composed of matter, mind, and God.

Jaspers would be quick to agree with Descartes about the hiatus between the living and the dead, and between both and the Deity, but he would insist with Samuel Alexander and Lloyd Morgan that other diremptions within the world are equally sharp and that it is closer to the truth to say that the world itself (*not* the universe or the All, which includes God) appears on *four* distinct levels, each of which is autonomous in relation to the others. Consequently science must deal with four very different sorts of stuff: *matter* (physico-chemical structures, the corporeal), *life* (the vital, organic), *soul* (the conscious, psychical), and *spirit* (mind as the seat of intentionality).[43] These four are independent

---

[43] In the author's terminology: "Die anorganische Natur *in ihrer alle Wirklichkeit umgreifenden Gesetzlichkeit*; das Leben *als Organismus*; die Seele *als Erleben*; der Geist *als denkendes, auf Gegenstände*

in about the same sense and to approximately the same degree as the Cartesians believed matter and mind to be. No point of interaction is empirically discoverable, and no means of interaction could be intelligible, although correlations between events at various levels are abundant.[44] The chief relation here is "founding," or, conversely, "being founded on." While each level follows its own laws, the lower have to be present before the higher can appear. "Every later sphere is founded (*fundiert*) on the actuality of the preceding one: life, on inorganic material and its laws, the soul on life, and the spirit on the soul. No later sphere can exist apart from its predecessor, but the earlier ones can well exist without the later."[45] A number of secondary relationships are worthy of note. If, as the devotees of emergence believe, these levels evolved gradually in time, then the order of dependence reflects the order of temporal development, and we may think of life as having emerged from dead matter, and the soul as having developed from life to give rise to spirit. From a pedagogical point of view the lower are seen to be easier to comprehend than the higher in at least one important respect: mastery of the lowest (or earliest) level requires no knowledge of the others, while study of the higher levels does entail knowledge of *it*. One can (that is) know physics without knowing biology or psychology, but knowledge of psychology involves the study of both the vital and the physical (endocrinology, neurology, anatomy and physiology of the sense organs, et cetera, plus optics, acoustics, elementary electronics, et cetera), while everything is grist

---

gerichtetes Bewusstsein. Jedesmal ist ein Sprung vom Einen zum Anderen statt einer Herleitung. . . ." PE I, 104-105.

[44] PE I, 106. In this connection, one may well note the popularity among psychologists of noninteractionistic psycho-physical parallelism during the past hundred years. Perhaps the "isomorphism" of gestalt psychology is, as E. G. Boring suggests, simply a sophisticated version of this old doctrine. See *Sensation and Perception in the History of Experimental Psychology* (New York: Appleton-Century, 1942), p. 84.

[45] *Ibid.*

for the mill of the world-historian. Correspondingly the upper levels admit of far greater complications than the lower. We proceed upward by addition and downward by subtraction. The first step downward involves dropping out external reference and responsible thought, the next omits conscious awareness, and the last excludes plants and animals to arrive at matter moving in space. By summarizing these levels together with a few of the famous philosophers who have shown extreme partiality for specific levels, we arrive at the scheme presented in the accompanying diagram.

Levels, Spheres, or Worlds	Essential Aspects	Sciences most Directly Involved	Philosophies Suggested	Typical Philosophers Concerned
Matter (*Materie*)	Measurability	Chemistry, Physics	Mechanistic-Materialism (Physicalism)	Democritus Epicurus Lucretius Hobbes
Life (*Leben*)	Objective Teleology	Biological Sciences	Vitalism, Biocentrism, Contextualism	Bergson Driesch Dewey
Psyche (*Seele*)	Conscious Experience	Descriptive Psychology	Psychologism, Phenomenalism, Subjectivism, Relativism	Protagoras Mill, Hume Pearson Berkeley
Spirit (*Geist*)	Intentionality (External Reference), Judgment	Social Sciences, Humanities	Personalism, Organicism, Idealism	Bowne Hegel Whitehead Blanshard

These stages or levels may be briefly characterized as follows: Matter is a "dead nature," made up of the quantitatively describable (an examination of the so-called primary qualities reveals the measurability and spatiality of the inanimate), whose motions are explicable in causal terms and predictable solely through subsumption under general laws. It must always be viewed *ab extra* and can never be understood in the sense in which human beings are understood. To us it is foreign, impenetrable, enigmatic, forbidding. But of

55

course it is by far the most extensive of all the spheres: "Every object in space and time is matter; only a few of these objects are living; of these still fewer prove through their expressions to be psychical. Of these latter a small proportion are capable of genuine spiritual communication."[46] Exclusive preoccupation with this level gives rise to mechanistic materialism—a theory to which we owe the mechanical world-view of the modern era, and which, when applied beyond its proper bounds, leads to falsifications, distortions and a curious blindness to the immediately given.

The living is that which can move itself, change its material constituents while remaining formally self-identical, develop from the simple to the complex, and even propagate itself. Most important of all, it is characterized by "objective teleology": a purposiveness observable *ab extra*, the denial of which leads to such incredible paradoxes as Lucretius' dictum that birds do not have wings in order to fly but fly because they have wings, and the claim of physicalism that animal behavior is entirely explicable in mechanical terms. The striking difference between this stage and the previous one is no more a matter of "proof" than, for example, the difference between the right and left hands, or the exquisite and the meretricious, and, from the standpoint of mechanistic materialism, this sphere is not even discernible.[47] "But he who has once seen life for what it is finds it not to be actual in the sense in which dead stuff is actual, but to have an actuality of its own."[48] Biologism uses the Aristotelian entelechy as a general principle of explanation, and thereby reduces psyche and spirit to the vital level and takes society to be an enlarged organism.

Anatomy and physiology in all their branches fail to supply even the slightest inkling of what is next to appear, for nowhere within these sciences is there any place for, or indication of the conscious awareness of, the psyche.[49] And from

46 PE I, 168.   47 PY 474-75.   48 PE I, 169.
49 From a Kantian point of view, *Seele* obviously means "soul." But in connection with the four levels, one is tempted to speak of

a biocentric standpoint it is natural to argue that there is "no evidence" of a "thing" named the soul, to call into question the existence of consciousness, and to ridicule the absurd "ghost in the machine" of an effete and antiquated tradition. As William James showed, contents of consciousness can be regarded as things in the world viewed in a special context, i.e. in relation to the viewer, while the supposed ego that observes them can be dismissed as too "diaphanous" to be observed.[50]

Those who accept as real this subject of traditional introspectionistic psychology do so, not because they can "defend" its existence through clever argumentation, because they know how to "verify" propositions about it, or because good English usage requires them to talk about it, but simply because, as Augustine and Descartes testified, everyone is intimately acquainted with it. Conscious awareness, after all, is acknowledged and described at length in a classic chapter of the celebrated *Psychology* of the author of the skeptical "Does Consciousness Exist?"[51] It is that to the momentary obliteration of which the applied science of anesthesiology is dedicated. It is the immediately given from which, to some extent and in some sense at least, all further knowledge derives. Anyone who wishes to take the halfway position that while he is sure of his own consciousness he does not believe in other conscious centers, since other "selves" would appear to be mere automata (i.e. anyone who chooses to consider himself a solipsist), may be left to argue without a hearer, not only because if he is right there can be

---

the "psyche" to suggest the science which relates to it. Both "mind" and "spirit" are commonly preempted for use in translating *Geist*. Note that in religious (but not in psychological) terminology *Seele* is an old-fashioned term for what now is called *Existenz*.

[50] "Does Consciousness Exist?" pp. 1-38 in *Essays in Radical Empiricism and A Pluralistic Universe*, ed. Ralph Barton Perry (New York: Longmans, Green and Co., 1947).

[51] William James, *The Principles of Psychology* (New York: Holt, 1890), chap. ix.

no one to argue with, but chiefly because solipsism is an outstanding example of the thoroughly incredible.

But why not stop with the psyche? Entities should not be multiplied beyond necessity. The answer is obvious if, with the introspective psychologists, we discover in the psyche nothing more than sensations, feelings, and images,[52] presumably taken together with the drives and desires which they inspire, and, accordingly, define psychology as the "science of feeling."[53] When external reference, judgment, and evaluation are missing, a further level must be supplied.

Soul, the subject matter of psychology, is less than and subordinate to spirit. Soul is lived experience, replete with sensation, feeling, drive, and desire, while spirit involves understanding and will, and aims at unrestricted comprehension and planning. Furthermore, the soul lives outside of history and derives from the genetic; spirit is enmeshed in history, derives from social inheritance, mirrors its own historical situation, and has no existence apart from society. "Psychic actuality, when compared with the spiritual, resembles a natural object." In contrast to the meaningful, intentional, normative, cultural, and historical which appear at the level of spirit, "it simply occurs as an event, subject to timeless laws and indifferent to historical development. But

[52] E. B. Titchener, whose psychology—surprisingly enough—was sometimes called "existentialism" or "existential psychology," carried this trend to highly instructive though perhaps absurd lengths when he explained why the psychologist "reads out all prior meaning, all interpretation, from the objects of his enquiry [bare sensations, images, feelings] and considers them for their sake, in their right, as they are." *Systematic Psychology: Prolegomena* (New York: Macmillan, 1929), p. 31.

[53] See R. G. Collingwood, *An Essay on Metaphysics* (Oxford: Clarendon, 1940), chap. x. Even today there is no perfectly satisfactory means of drawing a sharp line between feelings and sensations. Which, for example, is a pinprick? As Hume stated, seemingly with more regard for psychological fact than grammatical nicety: "Every impression, external and internal, passions, affections, sensations, pains and pleasures, are originally on the same footing." *Treatise*, I, 184-85.

58

it is a substratum of spirit."[54] Psychic expression, which is neither intended nor willed but simply *there*, is far simpler than the communication of spirit which is intentional, involves judgment, and raises and answers questions. "Psyche communicates directly only through vague feelings, through unselfconscious sympathy and antipathy, while spirit conveys something of itself when it communicates what is universal and objective."[55] Aggrandizement of the psychical at the expense of the spiritual leads to views like the elementistic and associationistic empiricism which stresses the certainties of sense, is baffled by our awareness of the self and our knowledge of the external world, and tends either to psychologize the normative aspects of logic and mathematics or to find in them nothing but the tautological.

Spirit will receive further consideration in connection with the so-called modes of the encompassing.[56] At present it remains simply to inquire into the meaning of the doctrine of levels or spheres, and its basis in fact. We cannot of course hope to deal adequately with the closely related problems concerning the nature of explanation (and, correspondingly, understanding),[57] and it must suffice here to show how this approach offers a means of accepting the irrationalities stressed by the empiricists and the nihilists, and, at the same time, containing or limiting them. On Jaspers' view the world is neither wholly intelligible, as the rationalists would have it, nor wholly unintelligible, as Hume's contemporary disciples at times appear to insist. Rationalities appear within each separate level, Humian irrationalities between the levels. Reason, however, predominates: *Existenzphilosophie,* though at times characterized as a variety of irrationalism,

---

[54] PE I, 170.   [55] *Ibid.*   [56] See below, chap. viii.

[57] Those who find the refutations of rationalism appearing in the opening sections of Hume's *Treatise* and *Inquiry* to be unanswerable may be referred not only to A. N. Whitehead's many critical comments on Hume in *Adventures of Ideas* (New York: Macmillan, 1933), but also to A. C. Ewing's *Idealism: A Critical Survey* (New York: Humanities Press, 1933), chap. iv.

could more accurately be viewed as a philosophy of reason.[58]

The understandable, rational, and intelligible is indeed present in the world. Within a given natural science we can understand events in terms of their causes and the natural laws under which instances are readily subsumed. We gain insight into certain sequences and are aware of understanding why they happen as they do; we find that they "make sense," and would be disconcerted if they occurred otherwise. Matters having to do with human motivation are understood in an even more intimate sense.[59] For, as Ewing says in explaining his ideal intelligibility: "It seems to me that in the psychological . . . sphere we do have faint glimmerings of . . . *a priori* insight . . . that we can see and to some extent really understand why an insult should tend to give rise to anger [and] why love should lead to grief. . . ."[60] Intelligibility is as easy to recognize as it is hard to analyze, and no account of the world that leaves it out could possibly be complete.

[58] In 1950 Jaspers not only insisted upon his allegiance to "the one eternal philosophy, the *philosophia perennis*" (EPT 16), but he also indicated that he preferred the expression "philosophy of reason" to "philosophy of Existenz" as a characterization of his own view (VF 49-50).

[59] For historical reasons the term "understanding" (*Verstand*) suffers from an excess of discordant overtones. It need hardly concern us that Spinoza used "understanding" for what Kant (and Plato) called reason, and vice versa. But it *is* confusing that while Jaspers often follows Kant in using "understanding" (*Verstand*) to refer to a scientific conceptualization of what is given in space and time, he has also learned from Dilthey and his followers (ca. 1900) to use "understanding" (*Verstehen*) to refer to a method by which human beings and societies—rather than inanimate objects—are understood. As Dilthey put it: "*Die Natur erklären wir, das Seelenleben verstehen wir* (We explain nature but we understand psychic life)." See Allport, *Personality*, pp. 539-42; Heinrich Klüver, "Contemporary German Psychology," in *Historical Introduction to Modern Psychology* by Gardner Murphy (1st ed.; New York: Harcourt-Brace, 1932), pp. 444-54. In a footnote in AP (pp. 250-51) Jaspers tells how psychiatrists took him for a radical innovator when in 1912 he first introduced them to this distinction although it had been a commonplace among students of the humanities for years. It was he who added the expression "*verstehende Psychologie*" to their vocabulary.

[60] *Idealism*, p. 176.

Unintelligibility is also unmistakably present, for many of the correlations to which we are accustomed prove to be totally inexplicable. No one can hope to understand, as Hume points out,[61] how volition produces motion in our limbs or how the soul (or brain?) can create an idea—"a real creation, a production of something out of nothing. . . . We only feel the event . . . but the power by which it is produced is entirely beyond our comprehension."[62] It is not that events at the various levels are unrelated. What is noteworthy here is the complete lack of intelligibility attaching to such familiar relations as obtain. There can be "no psychosis without a corresponding neurosis" as the contemporaries of Külpe and James used to say, but how the psychical can affect and be affected by the neural is beyond comprehension. "The unity of soma and psyche seems indisputable," as Jaspers tells us. However this kind of investigation is like exploring an unknown continent from two distant sides separated by impenetrable territory. "We only know the end links in the chain of causation from soma to psyche and vice versa,"[63] and can make nothing of what lies in between. "It seems, however, as if the further neurology advances, the further the psyche recedes; psychopathology on the other hand explores the psyche to the limits of consciousness, but finds at these limits no somatic process directly associated with such phenomena as delusional ideas . . . and hallucinations."[64] Very commonly the causes or effects of what lies across the gap are undiscoverable. But when they *are* discovered, they appear as related only in the manner described by the regularity view of causation which excludes "necessary connection" and admits only regular sequence or concomitance. Parallelism clearly obtains, but interaction is hypothetical.

Why should we accept this pluralism? Naturally it can no more be proven experimentally or logically than monism or the doctrine of the unity of science can be proven scientifi-

[61] *Inquiry*, Sect. VII, Part I.
[62] *Ibid.*   [63] APT 4.   [64] *Ibid.*

cally. One simply must see for himself: "This compartmentalization (*Gliederung*) cannot be deduced but only discovered. One has to ask where the greatest gaps actually are —those gaps that have repeatedly presented themselves in ever-increasing radicality . . . [in spite of] constant attempts to conceal them by invented transitions. They render the reduction of actuality to one single principle . . . impossible."[65] Detailed and reliable knowledge of this entire situation must wait upon such further progress of science as may lead to unanimity. "Our sketch of the situation represents only what is possible on the basis of the world-orientation that we have now achieved; no definitive insight into a fixed and final state of affairs is claimed."[66] This much we can already see, namely, that reductionistic attempts to explain one level in terms of another are mere *tours de force*. For example, we are not aided when psychic processes are accounted for in terms of quasi-mechanistic elements believed to follow three basic laws, or are "explained" in terms of what Skinner regarded as, in effect, "a queer make-believe physiology, a dummy physiology doing duty for truth when facts are missing."[67] Only confusion results when absurd attempts are made to identify the utterly disparate as Fechner did when he proclaimed the identity of mind and body after succeeding in placing a sign of equality between his measures of the psychical and the physical,[68] and as others do when they assert that harmonies are nothing but complex disturbances in the air, or that Communism is only a word, and a word is a sound.[69] Jaspers himself was well acquainted with such spurious claims: "As a physician and psychiatrist I saw the precarious foundation of so many statements and actions,

[65] PE I, 167.   [66] *Ibid.*

[67] This attribution appears in E. G. Boring's *A History of Experimental Psychology* (2nd ed.; New York: Appleton-Century-Crofts, 1950), p. 650.

[68] Boring, p. 280.

[69] See C. D. Broad's classic reply to this sort of obfuscation in *The Mind and Its Place in Nature* (New York: Humanities Press, 1951), p. 622.

and beheld the reign of imagined insights, e.g. the causation of all mental illnesses by brain processes (I called all this talk about the brain, as it was fashionable then, brain mythology; it was succeeded later by the mythology of psychoanalysis)."[70]

This point, which is not elusive, is inadvertently demonstrated every year in courses in elementary psychology. Following a chapter dealing with the phenomenology of (e.g.) color by describing visual sensations in terms of hue, saturation, and brightness, and systematizing them in the form of a circle, triangle, or double pyramid, typically appears a further chapter intended to supply causal explanations in physical and physiological terms. Waves in the ether (for corpuscles would be more difficult to fit into the picture) explain the observed colors by reference to wave length, amount of mixture, and amplitude of the waves, while the retinal rods and cones are made to account for the difference between the chromatic and the achromatic. The phenomena, of course, are explained, and the appearances are saved. But the point is that here—as elsewhere when there is a gap to be bridged—the only explanation is of the Humian variety: there is a (hypothesized) constant succession but no trace of necessary connection. We believe that one kind of event must continue to follow another regularly because we think it has done so in the past. But this supposed regular succession is at best simply an unintelligible conjunction that we must accept but cannot understand. We have no insight whatsoever into the reason why.

Summary of Conclusions Concerning Science and Philosophy

Bringing together the results of the present chapter we find that we have arrived at the following:

1. Philosophy is not science, and any attempt to prepare a scientific philosophy or to provide philosophic results that

[70] UPT 149.

are universally valid and inescapable is futile. And science is not philosophy, for the objective knowledge supplied by any of its branches relates always to what appears within one specific and narrowly circumscribed area of facts purged of values and uncontaminated by moral criteria. It is important that man should not confuse "the knowledge that he can prove with the convictions by which he lives."[71]

2. But philosophy today depends upon science for knowledge that is uniquely reliable: scientific proofs are coercive, universally valid, and objective. The conclusions which they support provide a proper basis for philosophical world-orientation.

3. Scientific coerciveness rests its logico-mathematical results upon indemonstrable assumptions, and leaves its factual conclusions open to a variety of interpretations. All findings are relative to the methods employed. And the vaunted objectivity of science is purchased by neglect of the qualitative and by inability to evaluate either itself or the goals which it serves.

4. To discover the limitations of science is to become aware of the immense area open to philosophic investigation and cultivation.

5. Science discloses both the rationality and the irrationality of our world. The former is prominent when each single scientific level is taken separately; the latter, when abrupt transitions are made from one level to another.

6. The unity which monism requires cannot be found within the natural world. "The foundation which is common to all must be more basic than anything that is accessible as an object to world-orientation. . . . Whenever we undertake to bring the four worlds together in thought, we simply think in analogies that are nullified by further study: life is regarded as mechanism, spirit as life, human society as organism. There is just no fruitful and cognitively defensible

[71] UPT 144. Cf. PE I, 135-38.

comprehensive theory of the world *in toto*."[72] Instead of seeking a world-hypothesis[73] that will unify and explain everything as a scientific hypothesis unifies and explains events in a limited area, we should look beyond the limits of scientific competence as did Plato, Spinoza, the mystics, Kant, and many others. To encounter a boundary is to know that something more lies beyond:

> Every limit encountered by scientific investigation provides an opportunity to transcend. There are two kinds of limits. On the *negative* side appears the irrationality of the incalculable—the unintelligibility manifested by physical "constants," atomic movements, and the so-called contingency of natural laws. On this side we are confronted by matter—the other that is not permeated by *Logos*. On the *positive* side it is *freedom* that appears as a limit. The sort of independently existing being that, because of its resistance, physical science could determine, though only negatively [as an unknown and unknowable thing-in-itself], now is assuredly present. The natural sciences (*Naturwissenschaften*) undertake to capture the cognitively impenetrable with their laws and theories; the humanistic disciplines (*Geisteswissenschaften*) submit the results and appearances of freedom to interpretation in terms of their own laws, norms, and meanings. But the final boundary is, for the natural sciences, the dark absolutely other, and for the humanistic disciplines the freedom of Existenz as a source of communication. This latter leads me to myself.[74]

---

[72] PE I, 107.

[73] Jaspers, who apparently is unacquainted with Pepper's defense of metaphysics in his *World Hypotheses*, again and again explicitly rejects the view that philosophy issues in "*Welthypothesen*" which are simply more general and less precise than the hypotheses of science. This entire approach seems to him positivistic. See PE I, 232, 235, 274, and III, 31, 135-36, 163, 214.

[74] PE I, 147.

chapter three

Institutions and Professions as
Guides through Life

༼ ༽

Schelling, as Jaspers reminds us, once said that "although man, at the beginning of his existence, finds himself thrown, as it were, into a stream (*gleichsam in einen Strom geworfen*) that . . . overpowers him completely, still he is not required to allow this stream to simply wrench him loose and carry him along passively like an inanimate object."[1] Without his consent he is brought into a world that he does not understand. Naturally he must try to "adjust" to the situation. But *how*?[2] Knowledge of the good life is not innate but acquired through experience. But at the outset he has had no experience. From what agencies can he learn, and are these agencies reliable? In brief, how is a member of our civilization to find out how to live?

This question does not relate to the educational system,[3] for the schools are not independent sources but transmitters to the oncoming generation of the mores, ethos, and lore of the group. Our present concern is not communication, but rather the value of our *modi vivendi* and the trustworthiness of the social arrangements that support them and promote their future betterment. Here we shall limit ourselves to a brief consideration of three topics that would appear to be highly indicative: the state and its laws, religion and the

[1] Schelling's *Werke*, XIII, 202, as quoted in SG 65. The idea of "*Geworfenheit*," however, can be traced back to Augustine. See PO 30.

[2] For Jaspers, "world-orientation," is not merely theoretical, but "concerned to know what it is possible to change as well as what already exists." PE I, 116.

[3] The reader who is interested in educational methods may well consult the following in English translation: GET II, 2; PWT 22-32, 243-54.

66

churches, and such medically oriented instrumentalities of counseling and guidance as are often substituted for the houses of correction of the former and the confessionals of the latter.

The State and Its Laws as Guides

Descartes, widely celebrated for the independence that caused him to begin his philosophizing with a sweeping rejection of scholastic thought, was content in practical life simply to accept the demands of religious and secular authorities, and follow the customs of his country. "In questions of action," he says, "I am guided by the state and the customs of the country, by the example of the best among my fellow men, and by resoluteness."[4] That much the same conclusion was affirmed two centuries later by another arch-rationalist speaks well for its viability. In a famous version of Hegelian *Sittlichkeit*,[5] F. H. Bradley tells us how the individual realizes himself only within the nation-state, conceived as a "moral organism" that is to a citizen what the body is to a specific organ. Within this "concrete universal" appears the "stern imperative" that supplies moral guidance. Hegelianism, in other words, asserts that virtue

> is not a troubling oneself about a peculiar and isolated morality of one's own; that a striving for a positive morality of one's own is futile, and in its very nature impossible of attainment; that in respect of morality the saying of the wisest men of antiquity is the only one which is true, that to be moral is to live in accordance with the moral tradition of one's country; and in respect of education, the one true answer is that which a Pythagorean gave to him who asked what was the best education for his son, If you make him the citizen of a people with good institutions.[6]

[4] A.T. IX, Part 2, p. 10, as quoted in DPT 156.
[5] *Ethical Studies* (2nd ed.; Oxford: Clarendon Press, 1927), p. 162.
[6] Hegel, *Philosophische Abhandlungen*, Werke I, pp. 399-400 (1932), as quoted and, presumably, translated by Bradley, *op.cit.*, p. 173.

However, since Hegel's era—and Bradley's—experience with totalitarian nations has opened our eyes to terrifying possibilities. Granted that it is as natural for the normal individual to interiorize the moral standards of his society as for the state to punish transgressors, still the almost inconceivably heinous atrocities committed on a huge scale by twentieth-century dictatorships have demonstrated anew that the demands of a state may be so flagrantly unjust that it is criminal to obey them. Thus it comes about that the law, far from providing reliable guidance for the individual who wants to know how to live, confronts him with a problem that may well prove insoluble. The law is to be obeyed, but not always, and the individual must decide on his own responsibility when exceptions are to be made and when not. That each should follow the dictates of his own private conscience is a formula for anarchy and downright social chaos, but at the same time the avoidance of freedom and responsibility through thoughtless and uncritical obedience to vicious *de facto* laws means abandonment of moral resolution. In any case, virtue must be its own reward. From a strictly nonmoral point of view, consistent obedience to law is time-consuming, troublesome, and costly; it constitutes a grave handicap in the economic and social struggles of contemporary life. But violations of our laws and customs committed for moral reasons may well be disastrous, for, as Reinhold Niebuhr reminds us: "Nations crucify their moral rebels with their criminals upon the same Golgotha, not being able to distinguish between the moral idealism which surpasses, and the anti-social conduct which falls below that moral mediocrity on the level of which every society unifies its life."[7]

Social Planning and the Welfare State

Those who are quick to recognize the fallibility of the *de facto* laws of actual states are often inclined to accept the utopian

[7] *Moral Man and Immoral Society* (New York: Scribner's, 1960), pp. 88-89.

notion of a future welfare state[8] that will apply intelligence to the challenging task of using large-scale industry, based upon science, to bring about a permanent and wholly gratifying improvement in the human condition. Now that the conquest of nature has been completed and the problem of production has been solved, it is tempting to suppose that nothing but willful perversity can prevent man from developing rational means to a humanistic millennium. There seems to be no limit to what could be done through social planning. If life on this earth is anything less than glorious, this must be put down to such alterable human tendencies as ignorance, apathy, greed, inability to apply what we already know, proneness to accidents, and insufficient and inadequate human engineering. And such things can readily be changed. War, it seems, could be replaced by a condition of perpetual peace. Medical science is already learning how to eliminate death—or at least to postpone it until senility, aided by analgesics, blots out all awareness of it.[9] Work can be rationalized and made enjoyable by appropriate mechanical means. The population explosion can be controlled through planned parenthood. Efficient use of manpower can be facilitated by aptitude testing and carefully programmed training. There is no limit to what man can do. Or so it appears. And yet:

1. There are ineradicable difficulties rooted in the human situation as such. Everything undergoes change without ceasing: since, on the national scene, the "same" causes never recur, the "same" effects cannot be anticipated. Every social situation is unique, and we must always expect the unexpected. We cannot say when the supply of our seemingly indispensable raw materials will be exhausted, or whether or not science will produce suitable substitutes when they are needed. Illness, famine, and "acts of God" cut down the

[8] PE II, 336ff.

[9] That such thoughts, along with "science fiction" actually occupy men's minds today is evident. See, for example, Review of *The Immortalist*, by Alan Harrington, *Time*, July 11, 1969, pp. 81-82.

population in astonishing ways. Inevitably a certain proportion of the population will suffer from congenital defects, accidental injuries, and chronic illnesses, and always some will have to undertake hard, tedious, and unrewarding tasks. And death will continue to await all however much anesthesia may diminish its terrors.

2. Social planning is further limited by the unpredictability and uncontrollability—even the caprice—of man himself.[10] Fashions, fads, and crazes upset the rational operation of the laws of supply and demand. Bad money drives out good money. Bureaucracy tends to perpetuate itself and enlarge its estate indefinitely. Programs to care for the indigent may in part defeat their own ends by discouraging saving. Wage increases intended to improve the lot of labor may harm labor by promoting inflation. Scientific progress increases the ability to destroy as well as the opportunity for positive achievement. As early as 1932 Jaspers wrote: "While we cannot as yet show how it could be done, it is by no means unthinkable that man will eventually prove capable of exploding the entire earth, leaving behind only a cloud of dust drifting through the universe."[11] A decade after the war, he found not only that "mankind as a whole can be wiped out by men," but that, since there is no way of safeguarding the use of the atom bomb in advance, "it has not merely become possible for this to happen; on purely rational reflection it is *probable* that it will happen."[12] In an indefinitely extended future, whatever is consistently thinkable is liable eventually to occur.

3. If, *per impossibile*, all the above-mentioned problems could be solved, man would still not be happy, for the novel, heroic, adventuresome, and extravagant easily outweigh such pleasure as humdrum security provides.[13] A life that is entirely thought out in advance is not challenging or even interesting. Boredom, ennui, the immense tedium that attends

[10] EPT 104.   [11] PE I, 118.   [12] ATT 3.
[13] PE II, 368.

the exclusion of all competition and the elimination of all hazards would render life futile and banal. No one really wants to live by bread alone. The world could be turned into a gigantic and efficient factory only to the great detriment of human beings. Leveling, loss of initiative, abdication of responsibility, and eventual dehumanization would result. Human wisdom is not sufficient to direct the course of world events.

4. While, as Aristotle said, one must live before he can live well, it is the *good* life, that is wanted. Without spiritual values (*geistige Werte*) life is a thing of rags and tatters. As sages and seers have long insisted, values achieved through art, literature, religion, philosophy, are incommensurably higher than the material and vital values. But still from the standpoint of the social planner, they constitute an *embarras de richesse*. For on what basis could one decide how the social income should be divided among the various cultural institutions? Is music superior to the visual arts? If so, what kind of music? Should we take from the museums to give to the churches, or vice versa? And is it possible to plan for artistic and philosophic creation and religious inspiration?

5. Finally, what is most terrifying about a planned society —whether that of Plato, More, Marx, or Orwell—is that man loses his dignity when he exchanges moral autonomy for passive and thoughtless obedience. In a world of this description, what a man is to himself and what he experiences religiously and philosophically are simply denied status. Socrates' tendance of the soul, the Stoics' freedom of thought, Jesus' Kingdom of Heaven, and Kant's good will disappear from view, to occupy a position in an immediately experienced but somehow unreal limbo that, being scientifically unknown and unknowable, must be brushed aside as illusory and inconsequential.

Sometimes it is supposed that what cannot be achieved by a single nation can be brought about by a world organ-

71

ization of nations. Up to now, attempts in this direction have not been reassuring. As Jaspers tells us in *The Future of Mankind*, when we compare the magnificent principles found in the Preamble of the United Nations Charter with the cynical and callous conduct of the member-states, we are appalled by the contrast. To the discerning eye the entire mise-en-scène proves to be a sham and a delusion, thinly disguised by pious attitudinizings and transparent hypocrisies. "Disappointment . . . increases with an examination of the reality of the organization created thus far. It culminates in the insight that the principle of falsehood, which has been the essence and the evil of all past politics, has come to prevail more ruthlessly than ever."[14] Talk about "the sovereign equality of all its members" is belied by the veto on Security Council resolutions held by five states, viz., China (i.e. Formosa), France, Russia, Great Britain, and the United States. While theoretically provision is made for the use of armed force, there is in practice no way to ensure its availability. Nations unwilling to recognize the principles of the charter are excluded—a provision that seems to apply only to Communist China. In fact, "executive power depends, not on the United Nations, but solely on the policies of the sovereign powers. The UN . . . seeks executive power to enforce its decisions, but there can be neither sanctions nor military intervention unless UN resolutions happen to coincide with the sovereign decisions of the great powers. . . ."[15] So great indeed is the contrast between pious pretensions and unsavory realities that

> UN debates lack the earnestness in which men approach inquiries supposed to find the right in disinterested objectivity. . . . As a rule, the proceedings are governed by brazen falsehood, or by more refined legal sophistry. . . . A cynical mood develops, an awareness of swindling all around. Uncomfortable facts are shamelessly swept under the rug; uncomfortable questions meet with silence.[16]

[14] ATT 142.   [15] ATT 144.   [16] ATT 146.

The conclusion would seem to be that the task of human betterment on an international scale is immensely complicated by the seemingly invincible selfishness and shameless hypocrisy of the representatives of individual nations. Those who incline to say: The UN is our last hope; what else is there? should note that the nonexistence of a viable alternative is not a commendation, but an invitation to despair.

Philosophy of Existenz and Christianity

Karl Jaspers' relation to Christianity is sufficiently involved to belie the simple trichotomy: for, against, or indifferent. He insists repeatedly that he is a Christian.[17] And still, as has been said of Montaigne,[18] he supports Christianity somewhat as a rope supports one who is being hanged, for he is outspokenly sympathetic with Nietzsche's proclamation of the death of God, as well as with Kierkegaard's "attack upon 'Christendom' " and, in the end, his commitments are to philosophical rather than religious faith. To understand his position we must observe a number of distinctions.

First of all, his Christianity was passively received as an ingredient in his cultural heritage. He was a member of a Protestant Church much as he was a citizen of Germany. He never underwent a religious "conversion"; he did not "decide" in favor of Christianity, but came to life, so to speak, as a member of a religious community. During his childhood he "had few contacts with formal religion,"[19] and he allowed himself to be confirmed only "as part of the proprieties, without religious emphasis, as a feast day that brought purely mundane presents."[20]

Because his Christianity was interiorized from the climate of opinion which enveloped his childhood, it was commonplace and matter-of-fact, and at the same time, deep-lying, intrinsic, and indelible. When, as a senior in the Gymnasium he felt that he ought to leave the church to preserve his in-

[17] PE I, 312; PHT 114; PO 52, 54.
[18] In Defense of Raymond Sebond, trans. Arthur H. Beattie (New York: Ungar, 1959), p. ix.
[19] PFT 286.   [20] PFT 287.

tegrity, he allowed his father to dissuade him—in spite of the falsehood involved—because the church was needed to sanction certain moral rules. Of his early years as a professor he says: "I did not dream that I might ever take an interest in theology. . . . When I lectured on religious psychology . . . I did so without personal involvement."[21] But if his Christianity was lukewarm, it was also penetrating, pervasive, and compelling. "We Occidentals," he says, "all belong to Christianity because it has been impressed upon us. Our Christian heritage inspires our souls, determines our decisions and intentions, and provides us with Biblical images and ideas."[22] To view our philosophy "from the standpoint of the ancient Greeks, not to mention that of the Indian and Chinese philosophers, is to become aware of a special Christian atmosphere that is so penetrating that we can feel it even in the thought of the sceptics and materialists."[23]

The term "Christian" is here used in a somewhat latitudinarian sense: "I do not believe in revelation, and so far as I know, I have never . . . believed in it," he says.[24] "We who do not believe that Christ was a God who became a man are also 'Christians.' Christians? The name is to be understood historically. It was as a result of a confused situation that Biblical belief acquired this name. Under the name of Christianity Biblical religion became fundamental throughout the West. . . . The historical name 'Christian religion,' old as it is, is misleading because it is too narrow."[25] To any theologian who says that just reading the Bible does not make one a Christian, I answer: "There is no person and no court of appeal competent to decide who is a Christian. We are all Christians (believers in the Bible), and Christianity is to be attributed to anyone who lays claim to it. We need not allow ourselves to be evicted from the house that our fathers have inhabited for a thousand years. What counts is the way one reads the Bible, and what comes of his reading."[26]

[21] PFT 286. [22] PO 52. [23] PO 62.
[24] PO 35. [25] PO 503. [26] PO 53-54.

It is from this standpoint that he can feel free to say, in his debate with the theologian, Rudolph Bultmann:

I realize that I am living in a context of Biblical thinking, that I was born in it, and breathe it, like all Western men, Jews, Catholics, or Protestants. I consider myself a Protestant, I am a church member, and as a Protestant I enjoy the freedom to ascertain my faith, the faith on the basis of which I like to think I live, without mediators, in direct relation to transcendence, guided by the Bible and by Kant.[27]

In a Christian era, adherents to a philosophy which concerns the truth by which we live cannot remain indifferent to Christianity or refuse to include such great religious leaders as Jesus, Buddha, and Lao Tzu in a roster of "great philosophers."[28] While Christianity rests its claims on extra-philosophical grounds, and will surely never be acceptable to the entire world,[29] still philosophers can no more ignore it than they can ignore science. When we view the matter historically, we cannot but recognize its far-reaching influence upon Western thought and the high moral and spiritual rank of many of its adherents. More important to us is its contribution to philosophical thought.[30] And finally: "We can not remain indifferent when the content of [its] revelations is of sufficient weight to have absolute significance existentially up to the present."[31] While the question of the

[27] FET 76. In this connection the following statement is enlightening: "Since tradition is bound up with organization, and the tradition of Biblical religion with churches, congregations, and sects, anyone who as an Occidental knows the ground on which he stands will belong to such an organization (Roman Catholic, Jewish, Protestant, or the like) in order to preserve his traditions and retain a point at which conceivably the *pneuma* could inspire the people were it again to become efficacious." PO 54.

[28] See the Table of Contents in GP.   [29] PO 7.

[30] An example: In talking to Bultmann he says: "I confess that it was only thanks to Paul and Augustine that I clearly understood what had for me been a purely philosophical impulse—the experience of helplessness in freedom." FET 73.

[31] PO 35.

relation between religion and philosophy is not now as prominent as it was during the Middle Ages, it is more baffling than ever because of the rival claims of science and the pernicious influence of the novel superstitions that science has generated.

The Church as a Guide

As we have seen, Karl Jaspers was a Christian much as he was a German: he never chose to be either, and he applied both terms to himself descriptively rather than eulogistically. Like Socrates who imagines "that the topics of praise should be true," and says that he is ready to talk of Eros only "if you like to hear the truth about love,"[32] Jaspers ignores didactic considerations and, at the risk of being considered offensive, deliberately and with malice prepense subordinates the will to believe to the will to truth. Perhaps here more than elsewhere we find a fulfillment of Nietzsche's ironic claim that in the end "the sense of truthfulness engendered by Christianity itself recoils from the falsehood and mendacity of all Christian world interpretation."[33] The question is not how much good the church may have done, but simply whether or not there is reason to accept Christian doctrine as the absolute truth and the church as a refuge and guide throughout life.

Certain relatively obvious points that have now become the common property of enlightened thinkers everywhere need not be elaborated upon, though they should be kept in mind. Pascal's wager, brought to American attention by James's "The Will to Believe," vastly oversimplifies the actual situation of the existing individual whose decision today relates to a number of world religions and many jarring sects and not Catholicism alone.[34] It will not do simply to ask "Should I or should I not be a Christian?" since for all of the wager a good Christian might awaken after death in

[32] Plato, *Symposium*, trans. B. Jowett (2 vols.; New York: Random House, 1937), I, 324.
[33] Quoted in NIT 15.   [34] NIT 48.

a Moslem hell, or find himself damned for not worshipping on Saturday. It is not possible, as Pascal appeared to believe, to avoid taking chances. And, as Spinoza and Locke (not to mention Paine) agreed, if a given revelation constituted indisputable evidence to the prophet or apostle who witnessed it, still to us it is only hearsay evidence which we are not obliged to accept.[35] And whether or not we agree with Hume that miracles have been observed "chiefly to abound among ignorant and barbarous nations," we must today recognize the proved unreliability of testimonial evidence, and ponder Hume's dictum that "no testimony is sufficient to establish a miracle unless the testimony be of such a kind that its falsehood would be more miraculous than the fact which it endeavors to establish."[36]

Turning now to Jaspers' own special approach, we shall find that however much the church may have achieved (and of this there can be no doubt) still, when the two millennia of its history are impartially viewed, it turns out to have been no more trustworthy or honorable than the state. It has been neither a good counselor nor a good example. In fact it has been repeatedly unreasonable, mistaken, dishonest, scheming, power-hungry, unscrupulous, and hypercritical.[37] It was no mere whim that led Dante, good Catholic that he was, to consign various popes and cardinals to eternal torments in the terrifying hell that his febrile imagination had created for them. Christianity is often found wanting, and any attempt at apologetics should observe at least the following charges.

[35] POT 56-57.

[36] *Inquiry*, Sect. X. The fallibility of testimonial evidence is, of course, notorious among twentieth century psychologists.

[37] In GPT I, 227-28 Jaspers remarks concerning Augustine, for example, that "he did not know the evil that the Church as a political institution was to bring into the world, more continuously, more consistently, more artfully and ruthlessly than any of the more transient world powers." As Paul Ricoeur says in PX 623, "the pages devoted to . . . Judeo-Christian or Islamic orthodoxy [insofar as they lay claim to exclusive possession of truth] are of a vehemence rarely found in the work of Jaspers. . . . The very principle of the revelation . . . is scrutinized with a great inner violence."

Revelation lies at the heart of Christianity. But how do we arrive at it? Not only was the truth not revealed *to us*, but what was proclaimed to the apostles has descended through human speech, and speech inevitably involves interpretation.[38] This point becomes especially troublesome when we recall that Jesus spoke Aramaic rather than New Testament Greek, and that this latter comes to most of us through translation. Christian revelation, unlike scientific knowledge, derives from unique historic events. But language is composed of general terms which in the nature of the case must fail accurately to depict the unique: "Thought cannot proceed without general concepts. But revelation is said to have been absolutely historical, and consequently it can be neither attained nor exhaustively conveyed by general ideas. All thought concerning revelation revolves around something that thought can not and will never be able to grasp."[39]

Assuming that inspiration produced the New Testament during the first century, how did canonization come about? That is, what principles of selection were employed by the Church Fathers? Did they choose those writings which were most widely promulgated, those which they took to be superior, or did they allow chance to decide? Are we to believe that God himself directed the selection as well as the writing of the books that now constitute the sacred canon?[40] And when church councils met for the sake of establishing church doctrines and extirpating heresies (as, for example, the Council of Nicaea which condemned Arianism in 325), were their decisions divinely inspired or subject to human error? If the latter should we not be impressed by the large number of able men who dissented, and inclined to wonder whether they received an impartial hearing, and what proportion of their writings have been permitted to survive?

Whatever the answer may be, there can be no doubt that Church dogmas were often repugnant to reason, or as St. Paul expressed it, "unto the Jews a stumblingblock, and

[38] PO 55.   [39] PO 56.   [40] PO 48.

unto the Greeks foolishness."[41] The *credo quia absurdum* of the Church Father, Tertullian, which resounded in Denmark during the mid-nineteenth century and has been revived in our time by Karl Barth and his followers, suggests the presence, at the very heart of the Christian religion, of a series of paradoxes or self-contradictions that cannot be resolved to the satisfaction of the human intellect.[42] The Unitarians find in the doctrine of the Trinity a compromise with polytheism that flatly contradicts the monotheistic insights of the Hebrew prophets and early Christians. The doctrine of the Incarnation seemed to Spinoza as absurd as talk about a round square or an infinite fly. And the predestinarianism of St. Paul and Augustine appears to be required by the omnipotence and omniscience which Christianity attributes to the Deity and totally at loggerheads with human conceptions of justice and fair play. Here we would seem to have a remarkable instance of Jaspers' claim that antinomies always appear when the human understanding transgresses its proper limits.

To those who are appalled by the admitted unreasonableness of Christianity, baffled at the discovery that seemingly rational human beings easily believe the incredible, and deeply and permanently offended by the attitudes of nominal friends who think them fairly and justly damned for failing to believe what they cannot believe, the church structures the situation in terms of divine election and irresistible grace: "It is not through thinking or experiencing or willing that I can manage to believe. For revelation belongs only to those to whom God gives the grace that enables them to accept it. Man does not seek God and, as it were, come to Him through his own strength. On the contrary, God himself chooses those whom he will have for his own."[43] By my-

---

[41] I Cor. 1. 23. The importance of this to St. Paul is clear from verses 18 and 19: "For the preaching of the cross is to them that perish foolishness; but unto us which are saved it is the power of God. For it is written, I will destroy the wisdom of the wise and will bring to nothing the understanding of the prudent."

[42] See, for example, PO 76-77, 81, 106, 495.   [43] PO 51.

self I can do nothing, for belief is independent of both knowledge and volition.

Unlike some other religions, Christianity presupposes that it has a monopoly on the truth by which one should live, and asserts that "it alone not only can make a universally valid claim, but is actually universal (catholic). Anything else that lays claim to be equally unconditional is untruth, blindness, wickedness."[44] But this is insufferable: "Only when the poisonous claim to exclusiveness is laid aside can biblical belief . . . actualize its true nature."[45] "For noble men and pure in soul are quite discernible outside of Christianity; it would be absurd for them to be lost, particularly if we compare them with certain of the most conspicuous Christians in history, who have been none too lovable or admirable in any human sense."[46] But more important still, exclusiveness means intolerance, and intolerance "stands forever in readiness to kindle new fires in which to burn heretics."[47] "Because intolerance against intolerance (but only against intolerance) is indispensable, intolerance against the exclusivist claim is necessary when it not only propounds a doctrine for consideration by others, but strives to force it on others by law, by compulsory schools, etc."[48]

On what sort of grounds did the early church make the decisions concerning doctrinal issues that had to be made if a generally acceptable creed was to be arrived at? Were the decisive considerations matters of inspiration, scriptural interpretation, reason, prudence, or political expediency? It would be difficult to rest such decisions upon the Bible, for "in the Bible seen as a whole, everything occurs in polarities. For every formulation one will ultimately find the opposite formulation."[49] A philosopher who deals with this question by examining the methods employed by St. Thomas Aquinas tends to find that his procedure typically "degenerates into a making of countless distinctions leading to endless discussion. Simple facts become blurred, one

[44] PO 83.   [45] PO 508.   [46] PHT 89.
[47] PHT 94-95.   [48] PHT 95.   [49] PHT 99.

carefully reasoned claim is set over against another, and both are annulled in favor of whatever vindication or condemnation happens to be required. The method also involves . . . being overwhelmed by citations."[50] Perhaps in this case as in many others, the simplest hypothesis ought to be chosen: The arguments are mere special pleading. The grounds underlying the churches' decisions are usually psychological and political rather than logical and/or spiritual. The "reasons" for the dogmas of the church are for the most part motives and strategic considerations rather than premises and evidences, and in case of a serious conflict it is the latter that must give way.

If, for example, we insist upon seeking logical or scriptural grounds for Augustine's willingness to persecute the Donatists who claimed that the sacraments are effective only when they are administered by priests in a state of grace, we are baffled, for the rejected doctrine is eminently reasonable. But when we view the matter politically, we understand not only his rejection of the doctrine, but also his readiness, contrary to his previous teaching, to invoke the power of the state to force the heretics to accept the orthodox view. In Protestant times this "shameful reversal of New Testament Christianity into its very opposite" assumed the cynical form: "*cuius regio, eius religio* (the denomination of the prince determines that of the country's inhabitants)."[51]

To take another example: the church could never quite bring itself to accept the predestinarianism of St. Paul, Augustine and Luther, for when strictly interpreted this doctrine implies the dispensability of the sacraments. But it also rejected the teachings of Pelagius who insisted upon free will in man, for if man is able to save himself, then again he can dispense with the sacraments. The upshot then was: "Neither predestination nor freedom, but an unstable semi-Pelagianism defended in the name of Augustine. . . ."[52] A sim-

---

[50] PO 85. [51] PO 87.

[52] PO 84. Note that while Augustine is concerned to show that God's foreknowledge is entirely compatible with freedom of the will,

ilar instability attached to the *anima naturaliter christiana* which permits us to believe that deserving pagans may enter the kingdom of heaven if they have had no opportunity to learn of Christ, for this view is limited by the contradictory view which admits of no salvation outside of the church (*extra ecclesiam nulla salus*). The former is needed in order to exhibit the "reasonableness" of Christianity, the latter to increase the power of the church.[53]

The church has often availed itself of immediate and forceful punitive measures to enforce its decisions. Its warlike character was obvious from the very beginning, and it is not surprising that "this religion of the church, as soon as it gained hegemony within the world, made many more martyrs by its deadly attacks on heretics and unbelievers than had ever died for it during the years when it was being founded."[54] But as though this were not enough, threats of eternal punishments to come were added. "The believers were coerced by the threat of the ban, the interdict, purgatory, and hell."[55] "Fundamentally, it amounts to this: a group of human beings that constitutes the church appeals to the Deity and uses this appeal as a means to its own worldly aggrandizement and self-assertion. Thus the

---

still he emphasizes divine election and predestination as does St. Paul. As Windelband puts it: "It will always remain an astonishing fact that the same man who . . . discovered in the will the vital ground of spiritual personality, found himself forced by the interests of a theological controversy to a theory . . . which regards the acts of the individual will as unalterably determined consequences, either of a general corruption or of the divine grace." *History of Philosophy*, trans. James H. Tufts (New York: Macmillan, 1926), p. 284.

[53] PO 84.

[54] PO 74-75. Compare the following statement by Joseph McCabe, as quoted by Harry Elmer Barnes in *The History of Western Civilization* (New York: Harcourt, Brace, 1935), I, 371: "The quarrel [between Arius and Athanasius, ca. 300 A.D.] made five or six times as many martyrs in fifty years as the pagan emperors had made in two hundred and fifty years; and to these we might add the massacre of the Goths in 378."

[55] PO 75.

human claim to power assumes the guise of the divine. . . .
Accordingly, communication, peace, and loyalty (*Treue*)
have been fatally injured by the political machinations of
the churches."[56] Imaginative and sensitive persons who cannot accept revelation find all this as excruciatingly painful
as it is incomprehensible.

> For almost two thousand years orthodoxy has threatened
> us with eternal death, condemning our self-deification, our
> pride, our presumption in setting man, i.e., ourselves,
> above God. These judgments fill us with amazement, as
> do the uncritical, curious assertions that condemn the
> nonbeliever to eternal torments and promise the believer
> eternal bliss. Is God absent from our lives? . . . [And] did
> not God side with Job against the orthodox theologians?[57]

In the end, we outsiders simply confront an ineluctable
mystery. We cannot see what those who accept the authority
of the church claim to see, and we can only be sure that the
ab extra view of Christian revelation must be *toto caelo*
different from the *ab intra* view which is available only to
believers. To us it is neither credible, intelligible, nor agreeable. Communication breaks down, *Verstehen* fails. We
alone know how desperately we have tried to reach an understanding, and how baffled we are when we cannot communicate what we find obvious. It was in this spirit that Jaspers, following a futile attempt to come to terms with Rudolf
Bultmann, whom he had admired for many years,[58] wrote:

> It is among the sorrows of my life spent in the search for
> truth, that discussion with theologians always dries up at
> crucial points; they fall silent, state an incomprehensible
> proposition, speak of something else, make some categoric
> statement, engage in amiable talk . . . and in the last anal-
> ysis they are not really interested. . . . People like us . . .
> strike them as merely stubborn.[59]

[56] PO 86-87.   [57] FET 48.   [58] FET 111-12.
[59] PHT 77.

83

Revealed religion, "where prayer, a cult, and revelation establish a community and give rise to authority, theology and obedience,"[60] as Nietzsche and Kierkegaard were quick to note, is dishonest and hypocritical. The typical believer will follow the path provided by the church only if it is not too inconvenient. And since he does not consider it feasible to live by pure and undefiled Christian doctrine (that of the Sermon on the Mount, for instance), "theology becomes a laborious invention of compromises, reinterpretations, and tergiversations calculated to conceal the conflict between well-known and generally acknowledged moral demands, and a set of practices widely at variance with those demands. Independent philosophic thinking, however, being committed to unwavering integrity, confronts us with the either/ or of complete acceptance or rejection."[61]

Every individual experiences an inner conflict between the desire for obedience with repudiation of independent responsibility on the one hand, and the urge to be free from creeds, cults, and authorities on the other. "This decision between religion and philosophy cannot be avoided unless one is willing to remain in the shady indefiniteness of apathy and indifference."[62] He who is not for us is against us. "Every form of the *sacrificio dell' intelletto* destroys one's dignity as well as his freedom."[63] Those who are unable to take the church as a guide may look to philosophy for another prospect—that of an independent search for value and truth within an ever expanding horizon.

The liberation which the way of philosophy offers is not easy, because it provides no tangible evidence, no guarantee, and no court of appeal capable of pronouncing a final judgment. To enter the company of philosophic minds means to have thereafter no example to follow, no authority to rely on, no truth to be passively received, and no historically given revelation to provide salvation.

[60] PE I, 296.   [61] PE I, 298.   [62] PE I, 301.
[63] PE I, 307.

He who philosophizes must confirm everything for himself, always taking full responsibility. No one receives him into the realm of philosophic minds; the venture is his own.[64]

While philosophy can enable us to see, we must always *look* for ourselves. "The unveiling of philosophic mysteries comes about as a result of our own philosophizing, and is never quite the same twice. While communicating with others within the realm of the spirit, everyone must seek and find for himself."[65]

Psychiatry as a Guide

Psychiatry, which supplies many of the elite with the guidance that they have failed to receive from either church or state, appears as a third and independent source. For if it seems to be simply a branch of medical science, its highly speculative contents, its many warring sects, its concern with ends or goals, and its total failure to arrive at a solid consensus show that science is at most its starting point. And its independence of morals and religion is notorious. For—apart from existential psychotherapy, which came into being as a revolt against the psychiatric orthodoxy here under consideration—psychiatry is a frankly secular approach which aims at "adjustment" or "mental health" rather than spiritual well-being, and, as O. H. Mowrer has made clear, typically emulates Freud in "championing the rights of the body [with its instinctual energies, especially sex and aggression] in opposition to a society and moral order which were presumed to be unduly harsh and arbitrary."[66]

The tasks of psychiatry may well seem endless and impossible to characterize in a few pages. But still, as Jaspers shows, a fair idea of its possibilities and limitations can be

[64] VW 965.
[65] VW 966. Compare the magnificent statement in UPT 136.
[66] *The Crisis in Psychiatry and Religion* (New York: Van Nostrand, 1961), p. 82.

gained from a rapid review of the stages or levels on which it can operate.[67]

1. First of all, it is easiest to work directly upon the body, viewed as a machine to be set right by surgery and drugs. While many mental illnesses are functional, some are undoubtedly organic, and these respond predictably to physicalistic therapeutic measures. Brain tumors can be removed surgically, various personality disorders can be treated by prefrontal lobotomy, while sedatives, analgesics, soporifics, and tranquilizers serve admirably in connection with certain temporary bodily disturbances. At this level therapy is quick, impersonal, effective, and sure.

2. The body, however, is not simply a machine. It is a living being, and as such endless and unsurveyable. The familiar expression "thorough physical examination" is simply a convenient euphemism for the most complete investigation that is feasible under given circumstances. While living beings usually respond favorably when suitably nursed, treated, stimulated with chemicals and exposed to well-tried remedies, there is always a risk, and the physician can never be certain that his curative measures will have the desired effects. Often the body improves of its own accord, and sometimes it fails to respond to the most reliable medicines. The whole matter is vastly complicated by the presence of the psyche. Efforts to show that all illness is organic have proved futile, and many disorders have to be regarded as "psychosomatic." But getting through to the psyche is a further task that requires remarkable sensitivity and tact on the part of the therapist. Here neurology, endocrinology, and pharmacy reach their limits.

3. Since the patient is an autonomous rational being, he wants to know why he is ill, and the doctor places his knowledge and his skills at his disposal. He examines the patient

[67] This section is based upon PE I, 121-29. Another version of the same topic, prepared especially for psychiatrists, is available in English in APT 795-800.

carefully and gives an objective account of his findings. But this leads to difficulties. The patient is intimately involved with his body and is not immune from fears and anxieties. He cannot be wholly objective. He interprets what he hears in his own way and his opinions and expectations have an unforeseeable influence upon his bodily functions. Only ideally is the physician treating a wise, courageous, and autonomous personality who can in all cases be depended upon to react reasonably. Furthermore, it is often the case that neither patient nor doctor can clearly distinguish the known from the probable, state in full the grounds on which the diagnosis rests, or foresee all the possibilities for the future. Often the physician is forced to withhold some of the facts for therapeutic reasons.

4. The patient's fears and the doctor's need for objective evidence of his own effectiveness often lead to an endless squandering of time and effort through the use of placebos which help solely by satisfying those suggestible patients who can be led to place confidence in them. Now the interchange between doctor and patient becomes a *circulus vitiosus*. To allay his own fears and arouse the patient's confidence, the doctor gives all his advice in dogmatic authoritative form intended to be accepted without question. From this point on, fear and authoritativeness tend constantly to influence each other for the worse: "The sensitiveness of the authoritative physician when his advice is not followed to the letter, and that of the patient when the physician is not self-confident, condition each other reciprocally. In such a circle things can so reverse themselves that the patient has to look after his physician on account of his sensitivity or stupidity, or the physician has to criticize the measures that he has taken to relieve the patient of his fears."[68] Usually the complexities and absurdities of this situation lead the therapist to abandon his candor, and undertake to "manage" the patient. Honest communication breaks down, and a further stage is reached.

[68] PE I, 124.

5. As though his medical knowledge were sufficient to enable him to survey the entire situation and introduce just the right causal factors, the doctor now uses words simply as stimuli to elicit desirable responses. No longer does he tell the patient what he knows and believes, but every single word and deed is carefully calculated to produce a given psychic effect. Trust is abandoned in favor of causal efficacy. "Following certain assumptions about human beings—that for the most part remain unclarified—along with conventional rules, and traditional notions concerning what is desirable and useful . . . he regards each of his acts as simply a means to an end. Now the two are completely estranged from each other. While the patient believes that he is enjoying a warm human relationship, the physician has increased the psychic distance to the point of complete breakdown of communication."[69] But this is to treat another human being as if he were a thing, or just another "case" to be subsumed under a general rule. If the patient finds out how he is being treated, he will take it as a personal affront. At this point we are forced to recognize the huge discrepancy "between that in man which stands over against us as a thing which we objectify in the empirical sense of the term, and the man himself as Existenz open to authentic communication. The former can be investigated, universalized and subsumed under rules; the latter, being historical (*geschichtlich*) resists generalization. The one can be manipulated through technique, nurture and art, the other develops through a mutual sharing of destinies."[70]

6. In dealing with the most challenging cases one finally reaches the limit of planned therapeutic measures, since problems arise that admit of no possible scientific solution. It would be easy to save the appearances if only this would satisfy the patient. Available are curative measures for bodily ills, scientific knowledge serving to provide a defensi-

[69] PE I, 125.   [70] PE I, 126.

ble world-orientation, and books offering rules governing social intercourse within polite society.

But the basic difficulties that confront serious and intelligent men and women lie at a deeper level, and it is in connection with these that one may readily lose his grip and fall, so to speak, into the abyss of pessimism, the void of nihilism, or the solitary waste of criminal egoism. Whatever well-indoctrinated professionals may claim, existing individuals need answers to questions that concern the human condition and the final meaning and purpose of life. Man cannot live by science alone, for sooner or later his religious aspirations and moral dilemmas demand to be taken into account and provided for.

The position in which the typical scientifically trained psychiatrist is placed is awkward, for he is faced with a dilemma. Either psychiatry is a science or it is not. If it is, then its practitioners must proceed objectively, leaving questions of value and obligation to moralists and religionists, for scientific objectivity requires a resolute refusal to deal with value and disvalue, right and wrong. But on this showing it is impossible to prescribe for the patient, since non-normative procedures cannot tell what a "good" adjustment is or how we are to distinguish better from worse behavior. If the aim is to improve the "mental health" of the patient, then this scientistic position must be avoided. But when it is recognized that the nature of the task requires the psychiatrist to recommend norms and standards by which his patients are to regulate their lives, then it must be admitted that this can be done only by virtue of extrascientific means such as moral insight, religious faith, and philosophical belief. Here the limits of science are transgressed and psychiatry with its many "schools" appears as a series of philosophies of life like cynicism, stoicism, hedonism, and optimism. Philosophy of life and religion have too big a contribution to make to the adjustment of the individual to be casually brushed aside.

When this level is reached (and of course it can only be

89

attained with a minority of patients), doctor and patient face each other no longer as a technician with his material, a teacher with his disciple, or as an authority speaking *ex cathedra* to an unschooled layman, but rather as two wayfarers on the path of life who exchange confidences and try to enlighten and encourage each other. The psychiatrist, being out of his field, can no longer afford to be dogmatic: he now appears before his patient as merely a knowledgeable and cultivated traveling companion concerned to assist him in finding his way. If he is a man of integrity, then, abandoning all pretenses and frankly admitting the limitations of his science, he will simply appear as his own authentic self and converse with the patient on terms of equality.[71]

At this point something which eludes scientific psychiatry is touched upon, viz., that which in the language of tradition is called the "soul," and which is now often known as "Existenz." This is the innermost self which, being a subject, can never be an object, and which, being free, and, consequently, a shaper of its own destiny, accepts responsibility for its acts and refuses to yield to the control of the psychiatrist. Here medical and psychological sciences reach their limit in an underlying source that can no more be observed than it can be defined or explained. It can only be "elucidated."

[71] This of course is what Carl Rogers, the founder of "nondirective therapy" has been insisting on for years. "When I'm being effective as a therapist," he says in an interview with Martin Buber, "I enter the relationship as a subjective person, not as a scrutinizer, not as a scientist. . . . I am able to sense with a good deal of clarity the way his experience seems to him. . . . Then it seems to me that there is a real, experiential meeting of persons. . . ." See *The Worlds of Existentialism*, ed. Maurice Friedman (New York: Random House, 1964), pp. 486-87.

chapter four

Existential Freedom

ᕬᕮ

As we have seen, world-orientation, whether undertaken on a theoretical level (chapter ii) or approached from a practical standpoint (chapter iii) leaves us in the lurch. Science, though astonishingly successful at achieving universally valid knowledge of objects within the world, cannot view the world as a whole, penetrate the veil of appearance, evaluate ends, or justify anything—itself included. When professional philosophers confront the basic questions, the result is not reliable knowledge, but such cacaphonies of incompatible views as are currently represented by the familiar textbook anthologies that, by making all positions readily available, render every position suspect. While any individual philosopher may claim to be a final authority, philosophy as such does not vouch for any set of ready-made and exclusive doctrines to be maintained with dogmatic finality.[1] No one who is keenly conscious of the extensive sweep of philosophy in time and in space, that is, who has carefully followed the serpentine movements of philosophy through history and confronted the vastness of the spectrum of contemporary philosophic persuasions (including the rationalistic, irrationalistic, positivistic, communistic, Hindu, et cetera) can easily believe that philosophy provides universally valid results. On the contrary, "This [much] is undeniable: in philosophy there is no generally accepted, definitive knowledge."[2]

When we turn from the question of what we can know to

[1] If terms like "orthodoxy," "heterodoxy," "heresy," "schism," "sound," and "unsound," have any place within philosophy, their ranges of application are certainly unstable. There is always ample historical justification for anticipating a time when whatever view is currently regnant can be brushed aside with the remark that it has "run its course," or "spent its force," or dismissed as "passé," "outmoded," "dated," or "old-fashioned."

[2] EPT 7.

91

questions concerning what we should do and what we can hope for,[3] we find ourselves again thrown back upon our own resources, for human society has—and can have—no suitable way of providing us with reliable answers. The social and political organizations of which we are members require more direction than they can give, and raise a number of problems for every one they solve. Psychologists, psychiatrists, and professional counselors whose business it is to promote "adjustment" and improve "mental health" through scientifically enlightened guidance, while entirely capable of purveying scientific facts and commonsense insights believed to be instrumental to the attainment of predetermined ends, can obviously lay claim to no special competence to deal with the basic questions that concern us most deeply.

Presumably the church has done more than any other Western institution to provide men with spiritual values and a way of life. But today it offers the perplexed individual a confusing plethora of conflicting authoritarian claims deriving from diverse interpretations of various revelations, purporting to come to us from a motley collection of unsophisticated witnesses whom we can never interrogate and whose credibility we are in no position to evaluate, concerning dogmas that are often intrinsically ambiguous and admittedly absurd.

One need not labor the point that any question that has many answers has no answer, and that when the foremost authorities disagree each man must be his own authority. The issues we are required to decide upon seem undecidable. Are moral and spiritual questions simply beyond our capacities, or is there something in man (whether it be called "will," "soul," "psyche," "anima," "spirit," "mind," "self," "persona," or "ego") by virtue of which he is capable of making fundamental decisions rationally, autonomously, responsibly, and unconditionally?

[3] These questions, taken together with the further question concerning the nature of man, are regarded as "the basic questions of philosophy" by both Kant and Jaspers. Cf. UPT 139; GPT 319.

The Kantian Background of Jaspers' Philosophy

Jaspers' statement that he ascertained the faith by which he lives "guided by the Bible and by Kant,"[4] is a remarkably telling index of his attitude toward the author of the three celebrated *Critiques*. Seldom has any philosopher been so strongly influenced by another. To be sure, Jaspers recognizes Kant's *lapsus judicii*. He lists his tautologies, vicious circles, and contradictions,[5] and even tells us that "all sorts of statements can be found in Kant; he even said that the world is conditioned 'by our brain.' Kant himself seems to have expressed all the distortions of Kantianism."[6] But at the same time he finds in the deduction of the categories of the understanding enough insights to found four typical schools of thought.[7] First of all, the *logical* insight points in the direction of the "absolute presuppositions" which R. G. Collingwood finds to be basic to the sciences of every era. Then the *psychological* insight leads to the interpretationism of Jacob Fries and Leonard Nelson. The *methodological* approach stresses with Poincaré the functioning of unverifiable hypotheses in all scientific cognition, while the *metaphysical* emphasis that led Schopenhauer to look beyond appearance to an underlying reality lends support to the combination of earnest dedication to worldly causes and serene detachment from them that has enabled seers of all ages to become involved in historic events without being overwhelmed by them.[8]

But this is merely a beginning. For, unlike many fellow commentators, he finds the crux of Kantianism in the "ideas of reason" which at once point the way to increasing scientific knowledge and supply the foundation for the "nonknowledge," or "philosophic faith" that illumines the area outside the bounds of science. Much as Plato's epistemology requires intellect to supervene upon thinking, and Spinoza's needs *intellectus* to supplement the work of *ratio*, so Kant's transcendental philosophy requires reason's ideas to organize the conclusions of the understanding. Reason, then, is a *sine qua non*, first as a capstone of science, and, second, as a marker

[4] FET 78.　　　[5] GPT I, 265-69.　　　[6] GPT I, 264.
[7] GPT I, 262-64.　　[8] See, e.g., EX 14-17.

pointing in the direction of those objects of faith and morality that the scientific understanding ignores.

Science, to be successful in its task of discovering and verifying laws of nature, must have at its disposal various assumptions or presuppositions that cannot be fully verified. The principle of parsimony, and the principle of limited variety, for instance, must be assumed even in the absence of cogent evidence. There are an indefinite number of such ideas.[9] Strictly speaking, they are not knowledge, but guides to knowledge, not conclusions, but means to the organization of scientific facts and theories. Without them science would stagnate. When ideas of reason are compared with the categories of the understanding, the contrast is striking:

Categories of the Understanding[10]	Ideas of Reason
Apply to perception	Apply to concepts and judgments
Empty without intuition	Not fulfillable in intuition
Limited to phenomena	Reaching out beyond phenomena
Determinate, precise, communicable	Indeterminate, vague, impalpable
Related to objects	Related to the extra-empirical
Productive of laws	Productive of principles
Constitutive of objects	Regulative of procedures
Definitive	Heuristic

[9] The distinction between "ideas" and the "principles" that accompany them is not always clear. Thus, for example, of the scientific group of ideas, A. C. Ewing finds it natural to write: "These [ideas] consist of principles. . . ." *A Short Commentary on Kant's Critique of Pure Reason* (Chicago: University of Chicago Press, 1938), p. 255.

[10] This list is based upon Jaspers' characterization of ideas and categories in the appendix to *Psychologie der Weltanschauungen*, especially pages 468-69. For a discussion of the topic in English, see GPT I, 279-83.

More to our present purposes, however, are the three famous metaphysical ideas that, while useful to science, are clearly basic to morality: the *soul*, the *world*, and *God*. Without being clear and distinct, verifiable, or rationally demonstrable, these ideas are inescapable in both science and life, for while they assist us in organizing and interpreting the work of science,[11] they also provide a mental context necessary for the moral life. These three ideas, to which Kant devoted very special attention, turn out to be precisely those which relate directly to what Jaspers takes to be the three chief domains of perennial philosophy: *Existenzerhellung*, or elucidation of the being that I essentially am, *Weltorientierung*, or orientation within the world, and *Metaphysik*, or the deliberate search for true being.[12] This is condensed and summarized in the accompanying schema.

Kant's Three Metaphysical Ideas and the Tasks of *Existenzphilosophie*

Theoretic Objects	Practical Objects	Fields Involved	Supporting Arguments	Existentialistic Undertaking
1. The Soul	Immortality	Psychology	Paralogisms	Existenz-Elucidation
2. The World	Freedom	Cosmology	Antinomies	World-Orientation
3. Total System	God	Theology	Existential Assumptions	Metaphysics

[11] The importance of the role played in science by the idea of the *soul* or *psyche* was brought out above in chap. ii. The idea of God, as Nietzsche emphasizes (see NET), furthered the radical and unqualified truthfulness which science requires. Also, by leading to the characterization of the world as God's creation, and hence an expression of His nature, it prepared the scientist to investigate every last detail with an elaborate thoroughness (VU 90-91). Finally the contribution of this idea to belief in the intelligibility of the world is obvious.

[12] These three ideas, of course, provide the titles of three volumes of the *Philosophie*. The present approach is amplified but not superceded by the account of the "modes of the encompassing" that first appeared in print in *Vernunft und Existenz* (1935). See below, chap. viii.

The world as object has been the topic of the two preceding chapters. The soul as subject—or Existenz—is the topic to which we now turn. Jaspers' metaphysics is reserved for the concluding chapter.

The Kantian Soul as It Relates to Existenz

The *Elucidation of Existenz* (Vol. II of *Philosophie*) begins as follows:

> If everything that cognitive orientation yields in the form of universally and necessarily valid knowledge is to be called "world," then the question arises as to whether being extends beyond the world, and thought beyond orientation within the world. The soul and God—or Existenz and Transcendence as we say when we exchange the language of mythology for that of philosophy—lie outside of the world. We cannot know them in the sense in which we know things within the world. . . . Although they are not known, they are not nothing, and while they are not accessible to science they can still be thought of.[13]

Here Existenz turns out to refer to what was once called by a more familiar name: it relates to (but is not identical with) "soul" (*Seele*) as it appears within religious and philosophical contexts. It is the modern equivalent of that which Socrates believed to be immortal, and which, as *res cogitans,* was regarded by Descartes as a substance separate from bodily substance. It definitely is *not* the soul or psyche that constitutes the traditional subject matter of the science of psychology, for what Jaspers wishes to "elucidate" is inaccessible to any possible scientific approach. It "is not an object" (*ist keineswegs Gegenstand*), never "becomes an object" to the psychologist through "meaningful gestures, behavior and actions,"[14] and is not to be represented as a stream of consciousness, a set of figures on a stage, a series of impressions, or the like. As Kant said of the "I think" which accompanies all perceptions, it is an underlying source

[13] PE II, 1.   [14] APT 9.

that cannot be given to introspection or phenomenological intuition. Like "things in themselves" it underlies appearance but nowhere appears. How is this possible?

Here it is important to see how narrowly circumscribed is the area open to psychological observation. Behavioristic psychology, which treats man as primarily a biological entity, can, of course, recognize nothing that belongs to inner experience. Freudian psychology relegates much of our inner life to an unconscious that can only be reached indirectly. Introspectionism, such as that of James, has to limit its investigations to the empirical self or "me," leaving the "pure ego" or "I" to the metaphysician. Interpretationistically inclined psychologists like Sherif, Cantril, and the late Egon Brunswik postulate an elaborate and spontaneous perceptual activity prior to, and concealed from, conscious awareness. Gestalt isomorphism appeals to underlying neurological processes which, though closer to us spatially than the physical objects which we observe, are never observable in healthy subjects. The Kantian idea of an innermost and uninvestigable self—a hidden source beyond experience which all experience presupposes—is widely shared.[15]

Not only is psychology given pause by unobservables, but it is incapable of dealing with some aspects of the inner man that lie directly open to view. Being, as R. G. Collingwood puts it, primarily a "science of feeling,"[16] it cannot recognize validity, truth, value, or the idea of the holy. There is, of course a branch of psychology devoted to the study of human thought. But, as logicians commonly recognize, when psychologists describe the process of thought, they must omit to consider certain fundamentals: Inference, for example, when logically considered, proves to be "not a psychological event at all. It is a relation between the forms

[15] At least this can be said if we can grant with N. K. Smith that the Kantian argument to presuppositions is, in effect, the familiar hypothetical method of science. *A Commentary on Kant's Critique of Pure Reason* (New York: Humanities, 1962), p. 36.

[16] *An Essay on Metaphysics* (Oxford: Clarendon Press, 1940), chap. x.

of propositions."[17] In experimental esthetics the psychologist may observe and record the value-choices of human subjects, but he may not, *qua* scientist, take cognizance of the values which are chosen. For the same reason, as Gordon Allport tells us, he may study personality but not character. The former, being "character devaluated," is open to scientific scrutiny. The latter, being "personality evaluated," has no scientific standing.[18] In the interest of objectivity science must ignore good and evil.

What is true of values obtains *a fortiori* of religious intuitions. One may, as it were, spend his life making a study of what, in the nature of the case, constantly eludes him. However industriously one may try to understand a given religion or weltanschauung, and however much he may come to know about it, still he will never see it as it is seen by its adherents.[19] Not even *verstehende Psychologie* can unlock the secrets of other men's most sacrosanct creeds.

> No one can gain an adequate view of a weltanschauung from an external standpoint, for it is only real to those in whom it develops and reaches fruition from an inner source. Consequently weltanschauungen are never seen as what they most truly are to those who possess and live by them. World views taken in their plurality are not genuine world views at all. They come to us as possibilities. But the heart and core, being wholly inaccessible to the method of *Verstehen*, is bound to elude us.[20]

At the very center of any given religion the nonbeliever inevitably finds an ineluctable mystery—an opaque, unintelligible essence—which defies understanding and invites a *sacrificium intellectus*. True religion, as experienced by the believer, is, and must remain, closed to scientific thought.

[17] Morris Cohen and Ernest Nagel, *An Introduction to Logic and Scientific Method* (New York: Harcourt, Brace, 1934), p. 19.
[18] See *Personality: A Psychological Interpretation* (New York: Holt, 1937), p. 52.
[19] PE I, 244.
[20] PE I, 242. Cf. PE I, 87, 244, 283, 292, 418-19.

Moral choice, related as it is to both values and religion, likewise eludes psychological understanding and is closed to psychological guidance. A responsible moral man may allow his psychiatrist to suggest improved ways of spending his spare time, better books to read, and even more gratifying patterns of sexual behavior, but he is normally unwilling to accept professional advice relating to his strictly *moral* obligations. He will not, for example, accept advice to relinquish divine service for golf, neglect his vocation for his avocation, or adopt promiscuity to improve his mental health. And not only can psychology not provide rules of right conduct; it cannot even understand strictly moral decisions. Psychological *Verstehen* stops short before unconditional acts—acts which are characterized by a sort of compelling necessity although they do not proceed from investigable causes. Why Antigone must bury her brother when her sister experiences no such compulsion, or why Socrates refuses to placate the jury or to escape from prison (as his friends advised him to do), can hardly be clarified in psychological terms. The unconditional commands of duty, which all of us as human beings experience, are no more open to specifically psychological investigation because found in the mind, than are the Pythagorean theorem or the law of gravity. "Psychologism" is as misleading in morals as in mathematics and physics. What is required here is not a scientific study of the psyche or soul, but an elucidation of Existenz.

What Existenz Is Not

Neither the desiccated language of science nor the ordinary language of common sense can say directly what Existenz is, for Existenz appears only to itself and to other Existenzen and is otherwise indiscernible. It is, however, easily possible to say what Existenz is not.

The much-touted assertion of the priority of Existenz to essence is not incorrect, but it is misleading insofar as it lays stress upon the universal and leaves out of account the all-important uniqueness, singularity, and unrepeatability of the individual.[21]

While Existenz is akin to the particular, it is not to be identified with "the brute presence of the individual in the world. . . . No mere fact [*Faktum*] constitutes 'Existenz.' " Nor, as we shall see, is it simply what the late scholastics called the "thisness" as opposed to the "whatness" of the individual.[22] There is more involved.

As we have seen, Existenz is not the psychological subject, the stream of consciousness, or anything that conceivably could be submitted to scientific observation.[23] It has "no tangible objectivity."[24] And of course it is not the animate body studied by biologists, for, like the traditional "soul," it serves to differentiate man from the brutes.[25]

Existenz should be regarded as the polar opposite of the *persona* or mask (the outward semblance), and of the role which is played. Being unique, it has more to do with individual variations than with the positions, behavior patterns, and costumes which society prescribes.[26]

As the moral center of the individual, Existenz is to be carefully distinguished from spirit (*Geist*) which is basically amoral. Existenz is responsive to duty. Spirit, guided by Kantian or Hegelian "ideas," proceeds esthetically through phantasy and scientifically through a reorganization of the products of the understanding: "Spirit actualizes as a totality a world which it has thoroughly penetrated in art, in poetry . . . in the vocations, in the construction of states, and in the sciences. . . ."[27]

Though impatient of legalistic restrictions and opposed to authoritarian controls, Existenz does not issue in the arbitrary caprice of anarchical behavior but in the highest moral decisions.[28] Since it underlies the self-identity that makes possible responsible behavior (e.g. reliability in connection

---

[21] PO 118-19. Cf. PE II, 4.   [22] PO 119.
[23] PE II, 1-2.   [24] PO 116.   [25] PO 115-16.
[26] VW 83.
[27] PO 115. Cf. PE II, 7; RE 62; NET 61-65.
[28] PE II, 2-4.

with promises and contracts, incorruptibility, undeviating loyalty), its expressions contrast sharply with the moment-to-moment existence of animalian man.[29]

Being among those "high matters" which Plato illumined but could not write about,[30] it can be touched upon only indirectly: "Existenz is not the particular, whose reality as an observable object is infinite, [although] the [expression] *'individuum est ineffabile'* applies to both. Rather it is the actuality that assigns itself an infinite task. It is not just a process within the world but a source from beyond that makes its appearance within the world."[31] Existenz is not a possession but a seldom actualized possibility, for it is in abeyance whenever ordinary habit patterns assume control of our conduct in the everyday world. "Existenz is not a state of being but a being able. . . . Existenz constantly has the choice of being or nonbeing. I *am* only in the earnestness of decision."[32] It falls most notably short of realization in those lukewarm, indifferent, and indecisive ones—those innocent bystanders trying to be all things to all men—whom Dante consigned to a "vestibule" especially prepared for the miserable nonentities who are not even worth damning.

Existenz cannot be aimed at directly or actualized by some deliberate methodical procedure. One does not say to himself: "I intend to *existieren* from this moment on." "It is not a goal but a *source*. . . ."[33]

It is distinguishable, though never entirely separable, from the present current of historical happenings—the *"Geschichtlichkeit"* which provides the arena within which it actualizes itself.[34]

Its behavioral and verbal expressions are never clearly and unambiguously identifiable by any rational method. Viewed externally, the result of a passionate moral decision is not

[29] VW 83.

[30] Glenn R. Morrow, *Plato's Epistles* (New York: Liberal Arts Library, 1962), p. 241.

[31] PO 119.   [32] PO 118.   [33] PE II, 5, 162.

[34] PO 120.

101

different from a coldly calculated act of inconsiderate selfishness. One may burn down a pagan temple to glorify the
Christian God or to gain undying fame; one may give his
goods to feed the poor out of love, or in order to improve his
"image."

During the war, when Jaspers had no position and no
social status, and, as a presumed enemy of the state, had
been deprived of political and social security, he penned a
paragraph that serves at once to summarize the above and
to point the way to a more positive approach. Freely translated, and with several deletions, it may be read as follows:

> Existenz *per se* cannot be objectively grasped. . . . Unlike
> life, consciousness, and spirit, it is never represented
> by its individualizations. Thus it may seem that everything
> is simply a play of empty masks, and that to the question:
> Who am I? no answer can ever be given, the roles being
> assumed by no one at all. But actually Existenz, though
> never empirically discoverable, constitutes the true self
> which enters into all the roles that I play. . . . It is present
> when I am authentic. . . . The question that concerns me
> as possible Existenz is whether I am to preserve my
> identity, become firmly united with and unconditionally
> attached to my historical roots, and thus gain awareness of
> the being that enables the eternal to be felt within the
> temporal, or to sacrifice my integrity, refuse to commit
> myself, fail to remain unconditionally loyal and true, and,
> ignoring Existenz, hold myself constantly in reserve as
> the insubstantial point of an innocent and uninvolved by-
> stander . . . who preserves an escape hatch for emer-
> gencies while going through the motions which his roles
> require of him—or merely runs on and on in the futile
> course of an empty and thoughtless bestial existence. Re-
> serve transforms everything into masks and roles—into
> mere standpoints and possibilities. . . . Existenz is the in-
> defeasible dark source of authentic being.[35]

[35] VW 83.

Existenz as Freedom: *Inadequate Conceptions*

Although the topic of Existenz is inexhaustible, and virtually everything in the remainder of this book relates to it, still it can, in summary fashion, be roughly identified with *freedom*. "While living beings are simply *there* empirically, Existenz has its being in freedom."[36] It is not the goal but the source of philosophizing, a source to which I transcend when I come to myself philosophically. "Existenz is constantly confronted by the choice of being or notbeing. I *am* only in the earnestness of decision."[37] The approach to Existenz, then, must begin with freedom.

Philosophers as well as scientists are prone to suppose that when we approach a topic such as freedom we should first arrive at a *definition*, then show that the definiendum *exists*, and finally *explain* its presence. We need to know *what* freedom is, *that* it is, and *how* it is possible. But in fact not even the first step of this procedure can be carried out: "If I undertake to get my bearings by passing in review all that is called by the name of freedom, I encounter a multiplicity of facts and definitions but no objective means by which to locate freedom and discover what it is and what it is not."[38] This we can easily see by examining a number of traditional conceptions of freedom. Let us begin by "objectifications" of freedom—conceptions which assume that freedom is a discoverable property of certain entities within the world, and pass on to a few typical extrascientific and metaphysical conceptions.

1. There can of course be no doubt that freedom is easily ascertainable "in connection with the relations of power

[36] PE II, 2.

[37] PO 118. Note that James Collins, in *The Existentialists* (Chicago: Regnery, 1952), p. 108, speaks of Jaspers as "shifting the entire meaning of existence [Existenz] to the act of moral freedom, which operates the other side of strict knowledge." Compare Kurt Hoffman's statement: "Existenz and freedom are interchangeable concepts for Jaspers. . . . If freedom and Existenz are two sides of the same thing, one must be as indefinable as the other." PX 100.

[38] PE II, 176.

obtaining among men within society and the state."[39] Czarist Russia allowed for *personal freedom* in private life, Germany under the Kaisers permitted the legal security of *civil freedom,* while the U.S.A. provides both of these in addition to *political freedom,* involving the right of the citizens to choose their leaders.[40] In other terms, we recognize and prize freedom of thought, of the press, and of assembly, in addition to freedom from want, freedom to achieve various ends, religious freedom, and so on. These "objective freedoms" are undoubtedly present to various peoples in varying degrees. But they are conditions of the appearance of freedom in Existenz, not existential freedom itself.[41]

2. Some would have us construe freedom as *self-determination.* On this view I am free insofar as I am self-sufficient and independent of external forces, that is, when my decisions are reached independently of outside influences and my acts derive from my true being. Freedom, thus understood, resembles the "free" fall of a body in space, or the growth of a plant. But this is ambiguous:

a. At its simplest, it amounts to a version of freedom that we have come to associate with such empiricists as Hobbes, Schlick, and Edwards. As Schlick states it: "Freedom means the opposite of compulsion; a man is free if he does not act under compulsion, and he is compelled or unfree when he is hindered from without in the realization of his natural desires. Hence he is unfree when he is locked up, or chained, or when someone forces him at the point of a gun to do what otherwise he would not do."[42] While this view has preserved its popularity in many quarters, existentialists are usually at a loss to understand it or to see how it could possibly deserve a refutation. Are we not *always* in one way or another "hindered from without"? And can a sharp distinction ever be drawn between being compelled and not being com-

---

[39] PE 166.   [40] PE II, 166.   [41] PE II, 167.

[42] As quoted from Rynin's translation of *Fragen der Ethik* in Paul Edwards and Arthur Pap (eds.), *A Modern Introduction to Philosophy* (New York: Free Press, 1965), p. 54.

pelled? How can one ever be "forced at the point of a gun" to do anything if he chooses to die instead? And, whether or not we are locked up, are we or are we not compelled to eat, to pay taxes, et cetera? Is not compulsion always a matter of degree? As Jaspers puts it: on this view "all existing entities [*Daseiende*, including animalian existence] can be viewed as both free and dependent. This makes freedom banal, by identifying it with merely psychological freedom of action and of choice." The limits of the former depend upon the extent of our power; those of the latter are diminished by such factors as fear, fatigue, depression, distraction, lack of time, et cetera.[43] Although this view contributes little to our comprehension of freedom, its apparent inadequacy does serve to challenge us to discover whatever further factors may be involved.

b. One might follow Nietzsche, who professes to accept Spinoza's denial of freedom of the will,[44] but still "views man as more than a being that passively undergoes alterations . . . [and] never doubts that man is [in some sense] free, and that he develops himself. . . ."[45] Such freedom as we have, Nietzsche believes, appears in *creative expression*—a primordial process which, as the ground of all essential activity, fulfills the highest moral demand and provides our supreme happiness.[46] Now the sense in which creative work at its best might be said to be freer than the humdrum repetitive routine of every day is fairly obvious. The spontaneity, lack of restraint, and exhilarating sense of exclusive authorship experienced in connection with creative thinking and artistic expression constitute at least a near analogue to what the free-willists are concerned to call to our attention. But we know little about creative thinking. And freedom, conceived in this manner, amounts for the most part to "being rooted in oneself." Its main thrust is negative. It means in

43 PE II, 164-165.
44 NET 156. Such references to Nietzsche should be understood *always* to relate to Nietzsche as *Jaspers* interprets him.
45 NET 154.   46 NET 151-54.

effect, "to cut oneself off from one's past (from fatherland, belief, parents, companions), to associate with outcasts (in history and in society): to topple what is most revered and affirm what is most strongly forbidden. . . ."[47]

c. The Stoics appear to provide more scope for human freedom, and to approach the topic in positive fashion. All that is within the mind is within our power, said Epictetus. In thought, at least, man is free. "Within our power are opinion, aim, desire, aversion, and, in one word, whatever are not properly our own affairs."[48] On this showing, internality is the hallmark of freedom, and freedom consists in independence and possible defiance on the part of a formal self possessed of human reason. This, however, is simply the pride of an empty self-being that fails to recognize the external derivation of its thought-contents and the dependence of the moral self upon the arena which the world provides.[49] It amounts to overlooking the constant interdependence of subject and object, and to positing a good will that wills nothing good. From such a standpoint, as Hegel pointed out, it is but a short step to skeptical disenchantment and moral nihilism.

d. Descartes, like the Stoics, locates freedom within the mind, as though he wishes to compensate for drawing "the soul in its dependence on the body into his mechanistic view of the world."[50] He regards each man as free—and even obliged—to refuse assent to all that is not certain, and to accept as true everything that is clearly and distinctly conceived.[51] But this is to betray an astonishing blindness to the actual human condition. Experience soon shows that the certainties he demanded as supports for practical decisions are unavailable, while the logically compelling conclusions which theories abundantly provide are irresistible. To refuse to act until I am certain of my grounds is suicidal: to reject what I clearly and distinctly see to be valid or true is unthinkable.

[47] NET 156.
[48] *The Enchiridion*, trans. Thomas W. Higginson (New York: Liberal Arts, 1950), p. 17.
[49] PE II, 167.   [50] DPT 153.   [51] *Ibid.*

3. Freedom may be regarded as mere indeterminacy, i.e., as absence of any cause whatsoever. Who can deny that an Epicurean atom might, without reason, swerve ever so little from its path, or that a Heisenberg electron might behave in an irregular and unpredictable manner? Tychistic events, below the threshold of observability, may, as Peirce insisted, be innumerable. This, however, would amount to nothing more than freedom of indifference—the *liberum arbitrium indifferentiae* that permitted Buridan's legendary ass, when placed between equidistant haystacks, to select without preference and reject without antipathy.[52] As F. H. Bradley has argued at length, freedom conceived in this fashion could satisfy no one,[53] and, as Jaspers comments, whatever arguments may be marshalled for it "are empty thoughts that prove nothing at all. . . . The appeal to freedom of the will is independent of the assertions and denials of freedom as thus understood."[54]

4. When defined in any of the above-mentioned ways, freedom is objectified, i.e., regarded as discoverable within the world of objects, and as explicable in terms drawn from this world. Social and political freedoms are matters of fact. Self-determination, however interpreted, relates (or is intended to relate) to natural processes directly or indirectly open to perceptual or introspective observation. And indeterminism receives its definition from the natural regularities to which it makes exception. Such approaches have proved inadequate. But this settles nothing, for freedom may still be explained *metaphysically* in terms of an "ultimate reality" that is immune to whatever strictures and cavils may issue from the findings of science.

a. Metaphysically an act is free when it is self-caused, self-sufficient, and self-explanatory. It is a first mover unmoved, a *causa sui*. While the "self-determinist" refuses to deny the universality of causal regularity, the metaphysician,

[52] PE II, 164.
[53] *Ethical Studies* (Oxford: Clarendon Press, 1927), Essay I.
[54] PE II, 164.

in defiance of the scientific world-view, attributes to each human individual the capacity to act entirely on his own, make fresh starts, and thereby to initiate and assume the responsibility for various new series of events that may prove to be unique, unforeseeable, and unaccountable. Neither empirically nor logically is such an idea defensible. Empirically, all events are found to have causally efficacious antecedents, and these latter form a chain of prior causes that leads on and on endlessly. Logically, it is nonsensical, since a cause, by definition, involves an effect other than itself. And from any standpoint it is unsound and untenable. "It can serve," says Jaspers, "only as a means of expression for elucidations in which it is no longer intended to represent objective reality."[55]

b. The Kantian approach, interpreted as a two-world theory, allowing the behavior of each individual to be strictly determined within the phenomenal world but basically free within the noumenal world, is misleading, for there is only one world. We cannot explain our acts in terms of a reality that underlies appearance, for when we attempt to do so, as Kant himself emphasized, "our thinking becomes caught in contradictions, because the intelligible ground of phenomena (which in this case we ourselves are) cannot be conceived objectively. . . ."[56] The search for freedom in a noumenal world must never leave out of account the fact that, in Kant's terms, "I have no knowledge of myself as I am but merely as I appear to myself."[57] Only the one world of phenomena is available for purposes of explanation.

c. Hegel, like Spinoza, finds that absolute freedom is the freedom of a totality that has nothing outside itself, and requires nothing further in order to exist. Within this whole the human individual is free insofar as he identifies himself with the encompassing that sustains him, and unfree insofar as he is confused, emotional, ignorant, and at loggerheads

---

[55] PE II, 188.   [56] GPT I, 301.

[57] *Critique of Pure Reason*, trans. Norman Kemp Smith (New York: St. Martin's Press, 1965), p. 169.

with his surroundings. But this is extremely misleading. Actually the individual is far removed from the assumed whole; he exists in the here and now and must deal constantly with the particular and contingent. The innocent acquiescence to which such passivistic conservatism leads condemns the individual to universalistic and totalitarian conformity. Self-reliance disappears, and with it Existenz itself.[58]

Even were the above survey exhaustive, it could not provide knowledge of freedom, for "freedom," like "religion" or "soul," lends itself to an unlimited number of definitions, no one of which is in any sense final. Examining the ways in which the words *Frei* and *Freiheit* (or cognate terms in English) are actually used is simply to be overwhelmed by a confusing disarray of terms, concepts, and precedents. And even if, *per impossibile*, one were to discover a fixed and final "real definition" of freedom, there would still be no way of finding out whether or not such a thing existed, for a thing's existence is never derivable from its definition, and the presence of freedom, as we have seen, is not verifiable.[59] The existence of free decisions and acts can be neither proved nor disproved. What the free-willist seeks is not a matter of knowledge (in the strict sense) but of belief or faith (*Glaube*).

The Approach to Freedom

"The question concerning the existence of freedom, when pursued as one pursues an investigation of an object, leads to a denial of freedom: it is because I am *not* an object that freedom is possible. The question of freedom originates in the self who wills its existence."[60] Consciousness of freedom is not a matter of inference but of experience, and arguments for freedom do not prove but rather affirm and assure.

[58] PE II, 194-95.
[59] Cf. William James, "The Dilemma of Determinism," *Essays in Pragmatism*, ed. Alburey Castell (New York: Hafner, 1951), p. 45.
[60] PE II, 175.

Much as Anselm's so-called ontological argument "was not a rational finding but the climax and foundation of his existence as a thinker,"[61] and Descartes's *cogito ergo sum* was not, as the *ergo* suggests, a proof, but rather an expression of an immediate certainty,[62] so our libertarian ratiocinations can never demonstrate but only emphasize, substantiate, and confirm what my acts disclose. "It is through my deeds and not through cognitive insights that freedom evinces itself."[63] One can be aware of freedom only because, potentially at least, he is already free: "It is from the possibility of my own freedom that I can raise the question of freedom."[64] One might say that this question is what Austin calls a "performative":[65] "Either there is no such thing as freedom at all, or it already has its being in the asking of the question. . . ."[66] We have here to do, not with demonstration, but with "the expression of a self who is aware of its own possibility as that of a being that decides concerning itself. In asking anything *of* myself, I am asking *for* my self."[67] We can never say directly what freedom is: "That freedom is not known and cannot by any means be thought of as an object remains the alpha and omega of its elucidation. I am sure of my own freedom, not through thinking but through existing, not through observing and questioning . . . but through achieving."[68] But still there are signs by which Existenz can hope to recognize the presence of freedom.

First of all, while cognition is not identical with freedom,

[61] GPT II, 100.

[62] DPT 67. The point is simply that no new knowledge is to be found here beyond the direct insight expressed. My existence is as directly given as my thinking.

[63] PE II, 176.

[64] *Ibid.*

[65] In J. L. Austin's terminology, a "performative" is an utterance that is tantamount to an act, as, e.g., "I take this woman to be my wedded wife" or "I concede the election." See *How To Do Things With Words* (New York: Oxford University Press, 1965), pp. 4ff.

[66] PE II, 176.

[67] *Ibid.* The last sentence reads: "*Es [das Selbst] fordert sich, indem es von sich fordert.*"

[68] PE II, 185.

it is indispensable to it. In the absence of knowledge there can be no choice, and restricted knowledge means limited choice. One who, to take an extreme but by no means impossible example, knows of only five or ten institutions of higher learning is unfree to choose any of the two thousand others. Even Spinoza restricted his determinism sufficiently to appeal to us to acquire knowledge with a view to extending our horizons and liberating ourselves from the influence of uninstructed feeling.[69] There is an obvious sense in which I become freer "as I constantly extend my world-orientation and gain awareness of limitless conditions and the opportunities for activity which they involve."[70]

In the second place, freedom involves a moment of impulse (*Willkür*).[71] That is to say, there is an ingredient of spontaneity which renders choice unpredictable. This is not to be eliminated by some mechanical procedure (e.g. tossing coins), for the procedure used would itself have to be chosen. And it cannot be explained away by the contention that choice is a contest of motives in which the strongest motive always wins, unless we are prepared simply to assume without question that whatever motive wins is the strongest. Impulse, spontaneity, and caprice, though by no means identical with freedom, are certainly among its ingredients.

At the moral level, I am, as Kant saw, free when the imperatives by which I live are expressions of my own demands. To be morally free means to preserve autonomy at all costs, to recognize no external court of appeal as final, and to do what I see to be right in my own unique situation. It means to accept only those norms which I find to be self-evident because they issue from my innermost self. Kant was not always clear on this. Insofar as he described the categorical imperative as a mere formula from which to derive specific maxims, as (for example) that I may under no circumstances tell a lie or appropriate what belongs to another, he "discloses the historical form of his thinking and

[69] GPT II, 330.　　　[70] PE II, 179.　　　[71] PE II, 177.

111

moves away from the source. . . ."[72] "To confuse [as Kant sometimes does] the wonderful purity of this source of ethical reason with the rationalist rigor of definitely formulated commandments and prohibitions destroys the very source which he raised to consciousness."[73] Here as elsewhere, formalistic legalism proves an impediment. What is essential is this: "When you act, bear in mind that the world is not as it is [in the sense of being fixed, final, unalterable, given once and for all], but that in your action you help to create it."[74]

Finally, the "idea" is presupposed.[75] It is not enough to act spontaneously in the light of my own norms with knowledge of what I am about. My act needs to be seen within a broader context. Nothing that I do can be disengaged from the restricted totality that is my life and the larger totality that constitutes human society. Without following Hegel in subordinating everything to life within the whole, as though each individual were only an organ or instrument within the nation or the world,[76] I must still recognize that it is with a view to a vaguely defined future within society that I must plan and act. The idea, as yet unfulfilled, provides an intimation of the entire setting within which my action is to take place, and stimulates a reflective process that can never reach a firm and final conclusion.

Choice and Resolution

Knowledge is never adequate and reflection can never complete its task. But as an existing human being I am often forced by the passage of time and events to interrupt my reflections and reach a decision on the basis of such inadequate and unassimilated knowledge as I have. Choice is not the resultant of a conflict of motives, not the product of a rational calculus (hedonic or otherwise), and not automatic obedience to law. It is an expression of my own innermost self—at once assertive and revelatory. In a summary that may well

---

[72] GPT I, 298. [73] GPT I, 299. [74] GPT I, 293.
[75] PE II, 179. [76] PE II, 194.

be regarded as definitive, Jaspers characterizes the freedom
of such a choice as

> objectively incomprehensible, but known to itself as a free
> source [*freier Ursprung*]. . . . Choice [*Wahl*] is the expres-
> sion of an awareness that through free decision [*freie
> Entscheidung*] I do not merely effect changes in the world
> around me, but also create my own being continuously in
> my historical situation. It is not that I must act in a certain
> way because I am here and of such and such a nature.
> Rather I know that in my acts and my decisions I am the
> source at once of what I do and of what I most basically
> *am*. Through resolution [*Entschluss*] I experience a free-
> dom in which I reach decisions not only concerning ex-
> ternal things, but concerning my innermost self. No longer
> can I be distinguished from my choice; I myself *am* the
> freedom of the choice. . . . Freedom comes to us as the
> choice of my self. . . . I *am* in so far as I choose; when I
> no longer am, I do not choose.[77]

Further elucidation of Existenz in terms of freedom can best
be undertaken in connection with morality and in the light
of considerations relating to communication, historicity, and
boundary situations. These latter topics will occupy the next
two chapters.

[77] PE II, 182.

chapter five

Communication

ᵔᵔᵔ

Jaspers shares with the Hegelians a tendency to stress
the dependence of the self upon social and linguistic intercourse between human beings. And he shares with the logical empiricists and linguistic analysts an abiding concern
with words, signs, and symbols. But in other respects he is at
loggerheads with both groups. Unlike the organicists, he re-
serves to each individual the final freedom to reject the communications of his fellows in favor of promptings from an
inner source. Unlike the positivists he insists that the
communication of universally valid and intrinsically intelligible scientific truth is so vastly different from that of
philosophic truth that to take either one as a model for the
other is misleading and stultifying. And he parts with the
linguistic analysts in his indifference to "ordinary language"
and his recognition of a kind of indirectly expressible "nonknowledge" to which the criteria that arise out of any specific language or group of languages are irrelevant.

His account of communication is crucial for his entire
philosophy. It supports his "elucidation of Existenz" by
exhibiting the limitations of scientific language, exposing
the deceptions perpetrated by ordinary speech, demonstrating the impossibility of expressing spiritual things in a
straightforward fashion, and by making plain the need for
what Kierkegaard calls "indirect communication." It provides a basis for an esthetic view which is unique to *Existenzphilosophie*.[1] It is essential to his scathing criticism of contemporary society.[2] It leads to a new appreciation of mythology and a rejection of demythologization in Christianity.[3]
And, as we shall see, it provides an indispensable background

[1] See, for example, PE I, 330-40; and PE III, 192-99.
[2] GET, Part I.   [3] See FET.

for his approach to metaphysical vision through the inter-mediation of what he calls "ciphers of being."

Anomalies of Scientific Discourse

While positivists believe that scientific language so far sur-passes other means of communication that it should serve as a model for all cognitively meaningful discourse, Jaspers in-sists that it is adapted neither to the demands of everyday conversation nor to those of philosophic discussion. Scien-tific communication is strictly *sui generis*. Even a brief sum-mary of its differentiae should serve to bring this out:

Only in connection with scientific abstractions is *clarity* of communication (whether conceived in Cartesian or in Hu-mian fashion) a feasible ideal, and it is unrealistic to require it in extrascientific areas. In the everyday world, as in philosophy, many of the items we refer to are too impalpa-ble, transparent, complex, or inaccessible to be clarified. We know what time is until someone asks us about it. We are aware that consciousness somehow "exists," but we find that it evaporates when attended to. We fall in love but think it unreasonable to do so. Though we cannot define civil rights, or, for that matter, rights of any kind, we still favor them. We can say what we think, but are unclear as to what thinking is. Clarity can properly be sought only among the artificialities of mathematics and science. Even the idea of clarity defies clarification.[4]

Scientific conclusions are universally valid and compelling. They are applicable without exception to all objects within their proper range, and they force themselves upon all intel-ligent and suitably trained subjects who are acquainted with them. One can no more reject a scientific proof than he can deny the clear evidence of his senses. But not so with com-mon sense and philosophy: extrascientific beliefs are histor-ical and fallible. They rest upon and must be expressed by means of notions acceptable in their own historical era. In

[4] See my *Philosophical Theory and Psychological Fact* (Tucson, Ariz.: University of Arizona Press, 1961), pp. 122-31.

our culture, for instance, Oriental doctrines are almost always enigmatic. And the Orient in turn can assimilate our science far more readily than our ideology. The commonplaces of other times and other nations are often esoteric to us.

Scientific communication presupposes truthfulness among scientists and would break down without it. Everyday communication enjoys no such privilege; it is carried on in an atmosphere of distortion, dissembling, and outright fraud (*vide infra*). When scientists disregard truth and publish spurious results, science is finished. When the man in the street or the politician presents specious arguments and false conclusions, no one is surprised or offended. Even idealistic philosophers are open to Nietzsche's charge of being unwilling at any price to see how reality is actually constituted.[5]

While the reasons that support scientific conclusions are factual and logical, those underlying common sense and philosophic beliefs are to a considerable extent motivational. Psychologism, though misleading in science, comes into its own in relation to daily affairs. The will to believe is no exception to a general rule, but a psychological force that cries out for recognition. To understand claims apart from motives is usually to miss the point. If, for example, the rope and the stake once facilitated the acceptance of Christian paradoxes, today the desire for belongingness—the urge to be like the others, to go with the crowd and get on the bandwagon—exerts an incalculable but very powerful unifying force.

Since the scientist is required to cultivate dispassionate objectivity, his communications are normally terse, precise, and unemotional. Science sponsors disinterested objectivity and a low temperature of argument. Many concerns of the nonscientist, however, are so vital and moving that a disinterested attitude toward them would be generally regarded as sheer affectation. Especially is this true of those philosophic insights that provide the truth by which man lives,

[5] NET 190.

determine what he is to become, and offer "the inner certainty in which a man's whole being participates." It is quite natural that communications that relate philosophically to man as man must "move us more deeply than any scientific knowledge."[6]

In summary, scientific language is not available for extra-scientific purposes. It is not that nonscientists ought to try to talk like scientists but perversely neglect to do so; there are good reasons why they *cannot* do so. Objectivity, in the sense of avoidance of emotional involvement, is to be attained only in highly artificial situations. Clarity, like unanimity, is a strictly scientific goal. And, contrary to popular prejudice, avoidance of deception, both of the self and of others, is an impossible ideal in life-situations. Further examination of everyday talk should serve to elucidate these statements.

The Deceptions of Ordinary Speech

The falsehoods to which altruism and egoism initially contribute are superficial. It is useless to make much ado over white lies and fish stories. But the final result to which these commonplace matters lead is significant. This appears when we explore the extensive context within which social lies function.

To minimize the friction which association with others entails, it is, as everyone knows, necessary that formalities be observed and pleasant sentiments regularly expressed. Regardless of one's feelings and intentions, an introduction calls for a handshake, a meeting after prolonged absence is a time for compliments, festive occasions require signs of good cheer, and the reception of even the least desirable of gifts involves an outward display of happy thankfulness. White lies are of course indispensable, but since no one attends to what everyone routinely recites, they are morally indifferent: "These are the untruths that, instead of serving to deceive both parties, merely bring about a tactful veiling of unpleas-

[6] EPT 8.

antness. . . . Speech tells our lies for us, providing everything from euphemisms to the various expressions which we have always on hand, and cannot fail to use without unintentionally and falsely conveying some degree of unfriendliness."[7] Such refinements of manners, which through early and prolonged training become second nature to the aristocrats of any society—the formalities of Chinese sages, medieval knights, and English gentlemen, for instance[8]—have a high degree of social utility and are not deceptive.

But a procedure that begins as a benevolent endeavor to spare people's feelings is readily enlisted in the service of self-regarding impulses. It is not enough merely to appear within society; one must make a good impression and forge ahead. One must improve his "image" and make the right contacts if he is to win friends and influence people. Character has low visibility, but a pleasant personality contributes enormously to one's effectiveness. The more successfully the self withdraws behind its mask, the more smoothly the plan succeeds. To save the appearances is to save all. One learns to use speech as a stimulus to elicit desired responses, not to express thoughts. We must "be nice to one another! Never ask penetrating questions! Smile!"[9] A tacit agreement is arrived at: each will carefully protect the other's illusions if the other in turn will protect his. "To come right out with the truth is considered tactless. In some situations a true assertion is tantamount to an open declaration of war. We enjoy peace only as a result of an agreement not to allude to fatal fundamentals. To bring these latter into prominence would mean to destroy a pleasant friendship."[10] A spade is no longer to be called a spade—it is not even to be mentioned. Why endure the truth when the false is more agreeable?

At this point the innocent attempt to avoid needless unpleasantness has developed into a nearly complete falsification of human relations. No one is what he seems to be

---

[7] VW 555.   [8] PE II, 96.   [9] PO 66.   [10] VW 667.

or seems to be what he is, and social realities, like Kantian *Dinge an sich* lie hidden behind an impenetrable veil of appearance. As Nietzsche viewed the matter, this "world, deprived of its substance, seeks its fulfillment in empty dramatics. The merely theatrical carries people away as though it were genuine, and everyone tends more and more to play a role instead of living."[11] An easily mastered etiquette assumes control of social behavior and constrains the inner reality:

> Not merely fashions [Jaspers tells us], but rules for social intercourse, gestures, phrases, methods of conveying information, incline toward uniformity. There is now a conventional ethic of association: courteous smiles, a tranquil manner, the avoidance of haste and jostle, the adoption of a humorous attitude in strained situations, helpfulness unless the cost be unreasonable, the feeling that "personal remarks" are in bad taste.[12]

Anyone to whom honesty, veracity, and authenticity are mere catchwords finds that

> the struggle [to be one's true self] brings risks which he cannot face. He only uses force when the big battalions are on his side, and shuns decision which involves danger. . . . A frictionless functioning of the enterprise remains the ideal of such persons. They are willing to merge themselves in the cooperative body, pretending that therein each member is supplemented and enlarged by all the others.[13]

Even the gray flannel suit of the organization man functions as a species of camouflage, providing privacy in public for the clandestine elaboration of devious schemes. The carefully cultivated "line" is preferred to the expression of genuine feeling, and the devious "pitch" of the salesman is more effective than any objective presentation. Every so-called reference has to be a "recommendation," and every public

[11] NET 241-42.   [12] GET 49.   [13] GET 81.

introduction a eulogy. Everything is artificial, affected, contrived, false, and misleading.

The disadvantages of this arrangement are of course unmistakable, and to authentic individuals they are insufferable. Where honest communication so completely breaks down that people can no longer know one another, everyone must go his own way alone. If Molière's Alceste, the "misanthrope" who prefers disagreeable honesty to dishonest agreement, seems a comic character within the setting provided by his own dissolute society, King Lear, who, having been corrupted by his own flatterers, can no longer recognize selflessness and loving loyalty in the person of his own daughter, is unspeakably tragic. If one gains complete conscious awareness of the artificiality of these social relationships, he tends to find the world stale, flat, and unprofitable; if he represses all such awareness he leaves himself open to the possibility of a shattering catastrophe.

Speech as a Weapon: Political Discussion[14]

What has been said of communication in society and business applies with even greater force to communication in politics. For in this area the tension between the veracity which morality requires and the social effectiveness indispensable to the attainment of desirable political ends is so great that a concern for the truth is a burdensome encumbrance while political success suggests deviousness and dishonesty. Insofar as the average citizen prefers the easy conscience that comes from ignorance to the guilt and anxiety that derive from an increased concern with horrendous social evils, the candidate for office cannot hope to win votes by proclaiming alarming truths. Thus it is that Jaspers, looking at Germany, finds few statesmen but many politicians, and can say of the latter that "they are opportunistic realists, mischiefmakers, cheats and blackmailers . . . [who] when exposed, escape into lies and jokes. By their actions they make a mock of Parliament,

[14] See PE II, 102-10⁵

which, being of their own kidney, scarcely notices it. . . ."[15] Among functionaries of this description, "the spirit loses its gravity": "Lacking a vocation, politicians of this type look on their task as a career, with promising prospects, a good salary, and the right to a pension. . . . They think without responsibility."[16] Paradoxically, as great a man as Jaspers' friend, Max Weber, was hopelessly handicapped in the political melee by his finest characteristics. He saw, as Jaspers tells us,

> that outward honesty is not compatible with political action; . . . that there is a political ethics, which follows from the statesman's responsibility for the actual consequences of his action in the world as it is. A passion for truth, a hatred of pettiness and low cunning, always stood in his way. A clear thinker, he knew what had to be done, but his ethical sentiment made him unwilling to lie, to dissemble, to cultivate the illusions, the veils over reality, that the masses require.[17]

It is simply not the case that truth is always victorious over falsehood or that in politics as in business honesty is the best policy. On these matters Machiavelli's doctrine would seem to be very nearly definitive. While a politician or diplomat must appear to respect the rights of all men, and must

[15] KST 54. No doubt many will say that Jaspers' position is too extreme and his outcry too shrill. It is as difficult—and as easy— to find evidence for his account of human mendacity as it is to support Schopenhauer's pessimism, Dewey's meliorism, or Lamont's optimism. Naturally it would be a simple matter to prepare a lengthy list of books and articles in support of any one of these philosophic balance sheets, but no limited amount of evidence would be regarded as final. It can only be hoped that a generation exposed from infancy on to the melancholy doctrine of original sin, aware of the propaganda methods of the Fascists and the Nazis, more or less familiar with the techniques of "brainwashing," and concerned about what at the moment of writing is called the "credibility gap," will give an impartial hearing to a view that must appear as simply a matter of fact to those Europeans who have been forced to live with the propaganda of the Italian, German or Russian totalitarians.

[16] *Ibid.*   [17] MWT 212.

seem always to be genial and in the highest good humor, this is merely a facade. "The art is to unite the greatest possible professed readiness for making concessions with a tenacious adherence to one's own secret goals."[18] Among diplomats, "stiff immobility is usually a social mistake. Forever arriving at new proposals and compromises—even though they actually make little difference and merely serve to keep alive an appearance of flexibility—serves to preserve an atmosphere of obliging compliance."[19] The breakdown of communication reaches its apogee when diplomats address each other in what Hegel called "the language of disintegration" (*die Sprache der Zerrissenheit*)[20]—a language that all speakers recognize as spurious.

To "Existenz" which, of course, involves sincerity, autonomy, honesty, and authenticity, this is insupportable. "Political socializing, made into a way of life, makes all possible Existenz disappear behind its veil. There remains a set of drives and impulses covered over by the smooth surface of a quiescent and well-ordered existence. Everyone counts in relation to someone else but not as himself. . . . Basically, self-contempt and a secret contempt for all the others reigns. Respect is accorded only to power, money, success and capacity to influence public opinion. . . ."[21] But at the same time, "to live behind a veil is the same as not living at all. Wherever Existenz becomes aware of itself, in every communication, in every unconditional act, the veil is pierced."[22] To appear *in propria persona* within society, however, requires both caution and fortitude: "A strong, self-reliant, and independent Existenz is . . . opposed by the masses as a deadly enemy of their own way of life; those who are dimly aware of the possibility of Existenz but do not choose it fear for themselves in its presence."[23]

[18] PE II, 103.
[19] *Ibid.*
[20] G.W.F. Hegel, *Phänomenologie des Geistes* (Hamburg: Felix Meiner, 1952), p. 376.
[21] PE II, 105.   [22] PE II, 388-89.   [23] *Ibid.*

Deception and Self-Deception

Some will reject this outlook summarily, believing that life among dishonest men would not be worth living. But of course this judgment is itself a first-rate illustration of the voluntaristic thesis which it denies. Some will urge that most people are observably honest and kind, and that what is here asserted is sheer calumny. But to the existentialist, this is simply another example of human gullibility: a striking instance of our incapacity to see how reality is actually constituted, i.e., to resist deception. Others will tell us that there is nothing new in the present approach and that we have long been sufficiently on our guard against human mendacity. But this is incoherent. For if we are not deceived then deception is not operating, and in that case there is nothing for us to guard against.

More impressive is the claim that *mutual* deceptiveness is not only contrary to fact, but downright impossible. For while one can occasionally deceive the unwary or be deceived by the crafty, people cannot be fooled by their own bag of tricks. We cannot knowingly be misled, for to recognize deceit is to be undeceived. Unless it is possible to deceive one's own self, people are not to be duped by the conspirators with whom they conspire.[24]

Self-deception, however, is not only possible but prevalent; it is a familiar and inexpugnable feature of daily life. Psychiatric terms which, like "rationalization," "sublimation," and "projection," have passed into the lingo of everyday life, refer to certain of its varieties. Freudians explain it in terms of a hypothetical unconscious mind, while existential psychoanalysts commonly take their cue from what Sartre calls "*mauvaise foi.*"[25] Psychiatrists have explanations aplenty. But acquaintance with self-deception is by no means limited to psychiatrists.

Kant saw not only that one could never be absolutely cer-

[24] ATT 152.
[25] Jean-Paul Sartre, *Being and Nothingness*, trans. Hazel E. Barnes (New York: Philosophical Library, 1956), Part I, chap. ii.

123

tain about his own motivation, but he went even further and maintained that "untruthfulness lies at the root of humanity. 'The lie—from the Father of Lies, who brought all evil into the world—is the real rotten spot in human nature,' " he said.[26] Hegel, whose *Phänomenologie* showed that "on the level of culture thought and language are in a state of mutual alienation, with the result that a sort of curtain intervenes between the individual's overt utterances and his inward reflections,"[27] prepared the way for Marx's claim that the supposed truths and values of the privileged classes were but deceptive reflections of intolerable unacknowledged material conditions. A number of Ibsen's plays (*An Enemy of the People* and *The Wild Duck*, for example) have reinforced the point by presenting a basically false society that lives by a mendacious tradition that promotes bad faith and is content to save appearances. And Nietzsche suggested Freudian "mechanisms" similar to those mentioned above when he showed that self-knowledge is difficult and self-deception inevitable,[28] and made clear that there are strong reasons why most people would prefer *not* to face the truth about themselves. Clearsightedness, he believed, must be frightful: "If anything were to unveil the essence of the world before our eyes, it would disillusion us most disagreeably."[29] On this view, as Jaspers tells us:

> Truth [i.e., the so-called truth of the community] is that which our conventional social code accepts as effective in promoting the purposes of the group. . . . Community members are obliged to 'lie' in accordance with fixed convention. To put it otherwise, they must be truthful by playing the group's game with the conventionally marked dice. To fail to pay in the coin of the realm is to tell forbidden lies, for, on this view, whatever transcends conventional truth is falsehood. To tell lies of this kind is to sacri-

[26] ATT 154.

[27] J. Loewenberg, *Hegel's Phenomenology: Dialogues on The Life of Mind* (La Salle, Ill.: Open Court, 1965), p. 226.

[28] NET 133.   [29] As quoted in NET 200.

fice the world of meanings upon which the endurance of the community rests.[30]

Far from being characteristic of humans merely, deceptiveness permeates all existence (*Dasein*). Capacity to deceive is even noticeable among members of certain infrahuman species. Through color and form and imitative behavior animals manage to escape notice, to elude their pursuers, or even to attract the ones they wish to devour. And chimpanzees have been known to deceive other creatures just for the fun of it. Such "organic mendacity," so to speak, is an essential ingredient in life.[31] To be worldly-wise is, among other things, to be acquainted with "this refined development of unconscious and semiconscious cunning, this indefinable something that thrives on ambiguity, that at one moment provides meanings and interpretations and in the next glides away as smoothly as an eel, this medium which deprives man of his self-being whenever he reveals himself briefly within the empirical world."[32] Lying pervades the social organization in its entirety:

> The fact that the average man is irrational, undependable, blind, and sensual means that actual social arrangements cannot survive without untruth. The *pia fraus* is well known to all great institutional religions—even when its use is officially denied. It is the same within the state. Authority cannot endure unless those in control insist upon the absolute validity of things which they do not accept in the usual sense. . . . It is worthy of note that Plato acknowledged this situation and [while condemning the lies of subordinates, regarded] the lies of the authorities as indispensable to the general welfare.[33]

Communication among Academic Philosophers

Philosophers, as Kierkegaard was quick to point out, are not disembodied intellects but existing individuals. In Plato's

[30] NET 187-88.   [31] VW 477-79.   [32] *Ibid.*
[33] VW 484.

nomenclature, they are propelled by appetitive and irascible as well as by rational faculties. Speaking on the basis of long experience with philosophy departments and students in Germany, Jaspers points out that the average graduate student—and especially the average candidate for a professorship—having a career in mind, is eager to promote his own cause. However, well-intentioned he is, he cannot, as Goethe once said in a similar connection, be required to gain insight into truths that threaten his life-conditions. While he may, for example, be persuaded that traditional philosophy is on the wrong track—just as the student of theology may conjure with Nietzsche's dictum that God is dead—he will never, after an appreciable expenditure of time and money, reject philosophy entirely, if doing so would deprive him of all hope of a career and make his life empty and meaningless. At this stage what is sometimes called "socialized anxiety" is operative. "The desire to safeguard one's own spiritual existence gives rise to a readiness to learn what is taught [by the dominant sect] in the school, as long as a chance at economic and sociological security is also involved."[34] One comes to identify himself with the group, and *camaraderie* and *esprit de corps* develop. "An openness and willingness to be corrected in terms of the criteria accepted by the school is accompanied by a readiness to exclude the strange and foreign."[35] That the student rejects what he has merely heard of and has never known at first hand is regarded as a good sign; it speaks well for his loyalty and singlemindedness. It is futile to disagree with him, for, feeling threatened by other standpoints, he becomes annoyed, impertinent, and uncommunicative, and refuses to see what is meant. "Unconsciously the truth is identified with his own interests. What counts as true to anyone with his capacities, his nature, his soul, and his academic background in this specific school constitutes the absolute truth."[36]

As these scholars mature and begin to practice their chosen professions, such obscuration of the truth becomes

---

[34] VW 497.   [35] *Ibid.*   [36] *Ibid.*

exacerbated. They find it natural to believe that "their own way is true and essential, and that whatever is inaccessible to them is false."[37] Various pressures force an authoritarian posture upon the German scholar, and instead of sympathetic understanding and tolerance he exemplifies "having to be right at all costs" (*Rechthabenwollen*), "refusal to see the point" (*Nichtsehenwollen*), and "inconsiderate self-assertion" (*Sichbehauptenwollen*). There are, as he sees it, two main kinds of philosophy: the kind that he has been taught, and its misguided alternatives.

While philosophic views are typically as hard to defend as they are easy to criticize, still a young scholar on the defensive can always rise to the challenge by making use of the many sophistical techniques available to philosophers everywhere.[38] One may boldly contradict his opponent, insist that what he says is irrelevant, or simply shout him down. When time is short one urges the opponent to give a brief reply to a question that requires a long answer and then expresses dissatisfaction. One changes the subject or avoids the issue by failing to understand, challenging what is merely incidental, objecting to the opponent's terminology, ridiculing, intimidating, or flustering him, et cetera. Or one surreptitiously misplaces the boundary that divides the fixed and final from the tentative and debatable by stating dogmas as facts and setting up sectarian standards as universally valid norms. Amphibole and equivocation are of course at the disposal of all, though they are less subtle and more easily detected than some other techniques.[39]

Since the presuppositions upon which a position rests are

[37] *Ibid.*

[38] Jaspers refers the interested student to the material given in the part of Aristotle's *Organon* that deals with sophistical refutations (most readily available to the American student in chapters in logic textbooks devoted to nonformal fallacies) and to Schopenhauer's *Über Eristik* (translated into English by T. B. Saunders under the title of "The Art of Controversy," in *Essays of Schopenhauer*, 1896), as well as to a forthcoming third volume of his *Philosophische Logik*, of which *Von der Wahrheit* is the first.

[39] VW 563.

usually implicit and unstated, one may readily confuse his opponent by changing them at will and drawing unexpected conclusions that come seemingly out of the blue. Having drawn an opponent into a commonsense frame of reference one can easily point out the patent absurdities of phenomenalism, epistemological dualism, ethical relativism, or what not, and then, since the scientific world-view has even more prestige, use it to suggest that these paradoxical doctrines may after all prove to be correct. Or, taking the offensive, the sophistically inclined philosopher may easily use the scientistic assumption that there is only one kind of truth—that which rests upon immediate sense experience and compelling rationality—to put all other kinds out of mind and then break off communication with the assertion that certain claims made by artists, moralists, or religionists are "meaningless."[40]

Confusion can always be compounded through the use of specious distinctions.[41] Following Hume's suggestion that "whatever objects are distinguishable are separable by the thought and imagination,"[42] one separates the inseparable (e.g. the cognitive and the emotive, words and their meanings), interprets differences in degree as differences in kind (extraversion-introversion, for example), ignores the overlapping of classes (thought and action, perhaps, or common sense and science),[43] and assumes that his distinctions correspond to distinctions within nature (as in the case of the "four cardinal colors"). Or one foists upon the unwary such attractive but impossible distinctions as essence-accident and/or analytic-synthetic.

In oral debate the eristic philosopher, depending upon the evanescence of the spoken word, may feel free to change his stance at will, and to impute to his adversary ridiculous

---

[40] VW 564.

[41] VW 565.

[42] *Treatise*, Book I, Part I, section 7.

[43] Cf. R. G. Collingwood's discussion of "the overlap of classes" in *An Essay on Philosophical Method* (Oxford: Clarendon Press, 1933), pp. 26-53.

versions of what he actually said.[44] And, of course, his freedom to be inconsistent is even greater when he goes from one
disputant to another. Speaking for the sophist, Jaspers says:
"For everything I prepare an alibi. What I say privately to
one is contradicted when I speak to another."[45] Above all,
one must never say too much; it is necessary to maintain reserve, avoid decisions, and know when to be silent.

"The technique of endless reflection, that uses conversation not to communicate but to vindicate its own vacuous
self, sanctions a kind of argumentation about what is presumed to be knowable and known that, in the absence of any
guiding idea, makes no progress whatsoever."[46] The speaker
introduces one set of rational formulae after another, or he
argues indefinitely within the frame of reference provided
by some set of concepts taken to be valid absolutely and
without qualification. If the conversation threatens to become
serious and to involve the questions and answers of a genuine discussion, he begins to withdraw, insinuating, perhaps,
that his opponent's remarks are meaningless, uninteresting,
irrelevant, or simply inconclusive.

The presence in thought of various universes of discourse, each of which involves special laws of its own, can
be made to contribute to the confusion.[47] For example, one
places objects of art within a physical frame of reference,
and then, by appealing to the laws of optics and neurology,
shows that it is nonsense to speak of "warm" and "cool"
colors, or that, as Berkeley insisted, it is impossible to represent distance. Or again, international politics is approached on an ethical level, with the result that we speak of
"a family of nations," and the "good neighbor policy," as
though nation-states were or could be subject to the ethical principles that relate to the conduct of individuals.[48] Or,
more rarely, rules of etiquette are called upon to settle phil-

---

[44] VW 573.   [45] *Ibid.*   [46] PE II, 111.
[47] PE II, 113.
[48] The example, of course, is suggested by Reinhold Niebuhr's
Moral Man in Immoral Society (New York: Scribner, 1960).

osophical arguments, as though serious discussion, criticism, and refutation were to be condemned as discourteous. Sometimes we hear that it is "not good form" to be too serious about anything, or that sympathizing with the communists "just isn't done." A prominent man can silence an accuser by merely pointing out that the accusation, if substantiated, would be very serious. A book that is abusive of a leading member of the regnant school of thought does not deserve to be reviewed. Pessimism should never be taught in the schools for it produces melancholia. Like the ghost of the elder Hamlet, one is now here, now there, and now gone: "What up to now was mere sociability I suddenly regard as a sign of true friendship or deal with officially, or, vice versa. . . . I enter into a sphere and leave it at will. When things become serious I slip away, having never really been there. Everything happens as though I were a selfless being with many souls."[49] At this point, of course, communication has completely broken down, and the discussion has become a shameless travesty of philosophic dialogue.

A Second Possibility: Philosophizing as a Cooperative Struggle for Fulfillment

Lovers of *philosophia perennis* tell of a better way. If to the dilettante philosophy is an accomplishment, and to the trained professional a means to a living and a reputation, to its own devotees it is a matter of unexampled urgency, having to do at once with each individual's experience of his world, his conduct in relation to his fellow men, and his full self-realization as a knowledgeable and responsible agent. As Plato says in the mythological language with which his *Republic* ends: when a man chooses a philosophy, his "whole fortunes are at stake. On this account each one of us should lay aside all other learning, to study only how he may discover one who can give him the knowledge enabling him to distinguish the good life from the evil, and always and

[49] PE II, 113.

everywhere to choose the best within his reach."[50] To become a philosopher is to forsake shadow for substance, to find a way out of the cave of ignorance into the light of knowledge, and to extend the horizons of awareness indefinitely. It is to discover a world not made with hands, or, in Spinoza's words, to learn to prefer the excellent rarities of the spirit to the honor, pleasure, and worldly wealth which the average man regards as the *summum bonum*.

Philosophy is not primarily an academic matter. Though fostered by universities, it no more "belongs" to them than do such other bearers of the fruits of the spirit as art, music, and literature—or, for that matter, morality and religion. It has no institutional reality, and even one who is hired to teach it "must not have the folly to wish to be recognized as a philosopher." Like the members of the "church invisible," the world's philosophers are not held together by any officially recognized tie, or identifiable by any credentials: "In philosophy's realm of the spirit there is no objective certainty and no confirmation. . . . Men become companions-in-thought through the millennia, become occasions for each other to find the way to truth from their own source, although they cannot present each other with readymade truth. It is a self-development of individual in communication with individual."[51] The great philosophers should be read as though they were contemporaries.[52]

While scientific statements relate to externals, philosophic communications have to do with beliefs that are constitutive of the nature of those who internalize them. That is why it is the duty of each rational man to use the utmost care in selecting the human guides who can best assist him: "Among the responsibilities of man are the philosophers, the philosophic writings, and the philosophy that he entrusts himself to."[53] One's character depends in large part upon his philosophy. But his philosophy depends no less upon his

[50] F. M. Cornford, trans., *The Republic of Plato* (New York: Oxford, 1945), p. 356.
[51] UPT 136.   [52] UPT 137.   [53] VW 572.

character: the two influence each other reciprocally. "Since, as human beings, we are more influenced by passion and empty intellectuality than by presently active love and circumspect reason, philosophers since antiquity have quite rightly made philosophic understanding dependent, not upon special capacity and unusual learning, but upon the basically ethical nature of the individual."[54] Character, personality, and world-view, though readily distinguishable, are not actually separable: "What I can conceive belongs to my innermost nature, what I believe constitutes my very self, the kind of God I accept is my true being, and I exist in the way in which I love."[55]

Seen from this standpoint, the typical debates of professional philosophers appear as little more than obscene caricatures of true communication. Admirers of the sages and seers of tradition, cannot but deplore the abandonment of truth-seeking in favor of debating, and the employment of subterfuge, concealment, and obfuscation when the things which matter most are at stake. But at the same time, ideal communication, such as was described by Diotima and practiced by Socrates and his followers, cannot be made to take place routinely, for, like ideal romance, its occurrence requires the coincidence of a number of special conditions.

First of all, such communication presupposes friendship between the communicants—not Aristotle's "friendship of utility" or of "pleasure," but his "friendship of goodness," calling, as it does, for the sympathy and disinterestedness of persons whose complete devotion to each other and concern for mutual assistance in the realization of potentialities precludes the presence of cant, hypocrisy, false modesty, envy, malice, ridicule, exhibitionism, condescension, depreciation, and the like. Not only is such friendship rare, but it cannot be deliberately brought into being by skillful practical activity. One may place himself in readiness and cultivate people, but there is no such thing as "making" friends, or even "finding" them. Friendship is not an object

[54] PE II, 113.   [55] VW 987.

to be sought or a product to be earned by skillful work. Like Christian grace it comes as a gift—an unmerited favor.[56] Unless each respects and trusts the other, honesty will go by the boards, and truth will be slighted. St. Paul concisely describes what is needed in his letter to the church at Corinth: "Love is never boastful, nor conceited, nor rude; never selfish, not quick to take offense. Love keeps no score of wrongs . . . but delights in the truth."[57]

Further, as Jaspers repeatedly remarks, the communicants must belong to the same "niveau"—the same level of existence. Of course there are always differences in capacities and achievements, but these can be allowed for among those of approximately equal rank. It was this requirement that Nietzsche held accountable for an increasing loneliness that weighed him down during the final years before his collapse. As Jaspers tells us in commenting upon two of Nietzsche's letters to his sister: "Never does he meet his equal in kind or in rank: hence, in the end he is forced to say: 'I am too proud to think that a human being could love me. This would presuppose that he knows who I am. Just as little do I believe that I shall ever love anyone: this would presuppose that I would, for once, find a human being of my rank. . . . (Mar., '85.)' Perfect friendship can exist only *inter pares* (July 8, '86)."[58]

In addition, various attitudes exclude the possibility of genuine communication. A few of the most common may be mentioned here:

Sometimes a friend rejects any communication that threatens to become critical, saying, "I am what I am" (*Ich bin nun einmal so*), "You can't change me" (*Mich kann man*

---

[56] The idea that the best things cannot be earned but come as gifts appears repeatedly throughout Jaspers' writings. The relation of this idea to the Christian idea of grace is made explicit on p. 295 of PO. Its derivation from the thought of St. Paul and St. Augustine is alluded to in his debate with Rudolf Bultmann. See FET 73.

[57] I Cor. 13:5-7, as translated in *The New English Bible* (Oxford and Cambridge University Presses, 1961).

[58] NET 86.

nicht mehr ändern), and the like.[59] In such a case the individual seems at one and the same time to seek and to reject communication. And he expresses his rejection in such a way that what he says contradicts the saying of it, for he manifests his freedom by freely denying it. Sometimes this simply means: "I prefer sympathy to communication."

Many a pat formula serves as a substitute for communication. Viewing the topic under consideration from a biased point of view, one refuses to recognize that it could be construed differently, and upholds his view by a tiresome repetition of unexamined shibboleths. This technique, a favorite with professional diplomats, executives, administrators, and bureaucrats, can be used to prevent others from going beyond externals. In public discussion it can be combined with a manifest tendency to regard the pressing home of searching questions as downright impudence.

One pleads a lack of the requisite specialized knowledge and, refusing to discuss or decide, turns the affair over to a specialist. Or again, he claims to possess the authoritative knowledge that makes further discussion futile.

Sometimes he prefers his own view and refuses to consider any other, saying, for example, "We would never be willing to admit that!" or "I won't allow anyone to take my religion away from me!" "It was in this manner that the Greeks distinguished themselves from the Barbarians: they were the ones who considered reasons and grounds. Even today naive barbarians say: 'You can never make me change my mind.' "[60]

Speaking positively, Jaspers describes the cooperative search for truth which he calls "loving struggle" (*liebender Kampf*) as follows:

> In such communication what is involved is not the blind love which fixes upon one object as readily as another, but the struggling love that is clearsighted. It calls into question, raises difficulties, makes demands, and, out of

[59] PE II, 87-88.   [60] PE II, 89.

possible Existenz, wrestles with the other possible Existenz.

The struggle involved is that of an individual for Existenz—at once that of the other and of the self. While at the level of empirical existence any weapon at all is acceptable, the use of cunning and deception is unavoidable, and the opponent is to be treated as an enemy on all fours with the entirely alien physical nature that resists all our efforts, the struggle for Existenz is infinitely different. It involves complete openness, unqualified renunciation of the uses of power and advantage, and concerns the other's self-realization as fully as one's own. In this struggle, both dare to dispense with concealment, to be completely themselves, and to submit to probing questions.[61]

What is here described is a precious and extremely rare experience which he may have at least approximated with his brother-in-law, Ernst Mayer,[62] with his student friend, Hannah Arendt,[63] and which he repeatedly achieved fully with his wife. It is not surprising that book after book bears the inscription: *"Gertrud Jaspers Gewidmet."*[64]

By way of further characterization, one may lay down a number of rules for *liebender Kampf*:[65]

Existential communication (somewhat paradoxically) cannot appear among the members of a self-sufficient group of like-minded people who believe themselves already to possess a fixed and final truth (e.g., the Parsees or the Amish). When nothing can be questioned, nothing can be philosophically discussed. "Only when I am exposed and deprived of the saving security (*Geborgenheit*) [of a social whole united by its sympathies, beliefs, and ways of behaving] do I experience the genuine urge to true communication."[66] And again: "For man, communication is a decisive source only

---

[61] PE II, 65.   [62] PFT 238.   [63] PFT 274.

[64] PFT 300. See, for example, the dedications in PY, PE, VW, and PO.

[65] PE II, 51, 66-67; PY 125-26.

[66] PE II, 106.

in the absence of the final and unquestioned security provided by selfless objectivities: by the authority of state and church, by an objective metaphysics, a life-order accepted as morally compelling, and an ontological grasp of being as such."[67]

Neither party can literally "help" the other, either by enabling him to believe, as did Christ when he dispensed grace, or by providing the truth itself, as did the dogmatic philosophers. Each is in doubt rather than possession, on the way rather than at the goal. One can only appeal and awaken, as did Socrates through the use of the maieutic method.[68]

Both discussants must recognize and control those psychological drives (e.g., egotism, envy, aggression) that hinder communication and lead in the direction of self-centeredness and isolation. These cannot be extirpated; they can only be unmasked and taken into account.

Since the communicants occupy the same niveau, respect is implicit in the struggle, and affirmation in the critical questioning. Each understands that to reject the other's opinion is never to reject *him*. This, however, must not be taken in the sense of a worldly "recognition" of the rights, privileges, and prerogatives that are "due" to anyone who has a certain character and enjoys a given status.[69] Such things, which are as important to the average man as food and drink, are irrelevant here. Rather, a basic and indefinable solidarity is presupposed.

All that is said is meant as a question to which an answer is required. However, the answer must not be a lengthy disquisition, a diatribe, a changing of the subject, a flat contradiction, or a mere coercive insistence. Bombastic harangue is not conversation, and contradiction is not refutation.

Chivalrous alleviations of difficulties may be employed with the sanction of both, but only temporarily. When they are retained indefinitely communication breaks down.

[67] *Ibid.*   [68] VW 847.   [69] PE II, 244.

Not only are all factual materials placed at the disposal of both, but the means employed are the same; each raises the same pressing questions about himself as about the other, for the two are not struggling against each other but making common cause in the struggle for truth.

Whatever argumentative means are employed by the one are placed entirely at the disposal of the other. All cards are laid on the table, and nothing pertinent is concealed.

Nothing that is felt to be relevant may remain unconsidered. What is not answered immediately is merely postponed but never ignored.

It is not superiority and victory that are desired. Such desires are experienced as disturbing, and they give rise to guilt feelings.

One must attend to the overtones, the nuances, and to what is merely implicit. Often the feeling-content is more revelatory than what is openly said, but emotional states are not to be summoned as reinforcements. And of course all tricks and sophistical procedures are regarded as destructive of mutual understanding.

For those acquainted with boundary situations (*vide infra*), communication is all-important: "When everything that is said to be valuable and true collapses before my eyes, those with whom I communicate or might communicate remain, and with them remains what to me is authentic being."[70]

Indirect Communication

Loving struggle is highly exceptional, as should now be evident: usually we address our elucidations to comparative strangers. In any case we are confronted by a further problem to which there is no apt solution: Existenz is the "absolute individual,"[71] and the individual is ineffable. If, as Aristotle pointed out, only the universal can be known and communicated, and, at the same time, only the individual is real, then that which *is* cannot be expressed. Strictly speak-

[70] PE II, 117.   [71] PW 378.

ing, the social sciences can never quite say what they mean (the individual), or mean what they say (the universal).[72] But, as such estheticians as Croce, Collingwood, Sullivan, and Green have long insisted, many things that scientific language, proceeding at the level of consciousness in general, cannot directly convey can be communicated indirectly through the arts. Much as science provides the understanding with knowledge of the universal, so art provides the imagination with suitable means of intuiting the individual. "*Au fond*, art is the illumination of Existenz through a kind of confirmation that brings the being of empirical existence intuitively to the fore."[73] It may be said to proclaim original truths of being,[74] when it conveys mediately what can never be said straight out.

Not only is Existenz confined to the individual; it is a profound and scientifically undiscoverable source. Being impalpable and *unanschaulich*, it cannot be directly expressed. Much as the modern theologian speaks of God in anthropomorphic terms even though he realizes that God is not a man, and thinks of Him as a person even though he knows that the analogy must in the end break down, the philosopher of Existenz must allude figuratively and indirectly to what his speech cannot directly and literally convey. "Existenz has no apprehensible objectification of its own. It relies upon three modes of the encompassing as media for its appearance": Life is known to the biological sciences, thinking is present to psychology and logic, and spirit (*Geist*) is objectified in its social and artistic products. But Existenz can convey itself through these three media only indirectly. That is why we must recognize an indefinite limit to the shareable and use vehicles of communication that are independent of the conceivable.[75] It is in this sense and for this reason that Lao Tzu's *Tao Te Ching* may be thought of as the first

[72] See Gordon Allport, *Personality: A Psychological Interpretation* (New York: Holt, 1937), chap. i.
[73] PE I, 331.
[74] PE I, 339. Cf. PY 378.   [75] PO 116-17.

great indirect communication: "He meant these written statements to induce the reader to transcend them, he meant them to guide us, through reflection, to the ineffable."[76] What cannot be said directly must be said indirectly or not at all.

In the third place, "doctrine is not life, and doctrinal communication is never a carry-over from life. Indirect communication, i.e., the experience of the direct as a medium in which something else is at work, proceeds as though it conveys life itself."[77] A thinker like Kierkegaard—or Sartre— may make philosophic insights available by presenting to our imaginations experiential sources that cannot be given to our sense organs. Rejection of a life of mere pleasure-seeking may derive in part from such vicarious adventures as are offered by *Faust, The Diary of a Seducer*, or even *Tender is the Night*. Awareness of the insincerity with which our society is permeated may be heightened and rendered articulate by a study of Molière, Ibsen, and Shaw. The most deeply moving of Shakespeare's plays may well do more to support "the tragic view of life" than any philosophic argument. Plato, in all likelihood, prepared his students for political philosophy by telling them of his experiences with Dionysius, the Tyrant of Syracuse. All theory is gray, and only the golden tree of life is green.[78] Unless one is as miraculously endowed as Faust, he can hardly hope, in his own person, to undergo sufficient experiences to make *Existenzphilosophie* meaningful. Sensory givens must be extended and made meaningful by the imaginings which signs and symbols convey.

Finally, indirect communication is deliberately employed by philosophers like Socrates, Kierkegaard, and Nietzsche who prefer the struggle for truth to possession of the truth, and dare not presume to tell their companions what to believe. Having no absolute truths to offer, they say nothing

[76] GPT II, 408.   [77] PY 378.

[78] Jaspers refers to Goethe, along with Kant, as an irreplaceable companion of his life. PX 844.

139

in straightforward fashion, but "merely stimulate people and make them attentive, unsettle them by rendering everything problematic, and refuse to provide any precepts, regulations, or doctrines about how they ought to live. They seem to create difficulties, wreak intellectual havoc, and lead people to despair, but to have nothing 'positive' to offer."[79] They do not want disciples, but prefer, by forcing people to seek truth for themselves, to emancipate them. Unsettling critical probing is used to bring to life by indirection what could never be conveyed through positive assertion. Philosophizing has to be provoked by the collapse of customary values and the discovery of insoluble vital problems, for genuine autonomy is possible only to those who have been stripped of their illusions and forced to confront unpleasant realities. This however is the topic of the following chapter.

[79] PY 376-77.

chapter six

Ultimate Situations

ᑫᑐ

Why philosophize? Why not be content with scientific knowledge and disregard the perennial perplexities of traditional philosophy? How can we recommend either individual or social support of an exhausting intellectual enterprise that produces no practical results, leads to no unanimity, provides no reliable knowledge, and solves no problems? If, as Jaspers tells us, "we are scarcely entitled to say that we have progressed beyond Plato,"[1] is there any reason to continue? What powerful motives serve to perpetuate groundless speculations whose apparent futility is notorious?

Philosophy, as Plato and Aristotle agreed, normally begins with *wonder*.[2] Whether or not wonder is compatible with the advanced status of a mature philosopher who, like Spinoza, prefers "that we understand the things of nature as learned men, and not stare at them in amazement like fools,"[3] this attitude is altogether appropriate to the inchoate beginnings of the life of reason, for it supplies an indispensable impetus. "I wonder . . ." marks the beginning of inquiry, just as "No wonder!" signifies the end. "Wonderment gives rise to question and insight";[4] without it philosophizing cannot get under way.

In the second place, as Socrates so well illustrated for the ancients and Descartes for the moderns, philosophizing is provoked by the disequilibrium of doubt. To be fully satisfied with one's present beliefs is to have no need of philosophy. It is when doubt erodes the values and principles by which people regulate their lives that philosophizing is called for. Any normal man can memorize erudite formulae and even learn to talk and act like a philosopher. But until he is

[1] EPT 8. [2] EPT 17-18.
[3] *Ethics*. Appendix to Part I. [4] *Loc.cit.*

jarred out of his everyday complacency, rendered dissatisfied with his present beliefs, and disabused of his prejudices, he can no more really philosophize than he can, to any good effect, see without looking or hear without listening. It is when we find that "our categories . . . become entangled in hopeless contradictions [and that] everywhere proposition stands against proposition"[5] that we are first enabled to engage in the radical questioning that leads to philosophizing.

In the third place—and this, being one of Jaspers' special contributions to the existentialist movement,[6] must here be considered at length—philosophizing is stimulated by so-called ultimate situations (*Grenzsituationen*), i.e., situations of profound import that, although often obscured and ignored, can never be changed. Unlike the problematic situations that we can easily manage, especially with the professional assistance of lawyers, pastors, counselors, and the like, these situations present insoluble problems that can be dealt with only in superficial and, in the end, futile ways. "There are situations which remain essentially the same even if their momentary aspect changes and their shattering force is obscured: I must die, I must suffer, I must struggle, I am subject to chance, I involve myself inexorably in guilt."[7] One can take out life insurance, learn to say that there is no death, employ anesthetics, acquire first-rate weapons, and so on, but he can no more banish death, agony, or combat than he can avoid the fortuitous or live without sin and guilt. Such frightful and unalterable situations, along with wonder and doubt, provide—insofar as we are fully aware of them—the most profound source of philosophy.[8] It is, of course easily possible to veil them, and indeed most people do so, thinking that concern with such things is morbid and futile. Unwillingness to face reality is intracta-

[5] EPT 18.

[6] See Edwin Latzel, "The Concept of 'Ultimate Situation,'" PX 183.

[7] EPT 20.   [8] *Ibid.*

ble. But intellectual honesty, "the presupposition of Existenz,"[9] is not on trial among philosophers. And, as Jaspers insists, "to experience ultimate situations and to exist (*existieren*) is one and the same thing."[10]

The Ultimate Situation of Historical Determinacy

The first ultimate situation to be noted is set off by its extreme generality from those most commonly mentioned. It is simply the familiar but seldom-considered limitation of each individual to a particular time, place, and status: "I exist in this specific historical time and sociological position; I am a man or a woman, and am young or old. I am dependent upon opportunities and chances."[11] Even though, like Miniver Cheevy, who loved the Medici and dreamed of Thebes and Camelot, we may prefer some other age to our own, we cannot escape from the here and now. The possibilities that we actualize exclude an unlimited number of others. Just because we are in a position to enjoy the remarkable advantages available in twentieth-century America, we cannot talk with Socrates, watch Leonardo paint, or hear Hegel lecture. The Germans of the 1930's used to say: "We, the living, have Adolf Hitler!"

My situation inhibits me in innumerable ways. It limits my freedom and narrows almost to the vanishing point the number of possibilities that I can hope to realize.[12] Repeatedly I find myself at the mercy of mere chance. "What I become and the tasks I take in hand depend upon what the occasion offers. My growth and development must accord with present sociological and economic opportunities, and the ties of love that bind me to my fellows depend upon accidental meetings within the everyday world."[13] Of course I can transform everything by viewing the operation of chance as actually an unavoidable, though hidden necessity.

[9] NET 202.
[10] PE II, p. 204. This crucial statement is repeatedly emphasized by Latzel in the above-mentioned article. See PX 186, 188, 189, 192.
[11] PE II, 209.　　　　[12] PE II, 211.　　　　[13] PE II, 216.

"But when the necessity becomes absolute it is as unbearable as mere chance. [Consequently] one tends to vacillate between the two: he escapes the arbitrariness of mere accident by thinking of necessity, and avoids necessity by dwelling upon the chances and possibilities that accident can provide."[14]

When the limitation to a specific time and place is regarded as constricting not only the individual's opportunities for action, but also the possible ways in which he can view his world, we approach what Jaspers calls "historicity" (*Geschichtlichkeit*). Not only is a philosopher not a disembodied intellect, standing outside of the spatio-temporal world of appearance, but he thinks in the language or languages present to him, with the conceptual tools taught him, and in relation to the problems which appear within his own culture. This is undeniable: "Contemporary knowledge always has a historical gestalt: the form in which we take possession of it, the selection which reflects our interests, the possibility of discovering this rather than that."[15] Descartes, to choose just one example, having rejected with contumely the scholasticism of his teachers, offered as his own a neo-scholasticism so similar to the rejected view that the reader is tempted to question his sincerity. So striking is Descartes's inability to step outside of seventeenth-century France and think as his successors did that at least one commentator— who, of course, has his own historicity to contend with—dismisses Descartes's theism as mere humbug.[16]

From this situation two important consequences immediately follow. First of all, since our way of structuring experience is demonstrably capable of changing radically, there being, as Jaspers puts it, "no theoretical reason why in the course of time new categories should not be discovered *ad infinitum*,"[17] the world as it appears to us should be regarded

[14] PE II, 217.   [15] PE II, 394.
[16] Laurence J. Lafleur, Introduction to Rene Descartes's *Discourse on Method* (New York: Liberal Arts, 1950), p. xx.
[17] GPT I, 254.

144

as only one of a large number of experienceable worlds. Not only is there no standard way of structuring human experience, but the possibilities are virtually unlimited. The phenomenal world is like a huge Rorschach inkblot test which each of us interprets in the fashion provided by his own society, though with striking individual variations. In the second place, every specific individual is blinded to many possibilities by the paucity of stimuli which the historical process places at his disposal. Some degree of tunnel vision is inescapable. Socrates, it seems safe to say, could no more have understood Moses than he could have anticipated the paradoxes of Christianity. And Kant could never have regarded process as reality or thought of time as a fourth dimension. The intellectual heritage of an age inevitably sets limits to its speculative accomplishments. "Whatever Existenz may experience as its transcendence is elucidated in its own present by that which it hears of its own past. I can no more fashion by myself the metaphysical symbols which convey the experience of transcendence than I can construct a private language."[18] Our thoughts come to us as a series of exegeses on unknown texts provided by our ancestors.

That we must renounce all hope of ever possessing the absolute truth and content ourselves with the search for truth, freely admitting that philosophy produces no universally valid results, has never been a popular view in the United States, for we are at once strongly motivated to reject it, and keenly aware of the paradox that its acceptance involves. Brand Blanshard surely speaks for the majority when, in spite of the vigorous defense of interpretationism in the second chapter of his *magnum opus*, he insists that "truth is the same for all men," and that "philosophy no less than science must order itself by objective fact." This he finds to be basic and inescapable, for unless "the sort of reflection that starts with facts, . . . and proceeds by logical inference from these facts" is employed, "philosophizing

[18] PE III, 19.

145

is surely futile."[19] And A. E. Burtt, who has spent many years studying Oriental philosophies, continues to look to philosophy for universally valid knowledge. "One need not forget, in stressing the unavoidable relativities," he writes, "that there is always a reality that is being perceived and interpreted."[20] Apparently we have access to this reality, for, as he emphasizes by means of an epigraph, "in the long run truth wins the race with falsehood and error—and it wins because it is truth."[21] It is natural to believe with Charles S. Peirce that there is an "opinion which is fated to be ultimately agreed to by all who investigate [and this] is what we mean by the truth."[22]

Nothing but familiarity, however, can have imparted to this view the appearance of glaring obviousness that it has for many. That there is a "reality" toward which our thought is tending, that truth will win in its struggle against error, and that philosophers will ultimately reach agreement—these claims are not demonstrable conclusions of logical or scientific reasoning but articles of philosophic faith. And no one who is not already deeply committed really believes that it is permissible to dismiss any view on the ground that its truth would imply the futility of philosophy—or any other disagreeable consequence—unless he can show on independent grounds that that consequence is contrary to fact. The unpalatability of a statement's implications proves nothing.[23]

In the second place, Jaspers, who, in spite of his existentialistic reservations, would appear to be more appreciative of Hegel than even the most idealistic and contextualistic thinkers in America, would subscribe in the main to the contention of the *Phänomenologie* that (as J. Loewenberg

[19] "Reflections on Economic Determinism," *Journal of Philosophy*, LXIII (Mar. 31, 1966), 169-78.
[20] *In Search of Philosophic Understanding* (New York: New American Library, 1965), pp. 120-21.
[21] Epigraph to *In Search of Philosophic Understanding*.
[22] *Collected Papers*, Vol. V, ed. Charles Hartshorne and Paul Weiss (Cambridge, Mass.: Harvard Univ. Press, 1934), p. 268, as cited by E. A. Burtt, p. 197.
[23] NET 441.

expresses it) "each [philosophical] persuasion, exemplifying as it does a determinate perspective of human experience, is relatively true, and, being the perspective it is, indefeasibly so. It is only when for any perspective the claim is made that it encompasses the entire truth . . . that absurdity ensues. . . ."[24] Though each philosopher, if he is to be effective at all, must feel that he is right and that his own view must prevail, he should also recognize (and this is not logically impossible but merely psychologically frustrating) that, objectively viewed, his own sponsorship confers no superior status upon its recipient. Mineness is impressive only to me.

In the third place, while Jaspers regards the plurality of tenable philosophic views as an incontestable primary datum—a basic fact of philosophical experience—he does not share the positivistic view that takes metaphysical theories to be simply quasi-scientific hypotheses of unlimited generality. To be sure, Stephen Pepper's study,[25] which explicated this contention when metaphysics was in the doldrums, would seem to have more than a little in common with Jaspers' *Psychologie der Weltanschauungen*. Both books stress the fact of perennial philosophic disagreement and accept as inevitable the resultant plurality of philosophic views. Both defend philosophic speculation, urge careful study of all recurrent types of philosophy, and deplore the intolerant exclusiveness and complacent provinciality that is often allowed to mar otherwise reasonable standpoints. But these areas of agreement are little more than incidental.[26]

To view philosophies, as Pepper purports to do, not "as creeds to be accepted or rejected, or as expressions of highly individual personalities . . ." but as facts—as "objects in

[24] J. Loewenberg, *Hegel's Phenomenology: Dialogues on the Life of Mind* (La Salle, Ill.: Open Court, 1965), p. 242.

[25] *World Hypotheses* (Berkeley and Los Angeles: University of California Press, 1942).

[26] If Jaspers is unacquainted with Pepper's own writings, he alludes repeatedly to the view that philosophy offers "world hypotheses." See PE I, 232, 235, and 274; II, 31-32, 53, and 136; VW 975, 979.

their own right to be studied and described in their own character, . . ."[27] as, for instance, the zoologist studies this or that species of animal, is to ignore Dilthey's now generally familiar distinction between explaining infra-human entities through subsumption under natural laws, and understanding the human spirit and its products by participating in its most intimate processes. Sticks and stones are *toto caelo* different from the genial fruits of the spirit that Pepper is concerned to observe.

Furthermore, the claim to examine world hypotheses as "facts" is incompatible with the function which these hypotheses are said to perform. For it is said that, like Kantian categories, these hypotheses formulate and confer meaning upon whatever is *before* the mind from their position *within* the mind. As Pepper says, they are like lenses: more easily seen through than seen. "Through the lenses of a world theory" we seem to see "the most obvious uncontaminated facts. . . . But where the pure fact ends and the interpretation begins, no one in the absence of a completely adequate world theory . . . could possibly tell. And the better a world theory, the less are we able to tell fact from theory, or pure fact from the interpretation of fact."[28] What is of paramount importance in connection with world views is that we do not merely think *of* them but think *with* them. Now if these hypotheses are the media through which we observe objects, then they are not at the same time the objects of our observation. We cannot properly be said to see our eyeglasses when we are seeing *through* them.

Jaspers makes the point more directly.[29] From Cicero on down, eclectics have advised us to become acquainted with the outstanding philosophies, test them carefully, and then, presumably using common sense—for at this stage we can have no philosophy—choose the best.[30] This, however, is unthinkable, for "either I already partake of a specific belief, in which case I cannot but view everything in terms of it, or I

---

[27] *World Hypotheses*, p. 2. [28] *Ibid.*, p. 81.
[29] PY 386; PE II, 418. [30] PY 386-87.

am devoid of belief, in which case I simply do not see any specific beliefs at all,"[31] and, as a result, have nothing to choose from. In other words, the truths of science are universally valid. But in philosophy, "every single manifestation in the world of the one absolute truth must be historical: it is unconditional for this Existenz [in its specific situation within the world] and for that reason it is not universally valid."[32] "The multiplicity of truths remains fundamental for Existenz."[33] From this there is no escape.

Much as every mountain appears different from different distances and directions, so every viable world-view presents various aspects to different viewers. Whatever the view may be, there are usually some individuals who are too far away to see it at all. This would seem to be what William James meant when he said that some "options" are not "live" to us. We do not reject them; we find them unthinkable. Presumably that is the way the seers of Athens reacted to St. Paul's eulogy of the Unknown God, and the aristocrats of Rome to St. Peter's fiery sermons. Early Christianity was indeed foolishness to the Greeks and a stumbling block to the Jew: viewed *ab extra* it necessarily appeared nonsensical and inconceivable.

Sometimes a view is close enough to be understandable though not to be acceptable. One may, like Hegel, succeed for a time in entertaining and criticizing from within numerous views to which he could never subscribe. He may, like Collingwood,[34] delight in re-enacting in his own mind what he recognizes as foreign to himself, or, like a perceptive sociologist use "the participant observer technique" to interiorize and study much that is alien.[35] To develop an understanding of a wide range of beliefs in this manner is to escape from narrowness and provinciality.

[31] VW 974.   [32] *Ibid.*   [33] PE II, 440.

[34] *The Idea of History* (Oxford: Clarendon Press, 1946), Part V, sec. 4.

[35] See, for example, K. Young, "Sex Roles in Polygamous Mormon Families," *Readings in Social Psychology*, ed. T. M. Newcomb and E. L. Hartley, *et al.* (New York: Holt, 1947), pp. 373-82.

Finally there is the one view that I *am*, in the sense that I have so thoroughly assimilated it that it belongs to me as completely as my weight, my mannerisms, and my profile. This is not a matter of conscious and deliberate choice: "That I have chosen an idea appears only from my living with it as Socrates lived as though there were immortality. It is just this life itself—not the intellectual decision of . . . sound common-sense—that *is* my choice."[36]

Specific Ultimate Situations: Conflict

It is no more possible to prepare a definitive list of specific ultimate situations than to enumerate all categories—or "category mistakes." But it may be said that *any* list should include at least struggle (*Kampf*), guilt (*Schuld*), death (*Tod*), and suffering (*Leiden*).[37] Of these four, the first two will be considered here.

Pacifists and practicing Christians may well imagine that after those who live by the sword have died by the sword, the surviving men of good will will beat their swords into plowshares and live on together in peace and amity. And dedicated Communists are inspired by the thought of a future era when, the state having withered away, laws and police-men will be unnecessary, and each individual will find his highest beatitude in eager cooperation with the members of his group. While this consummation is, indeed, devoutly to be wished, says Jaspers, it is incompatible with the human condition. Struggle, as political realists from Heraclitus and Callicles to Machiavelli and Nietzsche have recognized, is an inexpugnable part of life. When we omit loving struggle (*liebender Kampf*), which is in a class by itself, we find ourselves confronted by three quite different kinds: (1) the conflict over *Lebensraum* and material goods; (2) the competition for intellectual and spiritual advancement, and (3) the internal struggle to discipline the baser impulses and desires.

[36] PY 387.
[37] See EPT 20-22; PE II, chap. vii; PY 256-79.

1. At the level of everyday existence, conflict with others (covert when not overt) is inevitable. To live at all is to occupy useful space, to eat while many go hungry, and to hold a position that others desire. Any sort of success depreciates the less successful, who, quite understandably, are as displeased by the success of their rivals as they are pleased by their failure. Contention and strife can never be eliminated, and such unseemly emotions as envy, malice, jealousy, spite, and aggressive feeling will endure as long as the earth is populated. My life itself derives from the victorious struggle of my ancestors, and I shall be conclusively routed if in the end no one can regard me as his forefather.[38]

The virtue of fortunate circumstance, combined with the innocence of insensitive apathy, may serve as a protective covering and screen for those who believe in the omnipresence of cooperation. Members of the upper classes, by whom food, shelter, clothing, and gainful employment are taken for granted, often ignore the struggle or explain it away—at least until large-scale disturbances such as depressions, wars, monetary instability, and mass civil disobedience bring it forcibly to their unwilling attention. But our socio-economic knowledge, taken together with the psychology of individual differences, shows that the very existence of the intelligentsia and the cultural values which they support depends upon the dull and unrewarding labors of the congenitally incompetent. As Nicolai Hartmann insisted, the higher values do and must rest upon the lower. And these derive from excruciatingly tiresome labor. "Cruel and inhuman, and, at decisive points, enforced exploitation is the underlying condition, even though it may not be consciously recognized by the beneficiary. . . ."[39] Only in small groups or "enclaves"— the family, the church, the small homogeneous community —do we find mutual cooperation. Where huge organizations are concerned, it is only the slow tempo of the struggle that makes possible the illusion of enduring peace. As Nietzsche would have it, "Life itself is essentially appropriation, in-

[38] PE II, 235.   [39] PE II, 236.

jury, conquest of the strange and weak, suppression, severity, obtrusion of peculiar forms, incorporation, and at the least, putting it mildest, exploitation. . . ."[40]

To this situation, two diametrically opposed responses are possible. Pacifism says: "Resist not evil. . . . Love your enemies, bless them that curse you [and] do good to them that hate you." This, however, as its author's career shows, is so nearly a recipe for martyrdom that—except in special circumstances—it is incompatible with a full lifetime of effective action. In practice, nonresistance normally means allowing the worst elements to assume control. At the other extreme, with Callicles, Thrasymachus, and exponents of the survival of the fittest, one may advocate struggle, or even allow struggle to become all-important as it was "among the ancient Germans who found the meaning of existence in fighting as soldiers—no matter for whom."[41] But to struggle for nothing is to struggle in vain.

Benevolent theorists like Jeremy Bentham sometimes hope to exclude conflict by instituting a set of righteous laws that will make it worth each individual's while to cooperate with the others. But, as we shall see, "It has always been futile to appeal to a righteous law as to something known to possess universal validity. For a law is not justified as an abstract proposition, as the French revolutionists believed when they enthroned a goddess of reason. It can only be upheld when its unforeseen and unforeseeable consequences emerge."[42] We can never accurately evaluate our laws until we can view their consequences. But at no specific time can we be sure that all their consequences are known. And even if we could, it would not be possible to appraise them in generally acceptable terms. Authorities will always disagree about questions of right and wrong.

Finally the apostles of peaceful arbitration (mediation, conciliation, adjudication, et cetera) who believe, with President Roosevelt, that they can charm dictators, or with

[40] *Beyond Good and Evil*, trans. Helen Zimmern, sec. 259.
[41] PY 259.   [42] PE II, 240.

Governor Reagan that even the most violent emotions will subside when they discuss pressing problems while sitting "around a table in an atmosphere of good will,"[43] are using a method which is as deceptive as it is attractive. For normally disputes that call for arbitration are precisely those which are in principle insoluble by rational procedures. *De gustibus non disputandum est*: Where questions of ultimate values are involved, even the best informed and most selfless may be expected to disagree.[44] Not pat solutions but endless reflection comes of considering such questions as whether state funds are more desperately needed by universities or mental hospitals, whether education should be paid for by the recipients and their parents or by the community at large, or whether doctors of philosophy are as deserving of high salaries as doctors of medicine. In connection with issues like these, arbitration can only serve to disguise the underlying power struggle. Whatever the medievals may have thought, there is no such thing as a "fair price" or a "fair wage."

2. The various forms of *intellectual* conflict are hardly less ferocious. We can readily view the mental realm as a battleground of hostile spiritual forces[45] when we recall such well-known examples as Galileo's altercations with the Aristotelians, Leibniz' squabble with the Newtonians over the discovery of the calculus, Mesmer's struggles with the French physicians of his time, and, in our day, Gellner's much publicized quarrel with an editor who considered his book, *Words and Things,* too abusive to deserve a review—not to mention such current practices as ghostwriting and the exploitation of gifted graduate students. Presumably taking his cue from Hegel's famous chapter entitled *"Das geistige Tierreich und der Betrug oder die Sache selbst,"*[46] he describes

---

[43] *Time,* Feb. 17, 1967, p. 63.   [44] PY 220-229.
[45] Cf. POT, 128.
[46] *Phänomenologie des Geistes* (Hamburg: Felix Meiner, 1952), pp. 285-300. This has been variously translated as "The Intellectual Animals and their Humbug; or the Service of the Cause" (Royce),

the perennial contest. In this attenuated atmosphere "products of the spirit are brought together, compared, and allowed to challenge each other. While the *agon* of the creators invariably accompanies their birth, still [as though by way of compensation], when the underlying forces are genuine, the realm of the spirit in which each product is formed provides room for all with the result that nothing is destroyed."[47] On the spiritual level the conflict is beneficial for it stimulates and promotes: each critic places his own acquisitions at the disposal of his opponent. But there are secondary consequences and, in connection with them "the *agon* assumes the same forms of oppression, encroachment, and destruction that the struggle for existence exhibits."[48] Insofar as crass competitiveness takes precedence over the true goals of the spirit, everything is perverted and spoiled: "When it becomes a means of attaining material ends its very substance is falsified, for it mistakes itself."[49] Then confusion and misunderstanding become complete, for the underlying motives are indiscernible. One may criticize a colleague to find out what more he can say, to converse with him, to instruct him, to gain a hearing, to disparage him, or to completely discredit him. And equally numerous are the reasons why one may listen—or refuse to listen—to criticism. Since all may claim to act from the highest motives, all motives are suspect, and all accusations are groundless. The words are clear and present, but the speakers are hidden.

3. Finally, contrary to a popular impression, intellectual and moral growth depends upon internal conflicts. Existenz, obliged to realize its capacities and powers, as we are told, "is in a process of self-development that amounts to a struggle with itself."[50] Without self-discipline I can achieve noth-

---

"Society as a Herd of Individuals: Deceit: Actual Fact" (Baillie, first edition), "Self-conscious Individuals Associated as a Community of Animals and the Deception Thence Arising; The Real Fact" (Baillie, second edition), and "The Kingdom of the Spiritual Animals . . ." (Loewenberg). See Loewenberg, p. 168.
[47] PY 257.   [48] PE II, 234.   [49] *Ibid.*   [50] *Ibid.*

ing: "I eradicate certain possibilities in myself, assume control over my impulses, give direction to my natural tendencies, call into question what I have already become, and am aware that I only *am* so long as I do not regard my being as a possession."[51] This struggle with the self never ends. Each day, says Jaspers, I not only think of my achievements, but "I ask myself wherein I have erred, wherein I have been dishonest with myself, wherein I have evaded my responsibilities, wherein I have been insincere. . . . I find principles in accordance with which I resolve to judge myself, perhaps I fix in my mind words that I plan to address to myself in anger, in despair, in boredom, and in other states in which the self is lost."[52]

In short, *Kampf* is inevitable. We may imagine a Hegelian whole of things entire in which it has been eliminated. But the existing individual does not live within such a whole; where he lives conflict is an omnipresent reality. And this obtains even when a fortunate concatenation of material circumstances enables him to stand above the battle and merely enjoy the results. It is enough that he accepts this situation: "He has taken a stand and can no longer say that his Existenz is built upon love and 'nonresistance to evil'; like every other Existenz it is built upon dreadful exploitation, even though he personally has nothing to do with it."[53] And at the other extreme there is no escape, for as we have seen, the most intimate communication takes on the form of violent struggle. As Heraclitus would have it: "Men should know that war is general and that justice is strife; all things arise and [pass away] through strife."[54]

Guilt as an Ultimate Situation

One might more easily reconcile himself to conflict, sorrow, and death if he could hope always to preserve a clear conscience and avoid moral evil. If, like the ideal Stoic one could be wise and virtuous entirely, or, like Job, be "perfect and

[51] *Ibid.*   [52] EPT 123.   [53] PY 259.
[54] Fragment No. 62.

upright" and without sin even while enduring the most frightful tribulations, then he might accustom himself to genuine hardship, and face life with equanimity. But to the clear-sighted such things are impossible. Even an ideally moral man, willing at any price to pursue only the good, would inevitably fail.[55] Guilt is unavoidable.

"Every act has consequences within the world that are unknown at the time of the action. The agent fears for these consequences, for he knows them to be attributable to him whether he foresaw them or not."[56] Free action involves assumption of responsibility for much that we do not intend and cannot but regret. The conscientious surgeon whose error proves fatal will experience a heavy burden of guilt, as will a capable and well-intentioned driver who unavoidably kills a thoughtless pedestrian. What I do not intend and cannot condone may often quite rightly be laid at my door.

Even though by hard and conscientious work I earn all that I have and use, still I know that my life-conditions depend upon the unspeakable drudgery of unskilled laborers, as well as the unscrupulous pursuit of a "national interest" by public officials and other interested parties who care hardly at all for the welfare of backward and impoverished countries.[57] Whether I will or not, I am the beneficiary of various national policies that I could not conceivably defend on moral grounds. Indeed, I cannot even purchase supplies without spending money that the poor need more than I for goods that I need less than they.

[55] Jaspers does not, to my knowledge, consider the possibility that guilt and/or guilt-feelings are psychopathological phenomena requiring to be removed by psychiatric means. This view, discussed at length, for example, in O. H. Mowrer's *The Crisis in Psychiatry and Religion* (New York: Van Nostrand, 1961), would no doubt seem to him simply perverse. That dogs clearly express acute feelings of guilt should, it seems, suffice to show that this reaction is culture-free. And, as Mowrer insists, any uncontaminated moral individual must feel strongly that there are times when wrongdoers most certainly *ought* to feel guilty.

[56] PE II, 246.

[57] Cf. Reinhold Niebuhr, *Moral Man and Immoral Society* (New York: Scribner's, 1960).

"The real morality of actions," as Kant remarks, "their merit or guilt, even that of our own conduct, . . . remains entirely hidden from us."[58] Nevertheless, we see enough to arouse suspicion. Always, as Augustine says, there are "impulses, feelings, tendencies, that are in conflict with the conscious will. . . . Always the hidden motive."[59] The more Augustine concerns himself with his inner states, the more intensely he suffers from guilt: "He finds self-deceptions, as, for example, . . . when curiosity sets itself up as thirst for knowledge. . . . He is able to dispense with cohabitation but not with sexual dreams. He likes to do what is right, but in part he does it to make men love him. . . . All human life is perpetual temptation by the senses, by curiosity, by vainglory (the striving to be feared and loved). And we are [normally] unaware of it."[60]

I find myself attached to one person and would favor this one over many. But the many are also human beings who claim equality and should be given their due. If I am partial to my own, I am thereby led to neglect the general welfare and to place my concerns ahead of "the greatest good of all." But when I repent and, taking the brotherhood of man as my aim, learn to treat all men as I treat my brother, then I stand condemned for treating my brother as I treat all men.

Perhaps I propose to preserve my innocence by withdrawing from the entire situation. As a recluse I can live apart without harming anyone. But to do nothing is to neglect the worthy ends that I could help to promote. I am guilty of omissions as of commissions. The consequences of a failure to act may be quite as grave as those of any activity. And I am responsible for them.

The facts, of course, need not be faced; even ultimate situations are easily disguised. "What's the problem?" I say. "That's the way it is, and it can't be changed!" Or, again, "It's not my fault that things are as they are." And when forced

[58] *The Critique of Pure Reason*, trans. N. K. Smith (New York: St. Martin's Press, 1965), p. 475, note a.
[59] GPT I, 198.   [60] *Ibid.*

157

to recognize my responsibility, I can always remark: "It's no fault of mine that I am at fault."[61] In such a frame of mind I can ignore the unfortunate consequences of my acts, and avoid thinking of my moral condition.

In this, society is a willing accomplice. Men tacitly conspire to respect the life-lies of others so long as the others consistently reciprocate. Ministers in fashionable churches are careful not to offend their more wealthy listeners; only the poor are to be chastised. The mass media of communication enhance the meretricious rewards of immoral behavior, and psychiatrists continue to develop new techniques for eliminating feelings of guilt.[62] Members of the service professions earn their largest gratuities through shamelessly obsequious flattery of wealthy egoists, while politicians labor to improve their "images" in order to exchange charm for votes.

This view of our human situation is easy to brush aside. Such traditional measures as emphasis on neglected aspects, endless reflection, dismissal of the allegations as too extreme, or sheer inattention coupled with lapses of memory may easily be used to provide a different orientation. But still, no student of the social sciences can afford to admit to a lack of awareness of man's astonishing capacity for sham, hypocrisy, double-dealing, and corruption. And to the philosopher of Existenz, this is a matter of daily record.

The Ultimate Situation of the Questionableness of All Existence

"In every ultimate situation the ground is, as it were, removed from under my feet. Being, when regarded as empirical existence, cannot be grasped as a fixed and stable continuant."[63] Whatever is accepted as authentic being eventually succumbs to penetrating critical questioning, and even loving

---

[61] PE II, 248.
[62] See my Review of *The Crisis in Psychiatry and Religion*, by O. H. Mowrer, *Arizona Quarterly*, XVIII (Autumn 1962), 266-69.
[63] PE II, 249.

communication appears within the phenomenal world as struggle. "The questionableness of all existence means the impossibility of finding peace within existence as such. The way in which this latter, in all ultimate situations seems shattered through and through is its antinomical structure."[64] Contradictions are to antinomies what situations are to ultimate situations. Among the discrepancies and contradictions with which we are constantly confronted, those are antinomies that "are insoluable, stand at the limit of knowing and thinking, and, when properly comprehended, prove incapable of being dismissed as errors, mistakes, misunderstandings, or as merely apparent."[65] Antinomies, as Kant showed, mark the limits within which the understanding is confined. They indicate the presence of a boundary and demonstrate the impossibility of passing beyond it by conceptual means.

At the level of common sense antinomies are unnoticed, not because they are veiled, but because they have yet to appear. Inconsistencies, of course, are abundant—a fact which testifies only to the irrational insensitivity of the unphilosophical mind. If the proverbs in which the homely wisdom of our ancestors is encapsulated are laughably incoherent, it makes little difference. At this level a foolish consistency is indeed, as Emerson noted, the hobgoblin of small minds: while it is well to look before you leap, still he who hesitates *is* often lost. You can't teach an old dog new tricks, but it's never too late to learn. Since the vague and inchoate half-truths of the market place and the forum are indifferent to the standards of formal logic, an unrestrained proliferation of chaotic tergiversations and vacillations prevails. But since popular wisdom is merely the philosopher's *terminus a quo,* he can well afford to tolerate its odd caprices.

Science is a different matter. Typically it is self-consistent. But, as we are reminded, for instance, by the "dilemma of modern physics"—the question concerning the wavelike or corpuscular nature of the ultimate constituents of the

<hr>

[64] *Ibid.*   [65] PY 232.

world—contradictions sometimes appear, especially when the limits or boundaries of science are reached. Planck distinguishes physicists whose advances are retarded by an unwillingness to abide contradictions, from those others who continue to advance even at the cost of contradicting themselves, always hoping at a later date to make the needed corrections. "But," says Jaspers, in this case "the end is never reached, and the contradiction remains as a goad."[66]

When Kant took up the study of antinomies, he was not merely concerned to develop an argument for philosophic neutrality based upon a long history of disagreement among major philosophers. That the pros and cons of each traditional philosophic dogma have in fact been defended about equally well is as much a reflection upon man's forensic abilities as upon the inconclusiveness of *philosophia perennis*. Kant's basic conclusion was rather that the definitive limits of determinate scientific knowledge are demarcated by the series of downright contradictions that emerge when those limits are transgressed. We can think consistently about objects within the world, but not about the world in its entirety. "When we view the whole from the boundary marking the limit [of the scientific understanding], insoluble problems appear on every hand; only the specific and the relative can be completed. Worldly existence as a whole remains incomplete, for everywhere its suitable closure is hindered by the antinomies."[67] This is no less true —and it is perhaps more obvious—when we pass from the conclusions of theoretical reason to the claims of practical reason. Antinomies arise at once when we try to think coherently about the unconditional imperative of duty and the ultimate values with which duty is involved. To do what is right I must do what is wrong, for "in this boundary-situation one finds that the valuable is tied up with conditions that are disvaluable. Everywhere something unwanted must be taken into the bargain."[68] A few examples of antinomies,

[66] PE I, 257.   [67] PE II, 250.   [68] *Ibid.*

160

both theoretical and practical, should serve to clarify and emphasize this point:

The relativity of knowledge produces no serious difficulty for the social scientist but burgeons into an antinomy when related to the question of philosophic truth. It is more illuminating than disturbing, for instance, to learn from Ruth Benedict that "no man ever looks at the world with pristine eyes. He sees it edited by a definite set of customs and institutions and ways of thinking."[69] We readily understand about the many cultures, and are reconciled to the fact that the world of the barbarian is not our world. But when we turn from questions concerning the relativity of primitive cognition to the problems which the social scientist is obliged to raise concerning his own cognitions, we are puzzled, for if, as Benedict insists, no man sees things as they are, then certainly the scientist fails to see things as they are. This predicament becomes inescapable as we advance from anthropology to epistemology to find ourselves accepting as absolute the dictum that all knowledge is relative and insisting upon the fact that all facts are fabrications. If, as Nietzsche contended, knowledge is exegesis, then the knowledge that knowledge is exegesis is certainly exegetical.[70]

Again, the vast edifice of science is founded upon sense-impressions and is no more reliable than they. But, as scientifically oriented philosophers like Johannes Müller, Ernst Mach, and Karl Pearson have been quick to point out, science shows that these same sense-impressions are mind-dependent and illusory. Being composed of "secondary qualities," they cannot accurately represent objects.[71] In this way science uses sense experience to impugn sense experience; it relies upon the given to show that the given is specious.

Because the solution of merely theoretical problems can be postponed indefinitely, the antinomies to which they lead

[69] *Patterns of Culture* (New York: Pelican, 1946), p. 2.
[70] See NET 287-91; EPT 77-79.
[71] EX 56; cf. VW 30; EPT 77-78.

161

are easily overlooked. But the incessant demands of practical life involve antinomies which are not to be evaded.[72] In encouraging men to act resolutely and with conviction we are bound to support activities that contravene our own. In trying to be tolerant we increase our intolerance of intolerance. In promoting liberty beyond our boundaries we deny to other nations the freedom to reject freedom, forcing them, as Rousseau said, to be free. Within the domestic political arena, immoral means often prove indispensable to the attainment of high moral ideals: just to enter the contest one may have to buy votes, make false claims and promises, become obligated to unprincipled men, and/or assume disguises and play misleading roles. It is not that honest men are easily corrupted, but rather that the universal affirmative of morality is often forced to accommodate itself to the particular negative of someone's opposing self-interest.[73] Pristine and incorrigible innocence incapacitates its possessor for worldly effectiveness. When moral man in immoral society sets out to do his duty and promote values, he must cooperate with others, and, in doing so, knowingly participate in evil and voluntarily accept his share of guilt.

Reactions to Antinomies

A common reaction among academically trained thinkers is blank incredulity, followed by an affirmation of faith in the traditional laws of thought. One clings tenaciously and dogmatically to what he regards as strict consistency. Perhaps

[72] The prevalence of antinomies in practical as well as theoretical activities is emphasized in PY 232ff. Of course the antinomies that Kant made famous are only a few among a large group. One thinks of Zeno's paradoxes, Book I of Bradley's *Appearance and Reality*, and, of course, the thesis-antithesis dichotomy that Hegel and Marx brought to the attention of the entire learned world.

[73] An antinomical contradiction is of course not always of the sort represented by the traditional square of opposition. However, an exception to a general rule, being formally the opposition of an O to an A proposition (i.e. particular negative over against universal affirmative) may well serve as an illuminating example. Kant's belief that some acts are not determined, in the face of universal determinism which he concedes to science, is a case in point.

162

he mentally insulates conflicting views from each other to avoid direct comparison. Or he holds stubbornly to one member of each pair of opposites, supposing that spirited defense of the favored tenet is an adequate refutation of its contradictory.[74] Or he ignores what he cannot assimilate and refuses to allow his attention to be directed to it. At other times he abandons logic to champion his own claims as an authority. When this strategy no longer serves his purpose, he undertakes futile compromises, using stale old formulae such as "this as well as that," or "neither the one nor the other."[75] He calls attention to the form and ignores the content, and proceeds unthinkingly and without deviation as though on rails.[76] When worst comes to worst he panics and is at a complete loss.

In this last case he becomes confused and chaotic and is easily put to rout. "He wants something but cannot bear the means to it. He strives for a goal, but cannot accept its implications. When he wills an end, he also wills its opposite. . . . The more clearly he sees the ever-present antinomies, the more insecure he becomes and the more his conduct, his knowledge, and his very life are traumatized."[77] He lives by a series of accidents, and although he may forge ahead by making a display of consistency, he is *au fond* utterly faithless and irresponsible. "As a result of the complete blurring of all meanings he ends up with no standpoint at all. Instead of fashioning a shell (*Gehäuse*) of his own, he seeks out a ready-made position and comes to rest within the authoritative tranquillity of the church, or, if other things fail, among the disciples of a prophet."[78]

Ignorance of antinomies is hazardous and can even be fatal. He who fails to take antinomical conflicts into account is often "unable to yield to and move with changes in situations, opinions, and currently binding moral codes. . . . It turns out in the end, however, that his basic principles cannot survive indefinitely when the unrealistic modes of adjust-

[74] PY 240. [75] PY 240-241. [76] PY 354.
[77] PY 240. [78] PY 354.

ment which they entail consistently produce consequences that collide with the reality of constantly changing circumstances."[79] But not only are the apostles of consistency faced with enigmatic situations that they cannot comprehend, but they have to deal with the shameless and opportunistic Machiavellianism of the unreasoning realists: "Indeed the mere unscrupulous will to live and make one's way uses all principles indiscriminately as arguments that happen to serve its momentary purposes. What it wants is not truth but sophistical weapons. Consequently it welcomes the contradictory and yields to it completely."[80] Thus the consistency of "the good and the just" not only fails to conform to the natural disorder of things, but also collides head on with the shifting positions of crass and unprincipled expediency.

There remains a further possibility. Antinomies should prove a source of strength. In Jaspers' terms:

> He who evades an antinomy by ignoring the antithesis has to work against and in spite of it. But it is possible to derive strength from it. . . . An antinomy may inspire and strengthen the will in its struggle to approach a unity that can be realized only partially. The strength imparted has to be constantly renewed through shocks and inner disturbances that lead to the metaphysical and to an awareness of an infinite though nonobjective and unseen being. The forces operative within us are never fixed possessions that can be secured by formulae and prescriptions—they lead to the wager and to attempts at discovery. . . . Syntheses of antinomies exist only as living acts, endless and enigmatic from the standpoint of animalian existence and equally so when submitted to the impartial analysis of the disinterested observer. But this is where we enter upon the life of the spirit.[81]

[79] VW 517. The consistency with which his early position has been maintained is clear from this recent echo.
[80] *Ibid.*   [81] PY 241.

How is this possible? How can the antinomies that mark the limits of knowledge promote the growth of the intellect? First of all, as Socrates recognized long ago, antinomies are, in effect, hurdles that deter the weak and stimulate the strong. Philosophizing begins when one recognizes these barriers and deplores the consequent proximity of the horizon, the narrowness of his field of vision, and the vastness of uncomprehended outer area. It is from love of what we do *not* possess that philosophy develops.

In the second place, recognition of the discordant and the false is a mark of honesty and a presupposition of Existenz: "To experience ultimate situations and to exist is one and the same thing."[82] Believing with Nietzsche that "even among philosophers nothing is more rare than intellectual integrity,"[83] Jaspers regards readiness to recognize antinomies as a sign of honesty, and unwillingness to do so as a sign of conscious or unconscious mendacity in the service of dogmatism. Most misleading of all is the belief that reason guarantees one single exclusive truth for all men. One cannot subscribe to such a view without being dishonest.[84]

Finally, as Kant insisted, antinomies, together with circles and tautologies, prepare the way for speculative reason by disclosing the limitations of determinate scientific knowledge. The antinomies which arise when we pass beyond the objects of sense with which science deals to contemplate such extraempirical beings as the soul, the cosmos, and God, force us to abandon the clear, definite, and constitutive concepts of the understanding and avail ourselves of the indeterminate thoughts of which the "ideas" of reason are composed.

Beyond the limited realm possessed by science we find that where belief is inevitable proof is dispensable. Most of our beliefs, as James pointed out, neither rest upon nor need scientific demonstration. Abandoning the paradoxical claims

82 PX 186, 188, 189, 192.   83 NET 201.
84 PO 471.

of the skeptic which, as Hume said, admit of no refutation but produce no conviction, we make bold to assume what can never be known. Anselm's "faith," Pascal's "wager," Hume's doctrine of "natural belief," James's "will to believe," and Santayana's "animal faith" all testify to the indispensability of some form of nonknowledge to supplement the little that we can know. To set limits to the understanding is indeed, as Kant surmised, to make room for faith.

chapter seven

How Ought We to Live?

Whatever else we may know, there is no knowing how to live. Useful as science may be in connection with means, it offers little help with our choice of ends. The laws and customs of each nation provide a framework within which men can accomplish their purposes, but this framework is always subject to correction in the name of some higher principle, be it civil rights, the demands of conscience, the divine law, or what not. Advisers are generally available, but those capable of choosing wise advisers have little use for advice, while those who need advice have no way of knowing whose advice to heed. The church constantly offers practical guidance and moral support, but the plurality of tongues with which it speaks annuls the authoritarian exclusiveness to which it lays claim. In the end each individual is thrown back upon his own resources and forced to make his own decisions. The issues involved are momentous; each one's life depends upon his decision. But there is simply no rational way of deciding. Aristotle's golden mean, for instance, is incalculable; Bentham's hedonic calculus, unworkable. We have been thrown, so to speak, into a no-solution situation; the issues confronting us are undecidable. There is no method, no suitable procedure, no set of operations which, when properly employed, will solve the problems imposed by life.

But if philosophy can offer no ready solution, it is not irrelevant. If *Existenzphilosophie* rejects cut and dried formulations and broad generalizations, it does still strive after "the truth by which I live, and which I do not merely think, . . . a truth of which I am persuaded and which I actualize."[1] It agrees in substance with Max Scheler in asserting

[1] PE II, 114.

that the task of practical reason "is damned serious business" and in asking what good ethics is "if it is unable to give me directives how 'I' ought to be and to live right now in this social and historical context."[2] To come to grips with this ambivalent position, we must first examine the inadequacies of traditional ethical views and then consider Jaspers' positive proposals.

The Insufficiencies of Teleological Ethics

Whether we approach moral problems thinking in terms of scales of values and the *summum bonum*, or of rights and the unconditional demands of duty, we confront formidable difficulties. If we begin with the first, we take value to be fundamental, and view morality as a struggle to obtain the highest and best. This approach has the merit of being applicable in a wholly naturalistic setting, and it is sufficiently positive to suggest that life may be worth living to anyone who troubles to make it so. But it cannot be carried through. For, even apart from the well-known (and, I believe, fatal) problems that arise out of the conflict between the individual and society, it soon proves to be little more than a cheerful bluff.

First, the values in the world prove to be a motley lot, capable of being ordered in countless ways. There is "an endless series of values: health, power, fame, ability, enjoyment, science, bravery, sport, work, beetle-collecting, playing chess, and so on *ad libitum*."[3] These are normally dealt with by being placed in rank-order (i.e. in "value-hierarchies," or what Nietzsche called "tables of value"), in such a way that they reach an apex in a highest good, be it "happiness, pleasure, peace of soul, measure, virtue, life in accordance with nature, the useful, the vision of God, contemplation . . . activity and creation, the system of cultural values, etc."[4] But even what we call the very "same" values

2 Quoted in Herbert Spiegelberg, *The Phenomenological Movement* (The Hague: Martinus Nijhoff, 1960). II, 232.
  3 PY 221.   4 PY 226.

are differently interpreted in different eras. And since values are forever being created anew, every scale of values, and every *Lebenslehre* based upon one is subject to constant revision. During the Middle Ages, for example, extreme value-shifts took place. Constant, though often gradual, trans-valuations of values make any attempt to institute a final value-scale futile.

When we candidly examine the value-scales that have been actually set up, we are driven to scepticism. "Nietzsche once sponsored the series: science, art, and life, placing science at the bottom. . . . Kierkegaard accepted as fundamental the series of stages that he called the esthetic, the ethical, and the religious, holding that every stage included the previous stages within itself."[5] Max Scheler, who rejected Kant's ethics as purely formal, believed that phenomenological insight yielded (in ascending order): "sensuous values (pleasant and unpleasant); vital values (noble and base); spiritual values (beautiful and ugly, right and wrong); and at the summit, holy and unholy."[6] Different investigators arrive at different orders of rank among values, and there seems no possibility of gaining unanimity. Apparently the ways of arranging values are as personal and as arbitrary as the various arrangements of colors. There simply is no fixed and final scale of values, and no generally acceptable highest good.

Perhaps the view in question should be taken to mean, not that certain things considered valuable (riches, power, fame, pleasure, et cetera) should be pursued, but that values, whatever they may prove to be, and however they in the end may have to be defined, should take precedence over all other considerations. Duty consists in devotion to values, wherever they may be found. The good is to be realized within the world, and that is all. But this way lie frustration and despair: "Satiety and weariness, ennui and the desire for something new keep activity in progress even though it is impossible to reach a satisfying conclusion."[7] Incon-

[5] PY 224.   [6] GPT I, 297.   [7] PE II, 293.

siderate desire compels a senseless pursuit of a purposeless goal until life reaches its end and the entire process comes to nothing.

Finally, this view tends to neglect two characteristics of moral conduct that are often taken to be definitive, namely, those conveyed by that overworked Kantian term *"unbedingt,"* which means both *unconditional* and *unconditioned*. Many moral acts—teleological ethics to the contrary—are properly said to be *unconditional* in that they are performed without reservations, qualifications or selfish calculations. Thus we may say that "in love, in battle, in pursuing lofty tasks, we often act without regard for consequences, unconditionally."[8] And this applies to the moral law as well as to moral conduct: "The categorical imperative," says Jaspers, "lays claim to an unconditional validity."[9] But it is equally important to insist that a moral act that is unconditional has a source that is *unconditioned*. "Reason," says Kant, "as unconditioned condition of every voluntary act, . . . admits of no conditions antecedent to itself in time."[10] Or, as Jaspers expresses this same idea, this timeless intelligible source "is the 'cause of my actions as appearances' but is not itself appearance; it is not causally conditioned but free."[11] Like the theologians' ultimate ground of the world, the source resembles a *causa sui*—a prime mover unmoved. In order fully to appreciate the importance of these considerations, we must turn to the Kantian ethics.

Kant's Duty-Ethics

Kant, as every tyro in philosophy knows, developed an ethics of duty that neglects consequences, makes happiness secondary and pleasure irrelevant, and stresses the incommensurability of moral and material values. What counts

[8] EPT 52. Cf. GP 481.

[9] GP 481. Cf. Frank Thilly and Ledger Wood, *A History of Philosophy* (3d ed.; New York: Holt, 1957), p. 442.

[10] *Critique of Pure Reason*, trans. Norman Kemp Smith (New York: St. Martin's Press, 1965), p. 476.

[11] GP 496. Cf. 499.

from a moral point of view is the good will, i.e. the will to do one's duty out of respect for the moral law as expressed in the "categorical imperative": "Act only on that maxim whereby thou canst at the same time will that it should become a universal law."[12] In acting in this manner one acts freely and responsibly, knowing that he is entirely capable of doing otherwise. This view Jaspers takes to be true only when carefully qualified and restricted:

1. As stated it appears to be merely formalistic, as though morality were chiefly a matter of following certain rules. And indeed it has often been interpreted in this fashion.[13] But Kant soon makes clear that his formal requirement involves—or has for its content—a reference to a supreme end: "The central content of the categorical imperative," as Jaspers is quick to remind us, "is 'so act as always to treat man, both in your own person and in that of another, as an end and never solely as a means.' "[14] Furthermore, "Kant does not reject happiness; far from despising it or looking upon it with indifference, he affirms it as a fulfillment. But in none of its stable forms can happiness in this world yield the ultimate measure. It is subordinated to the condition of the ethical imperative."[15] The question is not how to become happy, but how to become worthy of happiness.

2. Kant—some of his apologists to the contrary—does in fact speak as though his imperative should show us what to do in specific problematic situations.[16] Seemingly it was intended as "a standard of material action in the world."[17] For example, I may never practice euthanasia on myself no

[12] *Fundamental Principles of the Metaphysic of Morals,* trans. Thomas K. Abbott (New York: Liberal Arts, 1949), p. 38.
[13] See, for example, W. G. Everett's *Moral Values* (New York: Holt, 1918), p. 297. The *locus classicus* is, presumably, Max Scheler's *Formalismus in der Ethik und die Materiale Wertethik* (3d ed.; Halle: Max Niemeyer Verlag, 1927), Part I.
[14] GPT I, 292. Cf. Kant's above-cited *Metaphysic of Morals,* p. 46.
[15] GPT I, 296.
[16] *Fundamental Principles of the Metaphysic of Morals,* pp. 46-48.
[17] GPT I, 297.

171

matter how hopeless my situation may be: "Certain actions
—such as suicide—'are such that they cannot without contradiction even be conceived as a universal law of nature.'
The right to suicide would signify the negation of life itself."[18]
Now of course this is to oversimplify a complex matter. That
when I follow moral rules I should not make exceptions in
my own favor is true but trite. That we can deduce the right-
ness or wrongness of actions from so formal a principle as
that of noncontradiction is false and misleading. "One may
very well ask," says Jaspers: "Is duty in fact always as clear
and unambiguous as Kant quite rightly takes it to be in
most cases? . . . Are the many concrete positive and negative
precepts of the moral life, in all their rational univocality
and rigor, as valid . . . as the categorical imperative itself?"[19]

3. Some of Kant's statements are so very drastic that they
seem to tell us more about his innocence of the ways of the
world than about moral conduct. For example, he "even
wrote a short treatise demonstrating that it is impermissi-
ble to lie under *any* circumstances. . . ."[20] It is entirely
proper, he claimed, to deceive beasts of prey, for they are
not rational. But it is morally incumbent upon us to tell the
truth in all our dealings with human beings—even when
the others refuse to do so, and go so far as to invent gross
deceptions to secure our undoing. But this is untenable:
"Where men wield total terrorist power, . . . am I not justified
in treating them as wild beasts? . . . Are men to be regarded
as human and rational beings simply because they belong
to the human species and are capable of thinking rationally?"[21] No specific moral laws have complete universal
validity, and "to confuse the wonderful purity of this source
of ethical reason with the rationalist rigor of definitely formulated commandments and prohibitions destroys the very
source which Kant raised to consciousness."[22]

[18] GPT I, 293. The inserted quotation is from Kant.
[19] GP 492. This passage is omitted from the English translation.
[20] GPT I, 298.   [21] GPT I, 299.   [22] *Ibid.*

4. Finally, Kant tends to think in terms of the ethos of his day. "There is a cleft between Kant's categorical imperative and his concrete ethical demands."[23] "Where he himself propounds a system of definite ethical principles, he discloses the historical form of his thinking. . . . The categorical imperative marks an eternal source; the concrete precepts are in good part an expression of the excellent, but historically contingent, ethics of eighteenth-century Germany."[24]

In summary, properly to appreciate the Kantian ethics we should supplement the first formal statement by the idea that everyone should treat all others and their rights with respect, and recognize that Kant did not intend to exclude happiness from consideration. We must also renounce any thought of using his principle as a guide to action, and overlook a rigorism so extreme that it would lead to a mechanical and thoughtless application of specific principles to concrete situations, regardless of the unique aspects of each one. And we must recognize that what is often objected to as "formalism" has value insofar as it serves to detach us from the situations and maxims characteristic of any specific historical era.

Given these modifications, two things must be strongly emphasized. First, morality is rooted, not in eternal scales of value or in the moral practices of any given society, but rather in the decisions of moral individuals. While one needs to know of the values of one's own time and of the scientific means available for their realization, and while everyone can expect to receive helpful guidance from the laws, customs, and religious institutions of his own group, still he must make his own decisions, and make them freely, responsibly, and resolutely in terms provided by the unique problematic situations with which he is confronted. The will to act impartially in treating every man as an end is, as Kant insists, autonomous, self-determining, and self-legislating. The moral law is not forced upon anyone; it is the rational expression of each individual's innermost will.

[23] GPT I, 298.   [24] *Ibid.*

In the second place, the self that decides is not the empirical self discoverable within the world of phenomena; it is the noumenal self. "The cause of my actions as phenomena" is not itself phenomenal, it is free.[25] Decision springs from a deeper level than any that is open to psychology. Free acts proceed from the unconditioned; freedom means, among other things, that "the beginning of a causal series lies in me."[26] To put it briefly, "Kant's insight is this: There is a condition of the good will that is itself unconditioned, discoverable through pure reason, independent of all material purposes in the world, a lawfulness that presupposes only itself."[27]

In stressing the uniqueness of every problematic situation and the consequent necessity of individual decisions, this profoundly modified Kantian approach appears as a forerunner of the "situation ethics" which today is appealed to in justification of such seemingly criminal offenses as Dietrich Bonhoeffer's participation in an attempt on the life of Adolf Hitler, and the courageous conduct of a concentration-camp doctor "who saved the lives of 3,000 Rumanian Jewish women by secretly performing abortions on them" to circumvent the Nazi policy of killing all pregnant prisoners.[28] When applied to sexual morality, to which it is sometimes thought to have a special pertinence, such an ethics repudiates old-fashioned rigid rules and plays down the fabled examples of ruined reputations, infected bodies, demented minds, and blasted hopes, in consideration of the shift in meanings accompanying altered social circumstances. It was presumably in something like this spirit that the committee of the British Council of Churches that authored *Sex and Morality* "refused to endorse the Biblical ban against fornication, which it found occasionally permissible, as when it is part of a 'total encounter' between consenting adults."[29] It has by now become evident that no finite number of rules can cover the

[25] GPT I, 301-302. [26] GP 458. [27] GP 481.
[28] *Time*, January 21, 1966, p. 55.
[29] *Ibid.*, October 28, 1966, p. 44.

practically unlimited set of varied and complex situations in which human beings find themselves.

Moral conduct as thus understood is less obviously gratifying and far more demanding than the laws and customs enforced by the group. One is not to give alms in secret in the hope of being rewarded openly; he is simply to give alms. Social recognition of private motives is out of the question. To the public, sincere trust, loyalty, and devotion, for instance, are indistinguishable from the shameless sycophancy of egocentric manipulators of human drives and emotions. Attempts to discourage, restrain, and punish evildoers in high places (as the currently notorious case of Senator Thomas J. Dodd illustrates) so closely resemble acts deriving from spite, hatred, malice, envy, racial bias, desire for revenge, or just plain sadism that anyone who seriously tries to inaugurate appreciable social reforms can expect to be presented to the public within a frame of reference that amounts, in fact if not in law, to calumny, defamation, and, at times, downright character assassination. And if the rewards are few, the demands are many, for no one who prizes rectitude can be content to respond only to the severely limited group of incentives which concern the average man. Devotees of virtue, like sincere worshipers of God, can never satisfy their requirements in moderation. Those who may properly be said to be beyond the good and evil of their tribes are not the unprincipled sluggards who ignore or deliberately violate the mores of their group, but the sages and seers who, like the refugees from Plato's cave, soon pass beyond ordinary norms to respond in socially unrecognized ways to things unseen.

"Whoso would be a man must be a nonconformist," as Emerson would have it.[30] The lack of social acceptance should not matter, for "I actually *am*, and do not need for

[30] "Self-Reliance," *The Development of American Philosophy*, ed. Walter G. Muelder, *et al.* (2nd ed. rev.; New York: Houghton Mifflin, 1960), p. 158.

my own assurance . . . any secondary testimony."[31] However, I can never appeal to my conscientiousness in vindication of my conduct, for not only is conscience unrecognizable, but it is generally regarded as a threat to society: "It is simply not accepted by the masses."[32] Luther's "priesthood of all believers," whether interpreted in religious or in secular terms, is anathema to most people: "The conscience that is independent and self-sufficient has up to now been hated by those able to sense it. The multitude recognizes conscience only when it is common to all, i.e. it does not recognize it."[33] That is why an original conscience is forced to preserve itself through silence, defending its acts in terms of whatever irrelevant standards the people can be induced to accept. "Appeal to conscience would [ordinarily] be as futile as appeal to feeling. . . . It would be taken as an expression of an unconditional challenge to fight it out. Conscience is an open and consequently not objectively fixated court of appeal only within existential communication from individual to individual, when it speaks freely and calls into question, in order, together with the other, to arrive at the truth."[34]

Thus, in summary, the self-reliant individual who is more than a creature of impulse and habit is finally forced to make his own decisions on his own personal responsibility. Within the world there is no higher court of appeal. While at a level below morality—at the level of mere *Dasein* (see Chap. VIII)—he simply follows inconsiderate and uninformed desire, as though values were objects of his own personal interest and duties were a hoax, at the ethical level he is guided by a conscience illumined by accurate knowledge of his situation and intimate acquaintance with the ethos of his community. He must act autonomously, for if there were objective indicators of the way he should go, he could not identify them, and if, *per impossibile*, he could do so,

[31] *Ibid.*, p. 159. That both Jaspers and Nietzsche were impressed by Emerson is clear from a number of statements in the long introduction to GP. See especially pages 34, 39, 41.

[32] PE II, 271.   [33] *Ibid.*   [34] *Ibid.*

he would still have to decide whether or not to submit to them. Freely and impartially to pursue the best that he knows in the light of principles that he would recommend to all is the most that is possible.

In view of the current widespread contempt of civil law and the prevalence of mass civil disobedience on the part of disadvantaged minority groups and outraged civil rightists all over the world, it appears that moral autonomy needs no recommendation to the now ascendant generation. And from a humanistic point of view, there is little more to be said. Jaspers, however, believes that when we trace conscience to its source, we encounter a force that lies beyond conscience. Can Kierkegaard have been right in supposing that from a fully developed ethical life a way leads on to a still higher stage? Just what *is* the source of conscience, and what does this source involve? Is there, after all, a significant sense in which the voice of conscience is the voice of God?

The Source

Paradoxically enough, it is when we are most free that we are most dependent. Acts that everyone would regard as spontaneous spring from an underlying source (*Ursprung*) that we can neither observe nor control. Let us consider a few examples that are sufficiently commonplace to be obvious. If dreams are our free creations, they are certainly not dependent upon our wills. They simply come out of nowhere, as it were, and force themselves upon our attention; we do not anticipate them, and we cannot prevent them. Much the same is true of speech; what we say simply "comes"; when it does not—when we are at a loss for words—we cannot force the issue. At times we speak easily, at other times we flounder and grope for words, while at worst we are speechless. Artistic, scientific, and philosophic creation is in the same case. The poet must consult his muse, the seer needs inspiration. Creative thinking, as Helmholtz, Poincaré, Wallas, and others have testified, is typically a matter of sudden and unheralded illumination after a suitable period of rumi-

177

nation or "incubation." The freest creations seem to come irrationally and even capriciously: they are just as much "given" as sensations.[35] When, for instance, the principle of specific gravity occurred to Archimedes, or the arrangement of the "Last Supper" to Leonardo, freedom was united with dependence and creation with givenness.

The voice of conscience is to be conceived along similar lines. When, to use Jaspers' example, Franz Neumann, the nineteenth-century German physicist, had to decide whether he ought to adopt the life of a farmer in order to remain with and care for his mother, or to leave his mother to pursue a demanding career in science, he spent many difficult hours trying to reach a decision. Then suddenly the awareness that farming was impossible for him came to him as though from an unknown source: "Such moments," he wrote to a friend, "come to me independently of my own activities, from outside, so to speak, and like a clear and intelligible voice calling to me."[36] In experiences of this description Jaspers finds "the consciousness of the absolute earnestness of Existenz in view of something final and inexpressibly important that lies in the act performed, and the responsibility that will rest nothing upon formulas, conventions, and norms."[37] The solution could not be forced, and when it came it did so suddenly and inexplicably. When the circumstances are unthinkably complicated the resolution is experienced by the individual as an almost miraculous gift.[38] It is "like a . . . communication of myself to myself; an appeal to my empirical existence from the source of my self-being. No one else is calling to me; I am calling to myself. . . ."[39] When I am already doing what is right, my inner-

---

[35] So true is this that one can just as well characterize sensory givens as our creations. If Hume finds it possible that sensations "are produced by the creative power of the mind," H. H. Price even goes so far as to say that "a colour-expanse . . . is created *ex nihilo* when suitable bodily and mental states are present." See Hume's *Treatise of Human Nature* (New York: Everyman, 1926), I, 87, and H. H. Price's *Perception* (London: Methuen, 1932), p. 113.

[36] PY 335. [37] *Ibid.* [38] *Ibid.* [39] PE II, 268.

most self need not speak: "Socrates daimon could only dissuade."[40] It is above all when conscience is silent because I am my true self that freedom coincides with necessity, and I willingly do what I must.[41]

Moral resolutions of this kind are phenomenologically or experientially immediate but logically and psychologically mediate.[42] At the moment of enlightenment the insight is directly present to the mind. It is simply given, and no further thought is required. But for all that it is subsequent to, and may be said to have been mediated by a prolonged period of reflection. It follows upon perseverative thinking, and invites explanation in terms of unconscious thought. What is directly *before* the mind is surely (as Bradley believed) a product of what is *in* the mind. As Jaspers expresses the point, "the existential resolution is not immediate like feeling and drive; rather it is first tested in unending reflection. It is a [logically] ungrounded immediacy, the actualization of which requires the fullest possible use of all available knowledge, experience, and thought."[43]

Somewhat surprisingly, perhaps, it is from this point that we proceed most directly to what Jaspers calls transcendence. I can will, and often do, but my will obeys no commands—not even my own. I wish, for example, to love my neighbor as myself, but I cannot effectively will to do so, for the will itself is not to be commanded or willed. Augustine, whom—together with St. Paul—Jaspers thanks for this insight,[44] tells us that he yearned to believe in Christianity long before he was able to do so, and when he finally succeeded, his belief came as a gift. As he describes the situation: "I did not that which with an unequaled desire I longed to do, and which shortly when I should will I should have the power to do. . . . More readily did the body obey the slightest wish of the soul . . . than the soul obeyed itself."[45] Freedom is a gift

---

[40] PE II, 269.   [41] *Ibid.*

[42] Cf. my *Philosophical Theory and Psychological Fact* (Tucson, Ariz.: University of Arizona Press, 1961), chap. ii.

[43] PE II, 270.   [44] FET 73.   [45] GPT I, 199.

that one can not boast of. "Therefore I am not absolutely free in my will, my freedom, my love. I am given to myself. . . . To myself I owe neither the outward conditions of my existence nor my own self."[46]

Here we confront an antinomy that refers us to something lying beyond. Free grace offered by an omnipotent God and unqualified human freedom provide a coincidence of opposites that points the way to a superhuman ground. Neither by itself will do. Were the source of grace an all-powerful transcendent being, then I could not will, but only automatically obey. But if there were no transcendence then the *ought* would lose its meaning, and only innocent and unaccountable free choice without guilt would be possible. A tension is inescapable: "Awareness of grace involves a repudiation of freedom in favor of the exclusive effectiveness of the divine will—as though this formulation allows for the possibility of guilt in the absence of freedom. Consciousness of individual guilt, however, preserves human responsibility by requiring freedom—as though guilt were possible without divine participation in freedom."[47]

Existenz and Transcendence

Existenz is aware that being without transcendence is uniformly unsatisfying. It is suggestive that Nietzsche, unlike most popular atheists, was in despair over the nihilistic conclusions to which he was driven. To renounce God, he said, means that "you will never again pray, . . . never again find peace in boundless trust. You deny yourself the opportunity to come to rest before a final wisdom, a final goodness, and a final power. . . . Man of renunciation, do you really choose to deny yourself all this? Who will give you the strength to do so? No one ever had this much strength!"[48] That "God is dead" was to Nietzsche an occasion for deep concern: "His atheism is neither a categorical denial of God's existence nor the indifference of an ungodly man whose disbelief consists in a disinclination to search for him. . . . His 'godlessness'

[46] GPT I, 200.   [47] PE II, 198.   [48] NET 435-36.

seeks to suppress the leveling and apathetic lie of pretended belief in God in favor of a genuine commitment to being."[49] However dead many of the traditional gods may be, and however misleading the idea of grace as originally formulated,[50] still, when Bruno chooses to burn at the stake rather than yield to the demands of the Inquisition, or when Luther says, "Here I stand; I cannot do otherwise," freedom is united with necessity and choice is, quite paradoxically,[51] beyond the control of the individual.

If, as Nietzsche believed, traditional religion is inadequate, it is not more so than the naturalism now fashionable. On a theoretical level, "philosophical world-orientation shows that the ground of the world does not lie within the world, for the world proves not to be self-contained. It would be impossible to know the world as an independent and self-sufficient whole standing by itself."[52] And from a practical standpoint, natural man has had little to hope for since the first atom bomb explosion. While there appears at present to be "no recognizable chance for a chain reaction to spread . . . to matter at large, thus disintegrating the globe," it is not only possible for mankind in its entirety to be "wiped out by men," but "on purely rational reflection it is probable that it will happen."[53] Given time enough, *some* man will do everything that man *can* do. In a word, the world without God is theoretically unintelligible and practically hopeless.

Existenz, unlike the scientific understanding, cannot demand proof. For it, as Paul Ricoeur tells us, "only the moment of choice, of anxious venture, of responsibility without guarantee or security, bears the stamp of authenticity."[54] In connection with the things of the spirit, we have only the wager, the will to believe, decision, and the cognitive uncer-

---

[49] NET 434.   [50] FET 74.

[51] This paradox is not recognized by Jaspers alone. Martin Buber, in *I and Thou* (p. 96) finds that "if I know that 'I am given over for disposal' and know at the same time that 'It depends on myself,' then I cannot try to escape the paradox that has to be lived. . . ."

[52] PE III, 3.   [53] ATT 3. Cf. PHT 131; PE I, 118.

[54] PX 615.

tainty of the leap of faith. Whatever the authors of traditional proofs may have intended to accomplish, still "all the proofs of the existence of God . . . differ essentially from scientific proofs. They are attempts to express the experience of man's ascent to God in terms of thought. They are roads of thought by which we come to limits at which the consciousness of God suddenly becomes a natural presence."[55] Faith (*Glaube*) is not knowledge but "nonknowledge." It relates to the unseen, which, though absent, is still hoped for: "A proved God is no God. . . . A certainty of the existence of God . . . is a premise, not a result. . . ."[56] At the boundary of science nothing remains but the leap of faith: "And in every case, the presence of gaps in the world structure, the failure of all attempts to conceive of the world as self-contained, the abortion of human planning . . . brings us to the edge of an abyss, where we experience nothingness or God."[57]

If proof is impossible, what then? On a theoretical level two ways are open to us: "formal transcending," which bears chiefly upon God's *existence,* and "reading the ciphers of transcendence," which relates primarily to his *nature.* These topics are taken up at length in the *Metaphysik*—the third volume of the *Philosophie.*

Nonknowledge and Cipher-Reading

Formal transcending employs the "negative theology" of the medievals[58] in order, by emphasizing the inaccessibility of the Deity to the senses and the finite understanding, to exhibit the constricting limitations of thought and thereby suggest the immensity of the outlying area. The theme is: "*It is thinkable that what is not thinkable exists.*"[59] Much as Hegel's dialectic is annulled when it attains the stage of absolute knowledge, scientific thought comes to nothing when it reaches the boundaries of the phenomenal world. As Kierkegaard never tires of insisting, "God is altogether other than man and man's world. His existence, therefore cannot

[55] EPT 42.   [56] PHT 32.   [57] *Ibid.*   [58] PHT 33.
[59] PE III, 38.

be proven nor His nature conceived."[60] Or, in Jaspers' words: "Everything thinkable is rejected as invalid by transcendence. Transcendence can be defined by no predicate, objectified by no representation, and attained by no inference, although all categories are applicable as means of saying that it is not a quality or a quantity, it is not a relation or a ground, and it is not one, not many, not being, not nothing, et cetera."[61] Such disintegration of thought which "conveys the 'that' but not the 'what' of the Deity," prepares the way for reading the ciphers, for it "provides space . . . that can always find . . . a fulfillment in keeping with its historical situation."[62]

Or again, the breakdown of thought may be signified by contradictions,[63] as shown by the antinomies of Kant and the *coincidentia oppositorum* of Nicholas of Cusa.[64] In any case it eventuates that "any category at all that we use in thinking of transcendence remains inapplicable so long as it is determinate, and becomes unthinkable insofar as it loses its determinacy."[65] God can no more be thought than can Kantian "things in themselves."

This *via negativa* would have little worth if taken entirely alone, for a "that" without a "what" is no more religiously available than an unknown and unknowable "x." However, the missing content is supplied when we learn to "read the ciphers of transcendence."

Anticipations of this idea are familiar to all, and as ancient as the Psalmist's proclamation that "the heavens declare the glory of God and the firmament showeth His handiwork." While Augustine could despise the world as the Devil's own realm, he could also enjoy it as the expressive creation of God.[66] Consequently it "points to the Creator. It is a place of parables, images, traces."[67] What cannot be said directly

---

[60] Louis H. Mackey, "Søren Kierkegaard: The Poetry of Inwardness," in *Existential Philosophers: Kierkegaard to Merleau-Ponty*, ed. G. A. Schrader, Jr. (New York: McGraw-Hill, 1967), p. 75.

[61] PE III, 38-39.   [62] PE III, 39.   [63] PE III, 40.

[64] GPT II, 123.   [65] PE III, 40.   [66] GPT I, 220.

[67] GPT I, 190.

can be said indirectly:[68] "The world is the making visible of the invisible God. The world unveils its Creator, so that He can be known as in a mirror, as in a riddle."[69]

Bishop Berkeley, who agrees with the negative theologians sufficiently to insist that we can never imagine or conceive of the Deity (though we may well have a "notion" of Him)[70] regards the universe as a language through which God reveals himself to us, that is, as a series of sensible signs that intend but do not resemble their object.[71] "It seems to me," he writes, "that though I cannot with the eyes of flesh behold the invisible God, yet I do in the strictest sense behold and perceive by all my senses such signs and tokens, such effects and operations as suggest, indicate, and demonstrate an invisible God—as certainly, and with the same evidence, at least, as any other signs, perceived by sense, do suggest to me the existence of [a human] soul . . . which I am convinced of only by a few signs or effects. . . ."[72]

And Nietzsche, who denied himself the luxury of believing in God, arrived, in his despair, at a cipher-language of nature which provided an identification of his being with the being of things. To this man whose loneliness was absolute, the landscape became mythical.[73] If at first he was merely overwhelmed by nature, "later it is as though nature and man's fate, sensual corporeality and true being, become fused. Not until his last decade does the world become transparent and nature assume a mythical guise. . . . Not only does he experience an intensified expression of the visible world, but he hears the language of being through nature."[74]

[68] GPT II, 154.   [69] GPT II, 192.

[70] See *Of the Principles of Human Knowledge*, par. 89.

[71] "Alciphron, or the Minute Philosopher," in Berkeley: *Essay, Principles, Dialogues*, ed. Mary Whiton Calkins (New York: Scribners, 1929), p. 360.

[72] *Ibid.*, p. 358. Cf. Ernst Cassirer, *The Philosophy of Symbolic Forms*, trans. Ralph Manheim (3 vols.; New Haven: Yale University Press, 1953), I, 139.

[73] NET 437.   [74] NET 372.

The difference between our awareness of things in the world and our awareness of the transcendent is not that the one is immediate while the other is mediated, for all awareness with any sort of cognitive import is mediated. The difference is rather that the former terminates in readily apparent objects that are easily distinguishable from the sensations and the concepts that refer to them, while neither Existenz nor transcendence has any special mode of appearance that can be viewed apart from the symbol through which it appears.[75] As Jaspers recently wrote, we have three things here to distinguish: concepts of objects, signs of Existenz, and ciphers (or symbols) of transcendence.[76] Here a brief outline may prove helpful.

MEANS OF AWARENESS	EXAMPLES	TERMINUS OF AWARENESS
1. Categories and Other Concepts (*Kategorien, Begriffe*)	Thing (*Ding*) Cause (*Ursache*) Event (*Ereignis*) Plurality (*Pluralität*)	Reality (*Realität*), i.e. Phenomenal Objects (*Phänomena, Erscheinungen*)
2. Signs (*Signa*)	Freedom (*Freiheit*) Resolution (*Entschluss*) Self-will (*Eigenwille*) Reform (*Umkehr*) Choice (*Wahl*)	Existenz, i.e. the Soul —the Intra-Personal Source (*Ursprung*)
3. Ciphers (*Chiffre*)	Physical Things: the Starry Heavens Mythical Events: Moses on Sinai Speculative Constructs: "Proofs" of God's Existence, et cetera	Transcendence as Actuality (*Wirklichkeit*) The Unconditioned (*das Unbedingte*) The Final Source (*der Ursprung*)

The first of these three levels is familiar. As we now easily understand, "the various phenomena of reality, such as appear in nature, psychic life, society, and history receive de-

[75] PO 156, 158, 162.   [76] PO 156-58.

scriptions that are universally valid. This presupposes an impersonal capacity for understanding [involved] in the sensuous capacity for perception. Every subject is convinced by what is pointed out to him because he sees as the others do. He can discover and allow for subjective deviations."[77]

Recognition of Existenz is different, for Existenz, having no embodiment of its own, must be revealed through discoverable "signs" within the world. A sign of Existenz, for example, is freedom,[78] i.e., such freedom as can be objectified, psychologically in choice, and sociologically in political freedom (liberty). This, together with other signs such as self-will and resolution, enables one to arrive at what, being nonobjectifiable, can only be elucidated.

Existenz gains access to transcendence through taking as ciphers certain of the representations, images, and thoughts that appear as objects of the understanding. While anything at all can function as a cipher, the ciphers that we have learned to employ derive in large part from our historical situation. Ciphers have a kind of meaning, but they never mean any specific "objects," for what they refer to can not be objectified. A similar account which Sartre gives of "natural symbols" illumines—though it could never confirm—Jaspers' account. In the view of Mary Warnock, "It is not at all difficult to understand what Sartre means by a thing's being a natural symbol. There are many things, especially perhaps natural phenomena, like the sea, or trees, which seem to us immediately to signify something, and about which it would be very reasonable to say that the distinction between the thing and its meanings disappears."[79] While "facts" are the same for all, ciphers, like natural symbols, are personal and unstable, and only meaningful or "transparent" to those who have learned to respond to them. As the iconoclasts have insisted, God may properly be presented through ciphers, but never pictorially represented.

[77] *Ibid.*   [78] *Ibid.*
[79] See *The Philosophy of Sartre* (London, Hutchenson, 1965), p. 104.

It is not that the religionist could speak more plainly, if only he would, but prefers to use the cipher-language of mythology for ornamental purposes; his message cannot be conveyed in any other way. Ordinary language simply cannot serve as a medium for the communication of religious truths. By the same token, no one can choose his own ciphers, for until he *has* his own ciphers he is too ignorant of divine things to be able to choose. We do not first become aware of God and then find the terms in which to express our awareness; we are aware of Him only in and through the ciphers that we possess.

Of course myths are in one sense knowable scientifically. Philologists and ethnologists collect them, classify them, and undertake to relate them to the historical contexts in which they originally appeared. "Metaphysical objects are externally visible to consciousness in general [i.e., to the scientific understanding] in the immeasurable riches of the myths, metaphysical views, and religious dogmas that history provides."[80] But only Existenz can discover what such things signify, i.e., can read them as they were originally intended to be read.

It need perplex no one that Jaspers is sometimes said to favor demythologization, and sometimes said to oppose it. If it is true that, as J. I. Loewenstein maintains, "Jaspers succeeds in freeing Transcendence from the last remnants of mythical imagery . . . by means of his basic idea of the Encompassing,"[81] so that he can actually "adopt the content of the religious tradition by demythologizing it,"[82] it is equally true that for him "all of reality becomes mythical" since "myths figure along with poetry and the plastic arts among 'the original spiritual intuitions, . . .' which render truth present."[83] For, as the controversy with Rudolf Bultmann made clear, Jaspers demythologizes only insofar as he

[80] PE III, 6.
[81] "Judaism in Jaspers' Thought," in PX 662.
[82] PX 658.
[83] "The Relation of Jaspers' Philosophy to Religion," in PX 662.

insists that "mythical ideas disclose their truth only after having been divested of their empirical reality."[84] A myth must never be taken literally, but, when taken figuratively, it is indispensable. "Philosophically speaking, the myth is the rational *a priori* form in which we become aware of transcendence. Psychologically speaking, it is the mode of experiencing the real."[85] Ciphers do not refer to anything corporeal. "Consequently the embodiment of the contents of ciphers is the fundamental confusion in our [dealings with] transcendence. When the actuality of transcendence is thus made a part of [bodily] reality, then it is lost to us."[86] "Even though corporeality strengthens the psycho-physical vital powers, it weakens truthfulness and consequently the strength of Existenz."[87] As Jaspers says on the concluding page of his *Philosophie*, "For Being simply to be is sufficient."[88] In other words, "It is enough that God is."[89] It matters little that we do not and cannot know His nature, that the transparency of ciphers permits us at best to "see through a glass darkly," and that the ciphers which our tradition places at our disposal must inevitably be markedly discrepant with those provided by other traditions. Just as moral man does his duty because he must and without regard to personal rewards and punishments, so religious man finds solace and support in transcendence even though his devotion leads to no direct consummatory vision or publicly identifiable advantage. It is for this that philosophy should prepare us, for to arrive at this point is to experience a change in our entire consciousness of being. Old things pass away and all things become new. At the end of his longest single volume Jaspers writes: "Philosophy awakens us and makes us attentive, it shows us what paths are open and starts us on our way, it fosters our maturity and enables us to expand our experience to its utmost limits."[90]

Any who find such a conclusion disappointing may well

---

[84] FET 86. [85] *Ibid.* [86] PO 163.
[87] PO 169. [88] PE III, 236. [89] EPT 39.
[90] VW 1054.

call to mind that it was this above all that enabled the Hebrews repeatedly to endure fiendish persecutions and horrible disappointments with magnificent fortitude. The fact that even without hope of rewards or fear of punishments in the life to come they could courageously endure the terrible cruelty of Herod, the calamitous destruction of their capital by Titus, and the subsequent exile and scattering, with all the interminable anguish that these events entailed, testifies to the astonishing power of selfless and ingenuous faith in the final source of all being.

chapter eight

The Encompassing

〜

Fundamental Philosophic Knowledge

From the days of the Milesian cosmologists to the present, philosophers have tried to pass beyond an investigation of things in being to a systematic knowledge of being itself.[1] Such attempted knowledge of being, which, due to a somewhat arbitrary decision of Andronicus of Rhodes soon came to be called "metaphysics," has hitherto appeared as "materialism (everything is matter and mechanical process), spiritualism (everything is spirit), hylozoism (the cosmos is a living spiritual substance), and so on. In every case being was defined as something existing in the world from which all other things sprang."[2] But this approach to the universe in its entirety by way of things within the world which stand over against us as objects has never recovered from the devastating critique of Kant, who showed once and for all that being per se, unlike things in being, is not an object, and can never become one.

The term "object," which in this connection is crucial, is, unfortunately, both vague and ambiguous. Dogmas aside, we are not quite sure where the subject ends and the object begins, and we hardly know whether to regard as objective the impressions that things make upon us, or the things that impress us. And, perhaps, as the classic doctrine of primary and secondary qualities would have it, each thing has both an

---

[1] In this respect Jaspers is close to the early Heidegger. As Gerhard Knauss tells us in his "The Concept of the 'Encompassing' in Jaspers' Philosophy" (trans. Matthew Cohen, PX 146), "If one were to seek agreement between Jaspers and the early Heidegger, for example, one could—making allowance for their different inferences—formulate it thus: the philosophizing of both thinkers revolves around the difference between 'Being-in-itself' (*Sein an sich*) and 'what is' (things) [*Seiendes* (*Dinge*)]."

[2] EPT 28-29.

objective and a subjective aspect. Finally we note that our language permits us to characterize *anything* as an object. Thus, somewhat surprisingly, Jaspers speaks, at least once, of the world as "something that becomes an object to me,"[3] and of the "encompassing [that] has become an object."[4] But the term can be given a precise meaning. From Jaspers' neo-Kantian point of view, an object not only stands over against a subject, as the German term *"Gegenstand"* suggests, but it possesses a number of extremely important characteristics:

(1) An object is distinct and distinguishable from other objects as well as from the subject. It is to objects that the principle, *omnis determinatio est negatio*, applies.[5] (2) Objectivity is a source of clarity, and to call (for example) the world and the soul objects is, among other things, to claim that they can be cognized clearly.[6] (3) Unlike transcendence and Existenz, objects are immanent. They appear only within the world, and they are susceptible of exhaustive scientific investigation.[7] (4) They are not things in themselves, for their formal aspects derive from the interpretive activity of the perceptual apparatus and the understanding.[8] (5) While they differ from illusions and hallucinations, they are phenomena—mere appearances.[9] In Kant's words, an object, though not mere *Schein*, is still *Erscheinung*. (6) Objects can be thought about without contradiction so long as they are not viewed in relation to the unconditioned. In brief, objects are those appearances within the world that, as a result of our categorization, are clear, distinct, regular, and consistently thinkable. Man himself can become an object only in part.[10] And the world and transcendence, with which

---

[3] EX 16.

[4] VW 604. Jaspers, in his "Reply to My Critics" (PX 798), having agreed with Earle that he has used the concept "object" in a narrower and a wider sense, goes on to say: "The form of my expression may, in some specific sentences, not have been too happy and this fact may justify the critic in his demand that I should speak more precisely."

[5] EPT 30.   [6] EX 14.   [7] EX 15.

[8] EX 16; PHT 28.   [9] EX 16, 19.   [10] EX 19.

philosophy is largely concerned, lack objectivity in all of the above-mentioned respects.

Philosophy's search for being, then, is by no means an investigation of objects in the world, as though it were a matter of deciding which things have the greatest explanatory value, or seeking the foundation of every discoverable structure. It is not philosophy but science that confronts physical things. Philosophizing, to begin with a helpful simile, is like climbing a mountain to enlarge the view, expand the horizon, and gain a heightened awareness of the immensity of the whole.[11] Typically, at the beginning, the visible area grows at an astonishing rate and occupies the center of attention. Within it, trivia disappear, innumerable relationships come to the fore, and the hope of unlimited expansion is constantly confirmed. But always, as it turns out, the horizon places a definite limit upon the extent of the visible. One can never remove the horizon though he can expand it by climbing higher. And the greater its distance, the more extensive it is and the more it is seen to conceal. Beyond the horizon lies a limitless expanse that, though unseen, is somehow patently *there*. If we allow the visible area to represent the scientific world within which we orient ourselves, the horizon to stand for the boundary that limits our orientations, and the territory beyond the horizon to signify the field allotted to philosophy, then we can think of philosophy as initially and basically an obscure but overpowering awareness of the untold immensity and portentousness of that which encompasses all that is present to us. Although philosophy tells us nothing specific and sanctions no creeds, it causes old things to pass away and all things to become new. In one sense it makes no difference, for it leaves everything the same; in another it makes all the difference, for it alters our entire consciousness of being.[12] While it shows us no new objects, still "it opens up to us infinite possibilities in which being may manifest itself to us, and at the same time it lends transparency to everything that is. It transforms the meaning of the

[11] EX 13.   [12] Ex 17.

world of objects, by awakening in us a faculty of sensing what authentically *is* in the phenomenon."[13] Something like this seems to be meant by Waismann when he tells us that "what is decisive [in a philosophy] is a new way of seeing, and, what goes with it, the will to transform the whole intellectual scene,"[14] for "at the heart of any philosophy . . . is vision."[15]

The Fundamental Operation and Its Results

In somewhat more literal and specific terms, passage from knowledge of objects within the world to awareness of what lies beyond the horizon and is neither subject nor object is a matter of performing a *"Grundoperation"*[16] which, for the most part, follows lines first laid down by Kant. Briefly, and with a minimum of technicalities, this "operation" or procedure might be described as follows.

Taking account of my situation, I find myself surrounded by many things, all of which belong to the world. These things I see to be mere appearances or "phenomena," for if the gestalten, meanings, relations, secondary and tertiary qualities, and so forth which I contribute to them were removed, nothing discernible would remain. I conclude that while I can know how things affect a cognizing subject, I can never know what they are in themselves. And, noting that I never perceive the world but only appearance of things within it, I conclude that the world is no object, but, as Kant said, an "idea."

Like the father of modern philosophy I soon discover that there is more within the world than the objects which sci-

---

[13] EPT 31.

[14] F. Waismann, "How I See Philosophy," in *Contemporary British Philosophy*, Third Series, 1956, as quoted in G. J. Warnock, *English Philosophy Since 1900* (New York: Oxford University Press, 1966), p. 88.

[15] *Ibid.*, p. 106.

[16] EX 14ff. See also VF 23; VW 37-39; PO 132. The term *"Grundgedankengang"* which Jaspers uses to refer to Descartes's thought-experiment has also been translated as "fundamental operation." See DPT 64, 79.

193

ence surveys, viz., the subjects to whom these objects appear. Subject and object are polar terms, and whatever is not known, directly or indirectly by some sentient being might as well not exist. Not only does the presence of objects presuppose that of sentient beings, but—and this is crucial —each sentient being is himself an "encompassing." If the realists were correct in pointing out that we are encompassed by our world, the idealists have been equally correct in insisting that the world is encompassed by us. The world is, in a perfectly meaningful sense, "my idea." Or, in Aristotle's terms, "The mind is, in a manner, all things." But the Cartesian dualism quickly proves to be an oversimplification, for the objective side must be added to, and the subjective side further divided.

Descartes clearly saw, though it required Spinoza to make his insight thematic, that the world is not self-sufficient or self-explanatory. The conditioned must be viewed in relation to the unconditioned. A clear grasp of the immanent leads to awareness of the transcendent. The world is but a manifestation of an underlying source, whose magnificence it reflects (*vide supra*). We are encompassed, not by the world alone, but by the world and transcendence.

On the side of the subject, distinctions are quickly multiplied. The Cartesian mind whose essence is thought is only a beginning. Prior to thinking—or the operations of the scientific understanding at the level of "consciousness in general"—is the crude empirical existence (the mere *Dasein* or "being there") of the unrefined and uncomplicated animal organism which, like a Leibnizian monad, embodies an extensive *Lebenswelt*, or world of lived experience. Not only is the organism (for the onlooker) within the world, but at the same time it embraces (for itself) a vast world of experience. Beyond both empirical existence and consciousness in general lies spirit and the social organism with which spirit is involved, and Existenz, which, as we have seen, is at once personal and transcendent. Finally, reason (*Vernunft*) is introduced as the bond which unites all the modes of the encompassing. Bringing the seven modes together, we find that (except for reason, which occupies a special position) they fall within two dichotomies that cut across each other. The world and transcendence fall outside the self, and are spoken of as "the encompassing that is being itself," while the rest constitute "the encompassing that we are." And again, both transcendence and Existenz lie beyond the world, and are, in a generic sense, "transcendent," while the remaining modes are "immanent." This can best be shown by means of a simple diagram.

The Encompassing

	The Encompassing That We Are (*Das Umgreifende das wir sind*)	The Encompassing That Is Being Itself (*Das Umgreifende, das das Sein selbst ist*)
The Immanent	Existence (*Dasein*) Consciousness in General (*Bewusstsein überhaupt*) Spirit (*Geist*)	World (*Welt*)
The Transcendent	Existenz	Transcendence (*Transzendenz*)

Reason (*Vernunft*)
as the Bond of the Encompassing in Us

There are of course various ways of exhibiting the relations between the modes of the encompassing.[17] Each of them distorts some matters while clarifying others. The accompanying outline is intended to suggest several of the directions in which the various modes point:

[17] This diagram is taken from VW 50. Cf. VW 48, 142.

Some Implications of the Modes of the Encompassing

Mode	Philosophy Suggested	Definition of Truth	Instrumental- ities Evoked
Existence (*Dasein*)	Naive Pragmatism	Practical Efficacy	Percepts and Images
Consciousness in General	Rationalism	Validity (*Geltung*)	Concepts of the Understanding
Spirit	Organicism	Coherence	Phantasies Concrete Uni- versals
Existenz	*Existenz- philosophie*	Communication	Discourse
World	Naturalism	Correspondence	Scientific Method
Transcendence	Theism	Adequacy	Myths Speculations Ciphers

In 1935, when *Vernunft und Existenz* appeared, it was not these "modes of the encompassing" but only their systematic formulation that was new. In Jaspers' thinking and writing they had long played important roles. In his *Psychologie der Weltanschauungen*, written at the time of World War I, oblique references to "the encompassing that is being itself" had appeared, though without emphasis or elaboration. According to this youthful version, the endless "is the enveloping (*das Umfassende*) within which every structured world-picture . . . is included."[18] This is said to provide a third alternative to the negativism of the atheists and the dogmatism of the authoritarians: "Between nihilism and shells [well insulated, systematized, and dishonest world-views]—between chaos and form—there is a mode of life which draws upon the unlimited in its entirety [*ein Leben aus dem Ganzen des Unendlichen*] that is not given to compromises, half-measures, and superficialities."[19] And at a later date, on one single page of the second vol-

[18] PY 149.   [19] PY 348.

ume of the *Philosophie*, he mentioned, more or less in passing, "the modes of the encompassing that we are." In scientific communication, he said, "I am considered only as the understanding of [the Kantian] consciousness in general (*Bewusstsein überhaupt*). But the possibility of such universal rationality is only the medium within which I remain possible as *Existenz*. . . . Man is never merely the formal I of the understanding, and never merely existence as vitality (*Dasein als Vitalität*), but the bearer of a content that . . . is actualized through a spiritual (*geistige*) whole."[20] In 1932, when the *Philosophie* was published, it remained merely to organize these concepts systematically.

One wonders how he arrived at his list of modes and whether it should be regarded as final. In a recent book he explained that he is far from dogmatizing about the details of this scheme.[21] What is intended follows from no principle, has no final guarantee, and should not be viewed as a finished system. It is advanced only as a tentative schema to be revised in the light of further insights. It is not a creed, but a representation of our situation, lying somewhere on "the boundary between scientific knowledge and existential philosophy."[22] It calls for suspended judgment, for it is itself "in suspension."[23] "My conception," he says, ". . . [arose] out of being receptive to the way in which I find myself in the world, [coupled] with the will to neglect nothing which occurs in my experience."[24] Not everyone will be satisfied with this, of course: "Dissatisfaction is bound to remain whenever such knowledge is measured by the absolute total knowledge which has so often been deceptively attempted." But this is unrealistic for "in order to be able to ask, we must first of all jump into the midst and begin factually to see where and how we are."[25]

Grundwissen, or fundamental knowledge, attained as a result of the recommended *philosophische Grundoperation* is then not knowledge of any specific set of doctrines or dog-

20 PE II, 53.   21 PO 148ff.   22 PO 149.
23 *Ibid.*   24 PX 801-802.   25 PX 803.

mas that could conceivably be written down in sentences and purveyed in outlines and synopses. Philosophy has no fixed and final set of truths to offer. The philosophy of the encompassing is not idealistic or realistic, and neither is it metaphysical (or ontological) in the traditional sense. "It says nothing about those things that we might well wish to know—whether there is a God and what he is like, . . . and what eternal being is."[26] Our "fundamental knowledge" is simply an attempt to make us aware of the human condition. "This belief conveys nothing specific that could exclude the creeds of others. It is simply the belief in the possibility of unlimited mutual understanding. It is the belief that says: truth is what holds us together."[27] Heidegger to the contrary, "Being, in its entirety, is no longer conceptually knowable in the form of an ontology; in the end it can only be elucidated as the encompassing space and as the spaces within which all being approaches us."[28] Our goal is not ontology, but "periechontology"—an account of the encompassing.[29]

The Modes of the Encompassing That We Are

Since we are already acquainted with "the encompassing that is being itself," the *world* as the subject matter of science having been considered in the second chapter, and *transcendence* as present to Existenz, in the latter part of the seventh, it remains to consider "the encompassing that we are or can be" (*das Umgreifende das wir sind oder sein können*), i.e., (empirical) existence, consciousness in general, spirit, and Existenz. These, as we first learn from *Vernunft und Existenz* (1935), may be regarded as constituting a series of levels or stages, proceeding from an animalian existence that, as Hobbes would have it, is solitary, poor, nasty, brutish, and short, through the stages of the scientific understanding with its generally sharable concepts and principles, and spirit with its magnificent speculative insights to the consummatory stage of Existenz. Within this

[26] PO 129.   [27] PO 150.   [28] EX 17.
[29] VW 158; PO 130, 306; PX 143.

series the lower levels are temporally prior and stronger, more durable and more independent, while the higher levels are comparatively weak, fragile and dependent.[30] To pass to a higher level is never to abolish the levels below, for always the higher makes use of the lower. The scientific consciousness cannot endure without vital existence, and spirit cannot proceed without *it*. Existenz has no being without the body, and can be effective only within the world.[31]

These various modes may be described as "encompassing" because, as we have seen, like the monads of Leibniz and the actual entities of Whitehead, they contain or represent the entire universe. All things in the world come to us as encompassed by first-person experience. "Prior to self-reflection *Dasein* finds itself in its world as lived experience. In the immediacy of its self-discovery it is . . . the reality in which all that is to be real to us must make its appearance, just as consciousness in general is the area that everything to be thought about must enter."[32] In terms made familiar by William James, *Dasein* can be said to be at once encompassed and encompassing, for there is a kind of "dualism connoted by such double-barrelled terms as 'experience,' 'phenomenon,' 'datum,' '*Vorfindung.*' "[33] The pure experience of the room in which you are is, as it were, "a place of intersection of two processes" and it can be "counted twice over."[34] In one context, seen as "the room in which you sit," the room, like yourself, is encompassed by the world. In another context, viewed as "your 'field of consciousness,' " or "state of mind" it belongs to the encompassing that you are.[35] The world is no more encompassing than consciousness.

[30] VET 88-90.
[31] The "soul" is not detachable. Jaspers writes: "Not only are all proofs of immortality fallacious and hopeless, . . . but it is precisely mortality that is open to proof." PE II, 224. Cf. p. 49.
[32] PO 114.
[33] "Does 'Consciousness' Exist?" in *Essays in Radical Empiricism and A Pluralistic Universe*, ed. Ralph Barton Perry (New York: Longmans, Green, 1947), p. 10.
[34] *Ibid.*, p. 12.   [35] *Ibid.*, p. 13.

The Basic Mode

In ordinary language, "existence," or *Dasein*, refers to what appears to have simple location in space and time as distinguished from ideal objects that do not. But this is not what Jaspers means; rather he uses the term to refer to sentient subjects aware of themselves and their environments. "It [*Dasein*] is being finding itself as being-there. This existence is expressed in the words 'I am there,' and 'we are there.' "[36] Although when viewed *ab extra*, as by a behavioristic psychologist, a living being appears *within* the world, when viewed *ab intra*, as by a participant observer using the method of *Verstehen*, the same being is seen to encompass the world. *Dasein* is primarily my existence as experienced by my self.[37]

When separated from the other modes, *Dasein* is remarkably primitive. It suggests the cynic's idea of man, the proletariat in Orwell's *1984*, or a human organism devoid of moral and religious values, as delineated by a rigorous behaviorist. For present purposes, *Dasein* may be viewed as virtually identical with Hobbes's man in a state of nature: a practicing hedonist entirely devoid of other-regarding impulses and concerned only to preserve and enhance his own being. For such a man, desire and aversion are the guides of life, and nothing can be good or bad apart from them. "The notions of right and wrong, justice and injustice, have here no place. . . . Force and fraud are in war [declared or undeclared] the two cardinal virtues."[38] *Dasein*, left to itself, can never believe that "the laws of nature are immutable and eternal."[39] No true religion is possible, but only a horrible travesty, viz., "fear of a power invisible, feigned by the mind,

---

[36] VW 53.

[37] VW 54. Cf. Heidegger's view that " 'Dasein' is always my own 'Dasein,' " in Werner Brock's "An Account of 'Being and Time,' " in *Existence and Being* (Chicago: Regnery, 1949), p. 14.

[38] Thomas Hobbes, *The Leviathan* (selections) in *The English Philosophers from Bacon to Mill*, ed. E. A. Burtt (New York: Modern Library, 1939), p. 162.

[39] *Ibid.*, p. 212.

200

or imagined from tales publicly allowed."[40] When illumined by "consciousness in general," *Dasein* may rise to the level of sociology to find in religion at most "a system of verbal abstractions, technically termed an ideology," perpetuated by a "specialized occupational group—the magic men or priests" and used as a framework around which "society builds a great complex of beliefs and rituals."[41]

At this level—the level of mere life—knowledge is but an instrument in the struggle of all against all,[42] and truth possesses neither certainty nor universal validity.[43] When scientific knowledge is placed at its disposal, *Dasein* prizes it simply as a means to selfish gratifications. Honest investigations that, like those of Dr. Stockman, Ibsen's "enemy of the people," run counter to the will of the ruling clique are ruthlessly condemned and punished. There are many purposes, but there is no final purpose, innumerable people but no free individuals. "The individual who goes his own way does not count. The exceptional man is obliterated."[44] Genuine truth has not yet appeared. It is present only in a figurative sense, conceived after the manner of a crude and popular pragmatism: "Truth is what promotes *Dasein*, what is useful; untruth is what injures, limits, and cripples it."[45] It is relative, alterable, personal, utilitarian, and arbitrary. It is, as James once put it, "only the expedient in our way of thinking."[46]

Consciousness in General

Dasein is above all noteworthy for what it lacks; it is a least common denominator and a *terminus a quo*. In its extreme deprivation it suggests the spiritual poverty of the blackboard jungle and the slave labor camp, with all the emptiness and tedium that accompanies living by bread alone.

---

[40] *Ibid.*, p. 152.
[41] Richard T. LaPiere and Paul R. Farnsworth, *Social Psychology* (New York: McGraw-Hill, 1949), p. 315.
[42] VW 316. [43] VW 608. [44] VW 610. [45] VW 608.
[46] William James, "Pragmatism's Conception of Truth," in *Essays in Pragmatism*, ed. Alburey Castell (New York: Hafner, 1951), p. 170.

Escape comes, not through obliteration but through supplementation: participation in the lower continues but is transformed when access to the higher is gained. Plato's discussion of the line which divides sense-perception from understanding, followed by the myth of the cave which illustrates it,[47] may be taken to signify (among other things) the leap from *Dasein* to consciousness in general. Suddenly, as though out of nowhere, appears a world of clear and distinct though invisible and intangible objects, such as species-concepts, scientific laws, and esthetic and moral norms. These, like the atoms of Democritus and the sphere of Parmenides, are immutable, eternal, and indestructible. They stand in unalterable, objective, and investigable relations to each other, and will always be available to the scrutiny of properly instructed human beings. Sometimes, as in the case of Galileo's law of falling bodies, the content concerns empirical fact. Sometimes, as in the case of the Pythagorean theorem, it is grounded simply in logical evidence.[48] But in either case, the contents appear precisely the same to all rational creatures, except, of course, when errors, misapprehensions, incorrect verbalizations, and the like are operative.[49] As Nietzsche discovered, the methodical attitude of science, which "seeks *certainty* rather than persuasion," furnishes unexampled cognitive security: "Scientific findings are indefeasible and capable of providing the means to new discoveries." Here we have something that is "calculable and determinate."[50] Although around the periphery of any science there are always many hypothetical propositions, the final conclusions of science are categorical. At the level of consciousness in general the scientific understanding provides clarity and distinctness, settles opinion and puts an end to doubt, and offers the sort of coercive certainty that constitutes knowledge at its best.

It is at this level that the simplest and most generally acceptable account of truth can be given. In terms of the old

[47] *The Republic*, Books VI and VII.
[48] VW 605.   [49] VW 65.   [50] NET 172.

formula, *adaequatio intellectus et rei*, it is a matter of agreement between a proposition and its object (*Meinung und Sache*).[51] That is, "We grasp unambiguous truth in the validity (*Geltung*) of statements that are founded upon the givenness of intuition and the evidence of logic."[52] Empirical statements must refer to the perceptible, measurable, and photographable. Logical judgments must be knowable with apodictic certainty.[53] Wholly apart from consciousness and thought there could be no truth: "A being that existed merely by itself without being known by itself or any other being would be neither true nor false."[54]

When judged in terms of clarity, communicability, and demonstrability, the truth of consciousness in general is truth *par excellence*. But when the existing individual applies extrascientific standards he finds that "the truth that is essential to us begins precisely where the statements that are coercive for consciousness in general leave off."[55] And the strictly scientific mind soon finds that it can understand remarkably little. At this level it is impossible to think metaphysically, come to terms with religion, understand literary criticism, appreciate art, apprehend the content of music, or make any sense of romantic love. The scientist may of course join Hobbes in dismissing the whole phenomenal world as "nothing else but original fancy,"[56] and urge with Bazarov, Turgenev's fictitious nihilist, that "twice two makes four and all the rest is rubbish." But this is to dismiss all values from the world and, since only values matter, to fall, as it were, into a void.

The Realm of Spirit

When we pass from the scientific to the spiritual level, we find that even the same words must be given new meanings. For example, it may be said that "spirit, like life, has pow-

[51] Wolfgang Stegmüller, *Hauptströmungen der Gegenwartsphilosophie* (Stuttgart: Kröner, 1960), p. 222.
[52] VW 605.   [53] *Ibid.*   [54] VW 606.   [55] VW 607.
[56] *The Leviathan*, in *op.cit.*, p. 132.

er, strength, intensity, force, and energy."[57] But these terms which natural science takes literally are here used figuratively.[58] And furthermore, while things within the world are explained in causal terms, "the investigation of objective spirit proceeds by means of understanding [*Verstehen*, that is, not *Verstand*] in terms of the category of freedom."[59] The life of the spirit is *sui generis*.

Having passed beyond *Dasein*, man gains an inkling of the things of the spirit when he confronts a series of urgent questions to which scientific findings are irrelevant—questions such as: "How do the liberal arts educate without providing knowledge of either facts or principles? What are beauty and ugliness and how is it that we learn so little about them from scientific (i.e. experimental) esthetics? What is virtue and how can it be taught? In what do the sacred and the holy consist? What kind of knowledge is required for a career in politics? How is the citizen related to the society to which he belongs? What is organization, and how does it differ from chaos? How do the members of a class differ from the parts of a whole? These and similar questions are meaningless to *Dasein* and indifferent to science. To answer them we must turn from the psychologists to the literati, from the sociologists and economists to the historians, and from the academic and scientistic philosophers to the moralists, art critics, and liberal theologians.

While it is impossible to give an adequate account of spirit in a few pages, some notion of what it involves can be conveyed in connection with the *Geisteswissenschaften* or humanistic studies of spirit, the "ideas" which spirit employs, the creative activities in which spirit engages, and the social institutions through which it objectifies itself.

Beginning with the first, we note that the present difference of levels corresponds to the difference, stressed by Dilthey and others, between the *Naturwissenschaften* or natural sciences which approach the opaque processes of infrahuman

[57] VW 73. [58] *Ibid.* [59] VW 73.

nature *ab extra*, and the *Geisteswissenschaften* or humanistic disciplines which view the motives, lived experiences, and attitudes of human beings *ab intra*.[60] The former explain what is alien and unintelligible to the human mind through subsumption under empirically discovered laws. The latter, making use of our remarkable though mysterious ability to momentarily entertain even those mental states which we cannot share, proceed by re-enactment, as Collingwood would say,[61] of the experiences of others in our own minds. To proceed in this fashion, as does the cultural historian, the practitioner of nondirective counseling, and the sociologist who uses the participant-observer technique, is to acknowledge the uniqueness of spirit, and to enjoy the intimacy of our acquaintance with the distinctively human.

Furthermore, spirit is the author of "ideas," much as the scientific understanding devises *concepts*, and Existenz issues in *faith* or *belief*. These ideas, as Kant was the first to show, furnish a background for our thoughts and actions. They are unlimited in number and available in all spheres. We have theoretical ideas (though no clear concepts) of matter, life, the *Zeitgeist*, the soul and God; and our behavior is guided by ideas of the physician, the university, the state, the world, and so on.[62] They do not constitute determinate knowledge, but rather the sort of indeterminate thought that serves as an atmosphere or tacitly held frame of reference within which our thinking can proceed. Like Royce's internal meaning and Blanshard's immanent goal of thought, these ideas serve a threefold purpose:[63] *psychologically*, they furnish motivation by tempting inquiry with intimations of what requires further investigation. *Methodologically*, they direct inquiry by revealing the most fruitful procedures. And *objectively*, ideas come to disclose a correspondence with nature—with

---

[60] "*Ideen über eine beschreibende und zergliedernde Psychologie*," *Gesammelte Werke*, V, 139-240.

[61] R. G. Collingwood, *The Idea of History* (Oxford: Clarendon Press, 1946), pp. 282-302.

[62] VW 613; PO 115.   [63] GPT I, 238; PY 478-83.

what Royce calls their "external meaning"—that fulfills the purpose of the investigation. Thus, for example, the maxim of parsimony encourages research by hinting at a simplicity that renders nature investigable, helps the inquirer avoid numerous *culs-de-sac*, and, presumably, calls attention to such unity as is present in the world.

Spirit, thus understood, is the seat of creativity. Catholic in its concerns, "spirit as wholeness actualizes a world thoroughly imbued with itself in works of art and in poetry . . . as well as in each profession and the constitution of the state."[64] On the subjective side, spirit appears as phantasy which "creates meanings, makes things intelligible through symbols, and provides speech in so far as possible."[65] When art confers powers of speech upon ciphers that refer to being, enabling them to convey what cannot be expressed in words, it becomes, as Schelling said, an "*organon*"[66] of philosophy. "To communicate a reading of ciphers in nature, in history, and in men is art when the communication is conveyed in an esthetic medium rather than speculative thoughts."[67] When, for instance, Homer and Hesiod, as Herodotus tells us, gave the Greeks their gods, they provided a language through which transcendence could be apprehended. That is why myths are indispensable: since "to demythologize would be to do away with an essential faculty of our reason, . . . the real task . . . is not to demythologize, but to recover mythical thought in its original purity, and to appropriate . . . the marvelous mythical contents that deepen us morally, enlarge us as human beings, and indirectly bring us closer to the lofty, imageless transcendence. . . ."[68]

On the objective side, spirit is the source of social organization, and, consequently, the enemy of individualism. This is its shortcoming. "Spirit allows everything individual to be taken up and absorbed within the universal that it exemplifies, and at the same time within the whole whose part it is. . . . As spirit the individual is not yet himself, but the unity of

[64] PO 115. Cf. VW 76, 617. [65] PO 115.
[66] PE II, 192. [67] PE III, 192. [68] FET 17.

a contingent individual with a necessary [concrete] universal."[69] On this showing every individual is entirely enmeshed in the social whole. Like the hand which, as Aristotle pointed out, would not continue to be a hand if separated from the body, each of us is regarded as an infinitesimal part of a larger whole from which our being, our nature, our function, and our reward derive. But each of us knows and insists that he is to some extent independent. And to the extent to which such independence is realized, organicism is proved inadequate, and spirit is found to be insufficient.

At this level the truth is that which brings about wholeness. My thought and conduct are true insofar as they participate in and are guided by the appropriate idea. Such truth has the character of persuasion, and is confirmed when it proves to be coherent with the totality of ideas. This is neither the truth of science nor the truth of existential philosophy.

Existenz and its Historicity

As we have seen (Chap. IV), the self is more than life and consciousness, and it aspires to more than the pursuit of truth under the guidance of ideas, the appreciation of visions supplied by phantasy, or even the Hegelian moral life (*Sittlichkeit*) within a civilized community. Still lacking is the moral center of the individual, viz., what Schelling, in harmony with Hamann, Jacobi, and Ranke called "Existenz," and persuaded Kierkegaard to set over against the Hegelian idea.[70] The esthetic stage must be supplemented by the ethical. Commenting upon the limitations of spirit, Jaspers, while still a young man, wrote that "through the absolutization of *Verstehen*, man is finally robbed of his personal Existenz. [To one who stops at this level] everything is important, and, consequently, nothing is important."[71] The man who "understands" but fails to *existieren* is "deprived of the awareness of the

[69] VW 81.
[70] Kurt Hoffman, "The Basic Concepts of Jaspers' Philosophy," PX 100.
[71] PY 182.

present, the meaning and unlimited importance of *Dasein* in the present moment, the consciousness of decision or responsibility, and, in a word, of living Existenz."[72] When finally attained, Existenz is not a result of philosophical argument, but a consequence of experiences that have to do with boundary situations,[73] encounters with nihilism,[74] breakdowns in existential communication,[75] and the like.

Although, as we have seen, Existenz cannot be objectified and has no mode of appearance of its own, each of its manifestations is necessarily rooted in some unique situation and concerned with some special task. Existence must appear in connection with *Dasein* which is always localizable within the spatio-temporal continuum. The soul is not detachable, and everyone has his place within the geographical environment and the historical process. We cannot live apart from the world or outside of history. Without the resistance supplied by specific objects in the present, Existenz could no more actualize itself than a bird could fly without the atmosphere.[76] And anyone who rejects the world entirely in favor of transcendence will, so to speak, lose his bearings and fall into a void.[77] "This union of my self with my *Dasein* as appearance is known as my historicity (*Geschichtlichkeit*)," Jaspers tell us. "Being fully aware of it is historical consciousness."[78]

From the presence of Existenz in the here and now, a number of curious paradoxes arise. In the first place, the affairs of this world are at once infinitely important and of no account whatsoever.[79] Regarded morally, empirical existence is infinitely important, and its conduct makes all the difference, for, as Kant saw, the value of virtuous conduct is incommensurate with that of all other things. But seen from the standpoint of transcendence the affairs of this world are as noth-

---

[72] *Ibid.*
[73] Edwin Latzel, "The Concept of 'Ultimate Situation' in Jaspers' Philosophy," PX 180, 188-89, 192.
[74] EPT 37.   [75] PE II, 440.   [76] PE II, 125.
[77] PE II, 123.   [78] PE II, 121.   [79] PE II, 122.

ing, for everything quickly passes away and is gone. To stand in this tension—to recognize at once the seriousness of our moral acts and the evanescence of all worldly events—is to be aware of historicity.[80]

In the second place, historicity involves a union of freedom and necessity. "I seem to myself to be unavoidably determined by what has already been decided, and still to be basically free insofar as I am capable of making my own decisions."[81] As a source I am free, but my freedom is always limited by circumstances. And in the end I must recognize that such freedom as I enjoy has been given to me.[82]

In the third place, historicity involves a synthesis of time and eternity. At this very moment, I may experience eternal truths, or become aware of events that, as Christianity has consistently maintained, remain momentous throughout all time. As summarized by Hoffman, "This moment, the authentic instance, that of decision, of intense communication, of transfiguration, this grain of eternity, as Kierkegaard has pointed out, must be opposed to the passing moment. Between the two, and subsuming both, historicity mediates. . . ."[83] The moving finger writes, and, having writ, moves on: "What has been brought into effect through decision is eternal."[84]

Finally, as we have seen, Jaspers asserts the historicity of truth itself. From his standpoint it appears as inevitable that "discursive thought can never arrive at a universally valid concept of Being, but only at one view of Being among others."[85]

It matters, for this philosophy, who asks the question as to the nature of this Being: man's concrete historical situation enters into the question and into the answer. In each individual, in all his insecurity and disquiet, philosophy must make a new start; hence it is always in process and

---

[80] *Ibid.*
[82] See above, chap. iv.
[84] Phil. II, 129. Cf. PO 238.
[81] PE II, 125.
[83] Hoffman, 102.
[85] Hoffman, p. 103.

always in suspension, it is never complete and final and can never be set forth in the form of a universally and eternally valid doctrine.[86]

Whatever may in the end have to be said about the theory of relativism, we cannot burke the fact of relativity.

Clearly philosophic truth, thus understood, is different from the truth of science. As philosophers "we wish to achieve awareness of the truth with which we live and die, the truth with which we come to be identified. It is this that constitutes the truth of Existenz."[87] At this level there can be no question of correspondence with an object, and no possibility of universal validity. As R. F. Grabau explains: "For the illumination of Existenz thus conceived there can be no objective criteria of truth. . . . Each Existenz is unique, unrepeatable, irreplaceable. Consequently, there is no guarantee that even at the level of Existenz the conceptual clarification which will prove true for one Existenz will also hold for another."[88] While the truth may ultimately be one, the oneness cannot appear to us directly. The truth of Existenz lies more in the act than in the content.[89] What counts is what happens to me in the thinking of such truth. "Existential thought is either true, and then it is indissolubly connected with the being of the thinker; or it is a content to be known like any other, and then it is false. The concepts of existential philosophy are such that I can not think them without being in them; scientific contents on the other hand are such that I can know them while I myself live in wholly different categories; what I am is irrelevant to scientific knowledge."[90] Truth at this stage is primarily authentic faith —existential awareness of a relation to transcendence.[91]

Insofar as Existenz is the drive to authenticity,[92] in the ab-

[86] *Ibid.*, p. 96.   [87] VW 619.
[88] "Karl Jaspers: Communication through Transcendence," in *Existential Philosophers: Kierkegaard to Merleau-Ponty*, ed. George Alfred Schrader, Jr. (New York: McGraw-Hill, 1967), p. 129.
[89] PHT 8-9.   [90] VET 90.   [91] PHT 28.
[92] Hoffman, p. 100, VET 62.

sence of which communication breaks down, one may say, as Jaspers does repeatedly, that truth is that which furthers communication.[93] To remain always in reserve, to be in "bad faith," to conceal one's beliefs, perhaps even from oneself, to say only those things that enhance one's image and further one's ends, to refuse to appear as a genuine self is to be fraudulent and false; to appear *in propria persona*, to avoid obfuscation, to expose one's convictions and stand by them, to seem to be simply what one is—these things are involved in being in the truth. Existential truthfulness consists, then, in avoidance of sham, cant, hypocrisy, sycophancy, perfidy, faithless treachery, and the nauseating lukewarmness of the indifferent. To be truthful is to have convictions and to be ready to stand by them.

Whatever the disadvantages, theoretical, practical, and pedagogical, of admitting that philosophical truth cannot compel agreement, and that what constitutes truth for one group is error to another, still there is no avoiding it. "Today a universal situation that has always existed in fact assumes crucial importance: . . . that my faith, precisely when I am certain, clashes with other men's faith; that there is always somewhere a limit beyond which there appears to be nothing but battle without hope of unity. . . ."[94]

In facing this predicament we may avail ourselves of certain metaphors, but all of them are misleading. We may say, for example, that the One discloses itself to us through its many aspects. But this merely presents a puzzle, since we cannot see how such discrepant aspects can meaningfully come together in unity. Or perhaps we believe with certain of the personalists that the "Existenzen" themselves constitute the One. But these are not aspects; the aspects, much rather, exist for them. We note that one and the same statue may look different from different angles. But the One is not in space like a statue, and we recognize that this is but a vague and misleading analogy. However we look at it the sit-

[93] Hoffman, p. 103.   [94] EPT 25.

uation remains unsettling and incomprehensible: "Even more than the boundary-situation, this marked discrepancy between the truths possessed by the various Existenzen produces the vertigo before the abyss that tears us loose from the grounds on which we stand and frees us through transcendence—unless our *Dasein* escapes by means of near-sighted self-deceptions that hold it fast in its obstinacy and overwhelming anxiety."[95] That absolute truth for man must be historically conditioned is inescapable: "Since it is impossible for man to attain transcendence as a knowable object in time that, like a thing within the world, is identical for everyone, it is inevitable that within the world every mode of the one absolute truth must in fact be historical: unconditioned for this specific Existenz, and, precisely for that reason, not universally valid."[96] To accept this is not impossible, though, psychologically speaking, it is extremely difficult. It is for this reason that Nietzsche, in spite of his agonizing loneliness and passionate urge to be understood, if only by a few,[97] still recommended through his prophet, Zarathustra, that every man be referred to himself, saying, "Now this is *my* way. Where is yours? . . . Faithfully follow your own path; in this way you will follow me."[98]

The Philosophy of Reason

Philosophia perennis[99] has consistently accorded the highest place in the cognitive hierarchy to reason. Plato, it will be remembered, who attributed to reason an immediate awareness of the Idea of the Good, wished it to direct the individual, and rational man, the state. Aristotle was convinced that the life of God was a life of reason and that, for men of the highest

---

[95] PE II, 440.   [96] VW 974.   [97] NET 85.
[98] NET 21.
[99] While this term has sometimes been employed in a dyslogistic sense (cf., e.g., PO 302), still Jaspers is on the whole inclined to eulogize the "simple, ancient, eternal philosophy" (*die uralte, ewige Philosophie schlechthin*) (VET 153; VE 113). It is typical that on p. 152 of EPT he tells us that "the one philosophy is the *philosophia perennis* around which all philosophies revolve." Cf. *ibid.*, pp. 16, 139.

rank, such a life was the best. The Enlightenment was, as every viewer of paperback covers knows, an age of reason. In Spinoza's thought—in spite of a troublesome verbal discrepancy[100]—the *intellectus* surpassed the scientific *ratio*, much as the Kantian reason, as *Vernunft*, guided and directed the *Verstand* by virtue of its overarching ideas. And Jaspers, who had originally inaugurated his own view as a philosophy of Existenz, began in 1950 to express a preference for the term "philosophy of reason" (*Philosophie der Vernunft*).[101]

Reason, for Jaspers, is at the opposite pole from the clear, objective thinking of the understanding. It is not a faculty which realizes itself in academic logic and logistics, or which presides over mere "relations of ideas." And it is not a suprascientific source of intuitive insight into eternal verities. It is the bond which unites the various modes of the encompassing.

Because of Jaspers' extraordinary awareness of fragmentation, the problem confronting him is unusually acute. The four modes of "the encompassing that we are" are separated from each other by wide gaps. And from these modes we attain to the world and transcendence only by a leap. *Dasein* and spirit are embodied in innumerable individuals. And while consciousness in general is by definition one, still, within the realm of appearance it is located in the innumerable beings who participate in it. Existenz appears only as a constant communicative interaction and opposition of diverse Existenzen. The world falls apart into numerous aspects, regions, and fields. The One speaks to us only through a variety of ciphers suggestive of the languages spoken on the Tower of Babel. Antinomic opposition is everywhere to be found.

Precisely because of the impossibility of finding a place for everything within one all-embracing organic whole or reducing all things in being to one level—because of the radical tensions, disharmonies, and incompatibilities—we need to strive for as much unity as possible. And this is the task of reason.

[100] **GPT 298.**   [101] **VF 50.**

While the scientific understanding is nihilistic in that it recognizes nothing beyond science, reason, intent upon the encompassing, seeks to preserve us from nihilism. Basically it demands an openness to all facts and a readiness to listen to versions different from our own. It calls for a release from all that is fixed, finite, and determinate, and comes to rest only when being is disclosed.[102] It strives to be impartial toward all peoples, all insights, all levels, and all fields of knowledge.

Jaspers' philosophy of reason was expected to reach completion in the promised *Philosophische Logik* of which the eleven-hundred-page *Von der Wahrheit* is only the beginning. Much as formal logic belongs to the understanding at the level of "consciousness in general," so philosophical logic relates closely to reason.[103] Further volumes of the *Logik*, dealing with categories, methods, and with science as such, have long been anticipated.[104] It is to be hoped that these are now in a sufficiently advanced state to admit of eventual publication—at least in part.

[102] See Stegmüller, *op.cit.*, p. 220.
[103] VW 9-11.   [104] VW 26.

Bibliography
Selected Writings of Karl Jaspers

ᔕᖇ

The abbreviations preceding the entries are those used in the footnotes. The letters are so chosen that the abbreviations stand in the same alphabetical order as the accompanying German titles. English translations (signified by the final *T*'s), when available, are listed together with their German originals. Complete bibliographies appear in PX, pp. 871-86 (through 1957), and WW, pp. 175-216 (through 1962).

AP   *Allgemeine Psychopathologie* (7th ed.). Berlin: J. Springer, 1959. First published as *Allgemeine Psychopathologie: Ein Leitfaden für Ärzte und Psychologen*, Berlin, 1913. Completely rewritten 4th ed., 1946.

APT   *General Psychopathology*. Translated by J. Hoenig and Marion W. Hamilton. Chicago: University of Chicago Press, 1963.

AT   *Die Atombombe und die Zukunft des Menschen. Politisches Bewusstsein in unserer Zeit.* Munich: R. Piper, 1958.

ATT   *The Future of Mankind*. Translated by E. B. Ashton. Chicago: University of Chicago Press, 1961.

DP   *Descartes und die Philosophie*. Berlin: De Gruyter, 1937.

DPT   "Descartes and Philosophy," pp. 59-185 in *Three Essays*. Translated by Ralph Manheim. New York: Harcourt, Brace and World, 1964.

EP   *Einführung in die Philosophie*. Zürich: Artemis, 1950.

EPT   *The Way to Wisdom*. Translated by Ralph Manheim. New Haven: Yale University Press, 1954.

EX   *Existenzphilosophie* (3d ed.). Berlin: De Gruyter, 1964.

FE   *Die Frage der Entmythologisierung.* Basel: Schweizerische Theologische Rundschau, 1953.

FET   *Myth and Christianity: An Inquiry into the Possibility of Religion without Myth* (with Rudolf Bultmann). Translated by Norbert Guterman. New York: Noonday, 1958.

GE   *Die geistige Situation der Zeit.* Berlin: De Gruyter, 1931.

GET   *Man in the Modern Age.* Translated by Eden and Cedar Paul. Garden City, New York: Doubleday, 1957.

GP   *Die grossen Philosophen.* Vol. I. Munich: R. Piper, 1957.

GPT   *The Great Philosophers.* Translated by Ralph Manheim. 2 vols. New York: Harcourt, Brace and World, 1962 & 1966.

KS   *Kleine Schule des philosophischen Denkens.* Munich: R. Piper, 1965.

KST   *Philosophy Is for Everyman: A Short Course in Philosophic Thinking.* Translated by R. F. C. Hull and Grete Wels. New York: Harcourt, Brace and World, 1967.

LP   *Leonardo als Philosoph.* Bern: Franke, 1953.

LPT   "Leonardo as Philosopher," pp. 1-58 in *Three Essays.* Translated by Ralph Manheim. New York: Harcourt, Brace and World, 1964.

MW   *Max Weber. Deutsches Wesen im politischen Denken, im Forschen und Philosophieren.* Oldenberg i.O.: G. Stalling, 1932.

MWT   "Max Weber as Politician, Scientist, Philosopher," pp. 187-274, in *Three Essays.* Translated by Ralph Manheim. New York: Harcourt, Brace and World, 1964.

216

NE   *Nietzsche: Einführung in das Verständnis seines Philosophierens.* Berlin: De Gruyter, 1936. 3d ed., 1950.

NET   *Nietzsche: An Introduction to the Understanding of His Philosophical Activity.* Translated by C. F. Wallraff and F. J. Schmitz. Tucson, Arizona: University of Arizona Press, 1965.

NI   *Nietzsche und das Christentum.* Munich: R. Piper, 1952.

NIT   *Nietzsche and Christianity.* Translated by E. B. Ashton. Chicago: Regnery, 1961.

PE   *Philosophie.* 3 vols. (3d unchanged ed., with added postscript.) Berlin: J. Springer, 1956.

PF   "Philosophische Autobiographie," in *Karl Jaspers: Werk und Wirkung.* Munich: R. Piper, 1963.

PFT   "Philosophical Memoir," in *Philosophy and the World,* pp. 193-314. Translated by E. B. Ashton. Chicago: Regnery, 1963.

PH   *Der philosophische Glaube.* Munich: R. Piper, 1948.

PHT   *The Perennial Scope of Philosophy.* Translated by Ralph Manheim. New York: Philosophical Library, 1949.

PO   *Der philosophische Glaube angesichts der Offenbarung.* Munich: R. Piper, 1962.

POT   *Philosophical Faith and Revelation.* Translated by E. B. Ashton. New York: Harper and Row, 1967.

PW   *Philosophie und Welt: Reden und Aufsätze.* Munich: R. Piper, 1958.

PWT   *Philosophy and the World: Selected Essays and Lectures.* Translated by E. B. Ashton. Chicago: Regnery, 1963.

PX   *The Philosophy of Karl Jaspers,* ed. Paul Arthur Schilpp. New York: Tudor, 1957. Contains Jaspers' "Philosophical Autobiography" and "Reply to My Critics," trans. by Paul Arthur Schilpp and Ludwig B. Lefebre (pp. 5-94), and various critical essays about Jaspers.

PY   *Psychologie der Weltanschauungen.* Berlin: J. Springer, 1919.

SG   *Schelling: Grösse und Verhängnis.* Munich: R. Piper, 1955.

TET   *Three Essays: Leonardo, Descartes, Max Weber.* Translated by Ralph Manheim. New York: Harcourt, Brace and World, 1964.

TNT   *Tragedy Is Not Enough.* Pp. 915-59 of *Von der Wahrheit.* Translated by Harald A. T. Reiche, Harry T. Moore, and Karl W. Deutsch. Boston: Beacon Press, 1952.

UP   "Über meine Philosophie," *Rechenschaft und Ausblick.* Munich: R. Piper, 1941.

UPT   "On my Philosophy," translated by Felix Kaufmann. Pp. 131-58 in Walter Kaufmann's *Existentialism from Dostoevski to Sartre.* New York: Meridian, 1956.

VE   *Vernunft und Existenz.* Batavia: Groningen, 1935.

VET   *Reason and Existenz.* Translated by William Earle. New York: Noonday, 1955.

VF   *Vernunft und Widervernunft in unserer Zeit.* Munich: R. Piper, 1950.

VFT   *Reason and Anti-Reason in our Time.* Translated by S. Godman. New Haven: Yale University Press, 1952.

VU   *Vom Ursprung und Ziel der Geschichte.* Munich: R. Piper, 1950.

VUT   *The Origin and Goal of History.* Translated by M. Bullock. New Haven: Yale University Press, 1953.

VW   *Von der Wahrheit.* Munich: R. Piper, 1947.

WW   Karl Jaspers: *Werk und Wirkung*, ed. Klaus Piper, Munich: R. Piper, 1963. Contains the original "Philosophische Autobiographie," a complete bibliography (to 1962) and articles presented to Jaspers by his students on his 80th birthday (February 24, 1963).

Index

～つ

227